PREVENTION IN MENTAL HEALTH CARE

Prevention in Mental Health Care: Time for a new approach focuses on the limitations in current psychiatric practice and research. Many professionals working in mental health care, as well as patients with psychiatric symptoms, are dissatisfied with what is currently offered by the discipline, with respect to the diagnosis and treatment of psychiatric disorders.

This book discusses possibilities and opportunities for change, and is the first to combine recent scientific research results with insights from philosophy and art. Illustrating these points with elaborate case studies, *Prevention in Mental Health Care* promotes a deeper understanding and a new model of mental health care, with an emphasis on prevention and natural recovery.

Prevention in Mental Health Care will be of use to qualified or trainee practitioners, clinical psychologists, psychiatrists, social workers, occupational therapists and nurses working with the current classification systems and treatment methods in psychiatry. Furthermore, the book will appeal to students, lecturers and researchers, as well as those with a general interest in mental health care.

Dorien Nieman is associate professor and Head of the Cognition Lab at the Department of Psychiatry, Academic Medical Center, University of Amsterdam, the Netherlands, where she has worked since 1996. She has (co)authored more than 80 articles in (inter)national journals, several book chapters and a book on topics such as psychotherapy, biomarkers, and the prediction and prevention of psychiatric disorders.

'Until recently, prevention in mental health was regarded as something for the future and, without clear biological markers, probably a fool's gold. Well, the future has arrived! This scholarly and well-argued book by Dorien Nieman covers the philosophical, scientific and pragmatic aspects of this new science. We learn from the history of public health that much disease is preventable without necessarily understanding all the biological and environmental risk factors, so long as we apply basic principles and pragmatic thinking alongside the available science.
This book is testimony to that and sketches out what a prevention paradigm might look like and illustrates with great examples. It is an outstanding contribution and will be widely read.'
—**Max Birchwood**, Research Director, YouthSpace & Professor of Youth Mental Health, University of Warwick, UK

'In this excellent book, Dorien Nieman reflects on the essential problems of contemporary psychiatry, eloquently bringing together philosophical, clinical and neuroscientific expertise. Dorien Nieman pleas scientifically for a dimensional perspective in psychiatry. Dimensions may be more difficult to grasp, but are more apt to reality. Clinically, she pleas for a more individual approach. We need to see the persons again behind diagnoses. Nieman illustrates nicely how these paradigm shifts may advance our troubled discipline. Psychiatry is notoriously difficult and fatiguing since we have to think and reflect continually on the possibilities and boundaries of our discipline. Dorien Nieman testifies with this book of her capacity of critical contemplation and is an example to all of us clinicians, philosophers and neuroscientists.'
—**Damiaan Denys**, Professor of Psychiatry, Academic Medical Center, University of Amsterdam, the Netherlands

'How can mental health transform itself so that these benefits can flow to people with mental illness and to society more broadly? Dorien Nieman addresses these issues in her ambitious new book on prevention and early intervention. She captures the views of many philosophers and shows how psychiatry, above all other medical disciplines, can realize a level of personalized medicine much greater than any other, in her discussion of the "authentic self".'
—**Patrick McGorry**, Professor of Youth Mental Health, University of Melbourne and Executive Director of Orygen Youth Health, Australia (from the foreword)

'Dorien Nieman belongs to the rare experts in psychiatric research who venture to publish not only scholarly articles but an erudite book as well. Whereas many focus on narrow research questions, Nieman does not eschew the basic topics of her field. Prevention in Mental Health Care: Time for a new approach is brave, comprehensive and profound. The volume candidly faces the vexed issues of psychiatric research and clinical practice. It does so in a critical yet inoffensive way, while also proposing possible solutions.'
—**Professor Trudy Dehue**, Philosopher and sociologist of science (more specifically, psychiatry and psychology), University of Groningen

PREVENTION IN MENTAL HEALTH CARE

Time for a new approach

Dorien Nieman

LONDON AND NEW YORK

First published 2017
by Routledge
2 Park Square, Milton Park, Abingdon, Oxon, OX14 4RN

and by Routledge
711 Third Avenue, New York, NY 10017

Routledge is an imprint of the Taylor & Francis Group, an informa business

© 2017 Dorien Nieman

The right of Dorien Nieman to be identified as author of this work has been asserted by her in accordance with sections 77 and 78 of the Copyright, Designs and Patents Act 1988..

All rights reserved. No part of this book may be reprinted or reproduced or utilised in any form or by any electronic, mechanical, or other means, now known or hereafter invented, including photocopying and recording, or in any information storage or retrieval system, without permission in writing from the publishers.

Trademark notice: Product or corporate names may be trademarks or registered trademarks, and are used only for identification and explanation without intent to infringe.

British Library Cataloguing-in-Publication Data
A catalogue record for this book is available from the British Library

Library of Congress Cataloging in Publication Data
Names: Nieman, Dorien, author.
Title: Prevention in mental health care: time for a new approach / Dorien Nieman.
Description: Abingdon, Oxon; New York, NY: Routledge, 2016. | Includes bibliographical references.
Identifiers: LCCN 2015041850| ISBN 9781138918153 (hbk) | ISBN 9781138918160 (pbk) | ISBN 9781315683805 (ebk)
Subjects: | MESH: Mental Disorders. | Psychiatry--methods.
Classification: LCC RC454.4 | NLM WM 140 | DDC 616.89--dc23
LC record available at http://lccn.loc.gov/2015041850

ISBN: 978-1-138-91815-3 (hbk)
ISBN: 978-1-138-91816-0 (pbk)
ISBN: 978-1-315-68380-5 (ebk)

Typeset in Bembo
by HWA Text and Data Management, London

To Edwin, Tristan and Florian

Let life happen to you.
                    Rainer Maria Rilke

CONTENTS

List of figures   x
Foreword   xi
Acknowledgements   xiv
List of abbreviations   xv

Introduction   1

PART I
Limitations in current psychiatric practice and research   5

1   Categorical classification   7
    Attention Deficit and Hyperactivity Disorder   10
    Case example: Lowell   17

2   Scientific research and its omissions   22
    Increase in mental illness and psychotropic medication use in the past decennia   22
    Outcome psychiatric disorders   23
    Case example: Agnes   28
    Stigma   30
    The current paradigm in psychiatry   31
    What is a paradigm?   32
    Scientific output   33

3 The nature of social contact   38
   Case example: John   41

4 Mystic experiences   43
   The ancient domain   45
   Case example: Marc   47

5 The mind–brain problem   50

PART II
Possibilities and opportunities for change in psychiatry   **53**

6 Transdiagnostic phenomenological symptom dimensions   55
   Case example: Liam   57

7 Biological markers in psychiatric disorders   59
   Cognitive impairment   62
   Treatment of cognitive impairment   71
   Case example: Steven   72

8 From clinical staging and profiling to prevention in psychiatry   76
   Clinical staging and profiling   76
   Treatment and underlying neurobiological mechanisms   83

9 Evidence for preventive treatment in psychiatry   87
   Case example: Mike   91

10 The stress–relaxation continuum   96
   Physiology of the stress–relaxation continuum   97
   Case example: Mira   98

11 Redefinition of health and illness in psychiatry   101
   Environmental factors   105
   Case example: David   106

12 The authentic self   110
   Martin Heidegger   110
   Friedrich Nietzsche   112
   Søren Kierkegaard   112
   Upanishads   113
   Baruch Spinoza   113

Joseph Campbell 114
Paolo Coelho 115
William James 115
Karl Jaspers 116
Mihály Csíkszentmihályi 120
Rainer Maria Rilke 120
Jean-Paul Sartre 122
Irvin Yalom 123
Carl Jung 125
Synthesis 126

PART III
Case examples   **132**

13 Thomas   133
    Discussion 138

14 Lizzie   139
    Discussion 144

15 Martin   146
    Discussion 154

    Conclusions and future directions   155
    Seeking help in low stigma settings 156
    Individual approach 157
    Wellness Recovery Action Plan 159
    Acceptance and Commitment Therapy 160
    Antipsychiatry 161
    New treatments for psychotic disorders 161
    The Open dialogue approach 162
    Biomarkers 163
    The role of cognition 164
    Primary prevention 164
    Essential and existential redefinition 165
    Paradigm change 166
    Conclusion 167

    Index   *171*

FIGURES

4.1	Religious adherence as a percentage of the world population in 2007	44
7.1	Biomarkers and clinical staging in psychiatry	60
7.2	The Complex Figure of Rey	63
7.3.	Antisaccade task performance in a control subject and a patient	66
7.4	Brodmann area 46	67
7.5	Mean antisaccade error rate in schizophrenia patients, healthy control subjects and patients with an at risk mental state (ARMS) for developing a first psychosis	68
7.6.	A global view of cognition and its disruption in psychiatric disorders	69
7.7	Average neuropsychological performance of the clusters	70
8.1	Grand average target waveforms	79
8.2	Kaplan-Meier survival analysis of risk classes of the prognostic index	80
9.1	The stress–vulnerability model	89
9.2.	Case conceptualisation – Mike	92
11.1	The normal distribution plot	103

FOREWORD

Patrick McGorry
Professor of Youth Mental Health, University of Melbourne and Executive Director of Orygen Youth Health, Australia

Humans are living longer than ever before. Health care costs for physical illnesses are rising exponentially, and put huge pressures on governments, families and individuals. Despite being seen these days as an intrinsic part of the health system, mental illness is an exception to these trends. People with mental illness die up to two decades earlier, ironically largely from physical illnesses. There is a massive underspend in the care of mental illness which may worsen as advances in hi-tech medicine suck more and more health funding into late life physical health care. People with mental illness have been short-changed, and may be at risk of further neglect.

Yet mental illness differs in another fundamental way, because of the timing within the life cycle that it strikes. Mental disorders are the chronic disorders of the young, with 75% of illnesses emerging by age 25. In a subset of cases they persist and will blight many decades of life, not merely the latter ones, where physical illnesses cluster these days. So mental health care should be, in sharp distinction to other major non-communicable diseases (NCDs) like cancer and cardiovascular disease, an enormous investment opportunity, not a cost burden to society. If many young lives are saved, and the wave of disability that would otherwise erode future fulfillment and productivity over many decades is reduced or prevented, then vast amounts of money would be saved. These savings would flow from other domains, notably social welfare, incarceration, public housing and homelessness services, higher tax receipts and reduced harm caused by drugs and alcohol. Evidence-based mental health care would provide a major return on investment if it were properly designed, built to scale and delivered expertly and effectively. Currently, even in rich countries, only a tiny minority of people, even with serious mental illnesses receive timely, sustained and comprehensive evidence-based care, even though this is eminently feasible. Psychiatric treatments prove just as effective as physical health interventions.

There are vital lessons to be learned from other NCDs such as cancer and cardiovascular disease, where improvements in mortality and morbidity have flowed from prevention, early diagnosis, sustained care as long as it is needed. We are just beginning to learn these lessons in mental health, but haven't applied them systematically.

How can mental health transform itself so that these benefits can flow to people with mental illness and to society more broadly? Dorien Nieman addresses these issues in her ambitious new book on prevention and early intervention. She launches a scathing and largely justified critique of current approaches to research and treatment, and argues for an honest appraisal of concepts and strategy to change the paradigms to something more useful and effective.

One of her key targets is the century old diagnostic system that remains central to international mental health care. Both the Diagnostic and Statistical Manual of Mental Disorders (DSM) and International Classification of Diseases (ICD) systems have virtually embalmed the Kraepelinian model for serious mental disorders, despite its demonstrable lack of utility and capacity to guide treatment or illuminate the aetiology of these conditions. This diagnostic model was formulated during the age of steam, before the first aeroplane flew, and reified and endowed its flawed concepts with the same status as classical physical illnesses such as diabetes and ischaemic heart disease. We don't build anything these days with nineteenth-century ideas and technology. The DSM and the ICD have become whipping boys for the widespread frustration felt by professionals and the public, yet they are merely the surface manifestations of a deeper problem, and their survival reflects our inability to formulate a better alternative. We desperately need new conceptual frameworks.

Dorien Nieman exposes the consequences of overvaluing current diagnostic concepts and equating syndromes in a hard reductionist manner with primary brain diseases. New drugs, which may be useful for a wide range of patients, can only be tested and licensed within a flawed diagnostic system. Agencies like the Food and Drug Administration are part of this conspiracy of self-deception, along with pharmaceutical companies, the American Psychiatric Association and the World Health Organization. If the emperor has clothes, they are fairly flimsy and fit poorly. All collude with this fiction to create a cartel whose grip will be difficult to break. In the USA in particular, and through its influence on many other settings, each diagnosis has its very own pill to treat it. New agents can only be studied within traditional diagnostic silos, and even the National Institute of Mental Health's 'Research Domain Criteria' will find it hard threaten this. This means that many people with early stage or mild to moderate disorders, who might benefit from simpler or even more expert transdiagnostic psychosocial care, are given medication as first rather than second line. Drugs might be useful transdiagnostically, beyond the probably spurious category that they were originally developed for and marooned legally within, but they may be restricted or even banned from use in other indications and patients. Such use is derided as 'off-label' and those who prescribe them are widely pilloried. Some of this off label use is undoubtedly risky, harmful and unnecessary, but some of it may well be helpful and essential, at least as part of a second or third line approach where psychosocial interventions alone have not resulted in recovery. This can all be seen as further symptoms of a flawed diagnostic system, which is of poor utility and highly uncertain validity. Of course, this weakness in concepts and strategy feeds controversies and ideological culture wars in our still immature and often savagely self-harming field. As Dorien Nieman recounts, the DSM-5 recently became a target. It was attacked as a symbol of the biological reductionism that effortlessly replaced the earlier and equally unhelpful psychological reductionism of psychoanalysis. These culture wars too are symptoms of a serious flaw in our field, namely a worrying lack of capacity to integrate different levels of analysis to create more sophisticated approaches to mental health care. Dorien Nieman takes a deep dive into philosophical and spiritual pools and wonders how these domains can be connected to neuroscience, psychology, personalized health care and the modern world.

The bulk of the book explores and describes some new and promising approaches to transcending these barriers and limited perspectives. It shows how the twin concepts of clinical staging and profiling, which are being effectively deployed in other branches of medicine, might help to make diagnosis a more useful and valid process to guide treatment, and particularly early intervention. The neurobiological changes that have been revealed in mental disorders do not map well onto the traditional diagnostic map as defined by polythetic DSM and ICD concepts. However many might well link to the stage of illness across diagnostic borders, and furthermore define subgroups that might respond to specific mechanism-related treatments. Even if it remains heuristic, such an approach brings psychiatry much closer to the holy grail of personalized or precision medicine. Finally, at the end of the book, Nieman shows how psychiatry above all other medical disciplines can realize a level of personalized medicine much greater than any other in her discussion of the 'authentic self'. She captures the views of many philosophers on this subject, but my personal favourite is Joseph Campbell, who drew on the universal 'monomyth' to characterize life as a 'hero's journey' during which predictable challenges and ordeals must be faced. Each individual has a unique life journey, which can be shared and personally understood by a skilled therapist. This is a great way to approach young people in the early stages of mental ill health, but would work well for most people in allowing the experience of mental ill health to be normalized without denying access to expert care and support. Tailoring the psychological therapy as well as biological therapies to that individual and to his or her authentic self, as well as his or her unique genomic complexion, is within reach. All it takes, and this remains a big task, is to integrate the multiple and fascinating perspectives of psychiatry and mental health. That's all.

ACKNOWLEDGEMENTS

I would like to thank the patients I worked with, whose stories form the basis of this book. This book is an attempt to improve outcomes for those who experience psychiatric symptoms. I thank Don Linszen, Arnold Ziegelaar, Bert Nieman and Marieke Speear for their valuable comments on the first version of the manuscript. Many thanks to my colleagues, family and friends for their support. I would particularly like to thank Damiaan Denys, Chairman of the Department of Psychiatry, for asking thought-provoking questions and the encouragement he gave me; Pat McGorry for all I learned from him about early intervention; Hiske Becker for interesting conversations about the topic of this book; and Annick Fransen for helping me with all sorts of matters. My gratitude also goes to Joanne Forshaw, Kirsten Buchanan, Aiyana Curtis and the entire team at Routledge. And last, but not least, many thanks to my husband and children for their love and patience which made it possible for me to write this book.

ABBREVIATIONS

ADHD	Attention Deficit and Hyperactivity Disorder
AMC	Academic Medical Center
ARMS	At Risk Mental State
DSM	Diagnostic and Statistical Manual for Mental Disorders
EEG	Electroencephalogram
GP	General Practitioner
ICD	International Classification of Diseases and Related Health Problems
NCD	Non-communicable disease
PKU	phenylketonuria
WHO	World Health Organization
SSRI	Selective Serotonin Reuptake Inhibitor

INTRODUCTION

Although in the western world, about 1 in 4 will suffer from a psychiatric disorder in a given year, and 46 per cent will meet criteria at some point in their life (Kessler et al., 2005a; 2005b), these disorders are still poorly understood. Mental illnesses account for a larger proportion of disability in developed countries than any other group of illnesses, including cancer and heart disease (Reeves et al., 2011). Direct and indirect financial costs associated with psychiatric disorders are huge (e.g. over $300 billion annually in the USA; Insel, 2008), not to mention the degree of suffering these disorders induce in patients and their families.

Many professionals working in mental health care, as well as patients with psychiatric symptoms, are dissatisfied with what is currently offered by the psychiatric discipline with respect to the diagnosis and treatment of psychiatric disorders. The main standard classification tool to diagnose psychiatric disorders and allocate treatment is the *Diagnostic and Statistical Manual of Mental Disorders* (DSM-5, American Psychiatric Association, 2013). This is composed of diagnostic categories based on expert consensus, not discrete medical diseases in the traditional sense. Many patients are confronted with several different DSM diagnoses and treatments before their symptoms improve. Despite a steep increase in psychotropic medication prescription, the number of subjects (especially children) disabled by psychiatric symptoms has risen substantially. The majority of individuals with severe mental illness (e.g. schizophrenia) still face a poor prognosis, despite the thousands of publications each year. The boundary between being mentally ill and being healthy is artificial, and so the list continues.

Psychiatry needs to turn to a new page. Research that continues to follow the presupposition that psychiatric disorders can be reduced to brain disorders is unlikely to lead to any progress in our understanding of mental illness and, subsequently, to an improvement of treatment. This book is for everyone with an interest in mental health care, including practitioners (psychiatrists, psychologists, social workers, occupational therapists and nurses), laypersons, students, lecturers and researchers.

Part I of the book focuses on limitations in current psychiatric practice and research. On the one hand, inevitable psychological difficulties that people encounter in their life are labelled as an illness and treated with psychotropic medication. On the other hand, curative treatment possibilities of severe mental disorders are scarce. Psychiatry is in need of new ways to diagnose and treat patients with (emerging) psychiatric symptoms.

Chapter 1 describes the limitations of the categorical classification systems used in psychiatry to diagnose mental illness. The second chapter discusses how the way scientific research is organized may have hampered progress in psychiatry. In scientific research, several topics are usually not addressed, but they may be important to comprehend psychiatric disorders. Three of these topics are: the nature of social contact, mystic experiences, and the mind–brain problem. These topics and their relevance for psychiatry will be discussed in the Chapters 3–5.

Part II of the book describes possibilities and opportunities for change, based on recent research in psychiatry as well as on insights from philosophy and the arts. Mental illness is complex because of the interaction between biological, social, existential and psychological components. In the past decennia, the search for the distinctive biological substrate of the DSM disorders (schizophrenia, ADHD, major depressive disorder, obsessive compulsive disorder, etcetera) has yielded little or no results. Examining the scientific literature on psychiatry reveals that although there are biological (cognitive, genetic, neurophysiological, neuroimaging, blood marker, etcetera) dysfunctions underlying psychiatric disorders, these are not specific for the DSM diagnostic categories, which have been defined top-down (by expert consensus). To gain insight into the biological component of mental illness, we should also use a bottom-up instead of a top-down approach (Chapter 6). The biological component should be studied 'transdiagnostically', across psychiatric disorders, i.e. without taking the DSM diagnosis into consideration. Chapter 7 (entitled Biological markers in psychiatric disorders) summarizes transdiagnostic research results concerning cognitive impairment. In Chapter 8, an alternative for the DSM is described: clinical staging and profiling. One of the most important developments in recent years has been the importing of the concept of clinical staging and profiling from general medicine. Clinical staging is common in many medical specialties and builds on scientific evidence that disorders evolve over time, and stages of disease severity can be discerned, including a subclinical prodromal phase. Profiling entails using variables in the diagnosis that have shown a personalized prognostic value, or can predict treatment response. Chapter 9 describes evidence-based and promising therapies that can be used in a clinical staging model. An important link between mind and brain is the stress–relaxation continuum, which as Chapter 10 shows can also be of value in a clinical staging model. In Chapter 11, the artificial definition of health and illness in psychiatry is discussed. In modern western societies, reflected in psychiatric practice, mental health is defined as a relative absence of depression, anxiety, psychosis, etcetera. With this definition, it is not surprising that 1 in 4 suffers from a mental illness. To come to a redefinition of health and illness in psychiatry, it may be important to take into account the true nature of social interaction, mystic experiences and the mind–brain problem, and not follow preconceptions of the majority. In addition, the authentic self may be an important concept to consider in psychiatry. In the last chapter (Chapter 12) the work of scientists, artists and philosophers who have written about the authentic self is summarized. With their insights, the concept and its relevance for psychiatry can be defined.

In Part III, the preceding chapters are illustrated with three elaborate case examples, written from a phenomenological viewpoint, and from the viewpoint of those surrounding them. Because subjective experience plays such an important role in psychiatric disorders, just a factual description of externally observable symptoms would provide too little information.

In the conclusion, the preceding chapters are unified. To understand and better treat psychiatric symptoms, alternatives to the DSM should be investigated. One such alternative is clinical staging and profiling. Furthermore, it has become apparent that merely investigating psychiatric symptoms by including patients with a certain DSM diagnosis in a scientific research design may not be the road to increased insight into psychiatric symptoms. We may need to consider these symptoms from a broader perspective, including insights from philosophers and artists. Combining these deep insights into human nature with promising new developments in psychiatric research may lead to a true understanding of mental health and mental illness and to improved treatments.

References

American Psychiatric Association. (2013). *Diagnostic and Statistical Manual of Mental Disorders* (DSM 5th ed.). Arlington, VA: American Psychiatric Publishing.

Insel, T. R. (2008). Assessing the economic cost of serious mental illness. *American Journal of Psychiatry* 165(6), 663–665.

Kessler, R.C., Berglund, P., Demler, O., Jin, R., Merikangas, K.R. and Walters, E.E. (2005a). Lifetime prevalence and age-of-onset distributions of DSM-IV disorders in the National Comorbidity Survey Replication. *Archives General Psychiatry* 62(6), 593–602.

Kessler, R.C., Chiu, W.T., Demler, O. and Walters, E.E. (2005b). Prevalence, severity, and comorbidity of twelve-month DSM-IV disorders in the National Comorbidity Survey Replication (NCS-R). *Archives of General Psychiatry* 62(6), 617–27.

Reeves, M.C., Strine, T.W., Pratt, L.A., Thompson, L. Ahluwalia, I., Dhingra, S.S., McKnight-Eily, L R., Harrison, L., D'Angelo, D.V., Williams, L., Morrow, B., Gould, D. and Safran, M.A. (2011). Mental illness surveillance among adults in the United States. *Centers for Disease Control and Prevention Supplements* 60(03), 1–32.

PART I
Limitations in current psychiatric practice and research

1
CATEGORICAL CLASSIFICATION

The frustrating lack of progress in psychiatric research and treatment may be partly due to the limitations of the dominant classification systems generally used in psychiatry: the Diagnostic and Statistical Manual of Mental Disorders (published by the American Psychiatric Association) and the International Statistical Classification of Diseases and Related Health Problems (ICD published by the World Health Organization). The ICD is an initiative of the World Health Organization (WHO), first published in 1948 and it is not restricted to mental disorders. Mental disorders are listed under chapter 5. A categorical system classifies a disorder as being present or not, depending on whether the patient fulfills a certain set of criteria (Chmura Kraemer et al., 2004) and is designed to make communication between researchers and clinicians worldwide simple and efficient (Sheehan et al., 1998).

The very first version of the DSM was published in 1952 (Grob, 1991). It was divided into two major categories: disorders that were clearly caused by an impairment in brain function (trauma, infection, intoxication, etcetera) and disorders characterized by the inability of an individual to adjust. The latter was divided into psychotic and neurotic disorders (Grob, 1991). The fourth edition is divided into 5 axes: clinical disorders, personality disorders and intellectual disabilities, acute medical conditions and physical disorders, psychosocial and environmental factors contributing to the disorder (problems at home, at work, etcetera), and finally a global assessment of functioning, which is scored from 0 to 100 and encompasses both overall functioning and severity of symptoms. Each disorder is characterized by a set of criteria that a patient must fulfill before receiving that diagnosis. The DSM is commercialized and encompasses an ever increasing number of diagnostic categories (more than 400 in the DSM-IV). A fifth edition has been published in June 2013 with new diagnoseses such as

'Voyeuristic disorder' and 'Tobacco use disorder', i.e. smoking. Over the years, more and more objections to the DSM have been raised.

In psychiatry, nosology has been defined by the DSM (and ICD) since the Second World War. It is important for any researcher to realize that the DSM does not take into account any (hypothesized) cause or process supposed to underlie the diagnostic categories. The DSM system defines 'diagnostic categories' by operational criteria based on the presence of symptoms, without reference to supposed psychological or biological processes associated with the diagnostic categories. As such, the DSM categories do clearly not resemble mature medical diagnostic concepts validated by an underlying biological disturbance. This, of course, does not imply that DSM concepts are completely arbitrary. They have been chosen because of their apparent clinical validity, reinforced over a century of psychiatric thinking and practice (van Beveren and Hoogendijk, 2011).

However, the key concepts, notably schizophrenia, were developed in late stage samples from tertiary settings and before modern treatments were developed. They were essentially descriptive, with an attempt to capture prognostic utility which proved challenging. Consequently, they have not only a weak relationship to treatment selection (one of the major purposes of diagnosis), but also poor utility when retro-fitted to the early stages of mental ill health. Critically, they set the bar too high for commencement of treatment and provide little guidance as to safe and appropriate care. Although the DSM has improved the reliability (under research conditions only) of categorical diagnoses, these diagnoses represent expert consensus with all its failings, and not discrete valid medical diseases in the traditional sense (Nieman and McGorry, 2015). In the case of medical diseases, e.g. ischemic heart disease, diabetes or glioblastoma multiforme, it is possible to have the disease without symptoms. In contrast, is not possible to have a psychiatric disorder without symptoms (Borsboom and Cramer, 2013).

The DSM works under the assumption that psychiatric disorders are discrete entities that have natural boundaries delimiting them (Dalal and Sivakumar, 2009). However, over the years, comorbidity has proven otherwise. The DSM allows multiple diagnoses per patient, which reflects the fact that disorders such as anxiety and depression often go together. Surveys have shown that comorbidity is more frequently present than absent. In the United States 51 per cent of patients diagnosed with major depressive disorder suffered from at least one comorbid disorder (Maj, 2005; Kessler et al., 2011). In Spain, 30.3 per cent of all patients surveyed had more than one current mental disorder (Roca et al., 2009).

The DSM also assumes the concept of multiple parallel pathways each leading to distinct diagnostic categories. This assumption is not supported by longitudinal clinical nor neurobiological studies (Hickie et al., 2013; Lichtenstein et al., 2009; Sullivan et al., 2012). How do psychiatric symptoms develop? Data from studies that assess patients longitudinally from childhood or adolescence show that symptoms are shared and sequenced across disorders (Merikangas et al., 2012; Kelleher et al., 2012). Mental disorders are not fixed and independent entities, but each diagnosis is robustly related to other diagnoses in a correlational structure that is manifested both concurrently and in patterns across time (Lahey et al., 2014). Prototypically, anxiety disorders that are evident in children before the age of 12 years predict later depressive, bipolar and psychotic disorders (Kim-Cohen et al., 2003). This sequential pattern opens up the opportunity for prevention of secondary disorders. Stress, and its accompanying physiological changes and anxiety, may be at the core of many psychiatric disorders, as corroborated by aberrant oxidative stress and inflammation biomarkers in evolving severity (Kuloglu et al., 2002; Bouayed et al., 2009; Dean et al., 2011; Nieman and McGorry, 2015).

Another hotly debated topic when discussing categorical diagnosis is the fact that DSM imposes very specific thresholds, above which a patient qualifies to be diagnosed with the disorder. It can be a time frame, such as presence of a certain severity or number of symptoms in an uninterrupted fashion for an arbitrary period such as two weeks. Someone who has had the symptoms for 10 days will not be considered ill and thus will not receive treatment, whereas someone who has had them for 15 days might receive the same treatment as a patient who has suffered for a year. Although the DSM was not primarily created for making treatment decisions but for facilitating communication and research, in many countries it plays an important role in treatment allocation in clinical practice. This can lead to some patients with a need for care not getting treated at all, as well as to possible over-treatment of others (Helzer et al., 2006). Yet this is obviously a set of somewhat arbitrary decisions, and represents a spuriously objective definition of the boundary of 'need for care'. We do not have such thresholds for conditions such as allergy or rheumatoid arthritis. The threshold here is lower, though intensity of treatment will vary.

Furthermore, recent studies have raised the stakes when it comes to sub threshold symptoms reported by patients: they have shown that particularly in psychosis, depression and anxiety, sub threshold conditions can impair psychosocial functioning and may lead to the full blown disorder as arbitrarily defined. This shows that the criteria listed in the DSM may be insufficient when it comes to detecting patients in need of care (Shankman et al., 2009; McGorry, 2010; Karsten et al., 2010). On the other hand, there has been concern about broadening the boundaries of mental ill-health (Frances, 2013). A definition of need for care or an approach to prevent any harm arising from 'soft entry' is needed and in fact achievable (Nieman and McGorry, 2015).

Finally, DSM diagnoses are polythetic. A polythetic class is defined in terms of a broad set of criteria that are neither necessary nor sufficient for class membership. Each member of the category must possess a certain minimal number of defining characteristics, but none of the features has to be found in each member of the category. For example in the DSM, 9 criteria are listed for a major depressive disorder but only 5 are required for the diagnosis, and thus two patients can receive the same diagnosis while sharing only one symptom (Hyman, 2010). In addition, sleep difficulties are listed under major depressive disorder, post-traumatic stress disorder, generalized anxiety disorder and a number of other diagnostic categories. This way of defining classes (polythetic) is associated with Wittgenstein's concept of 'family resemblances'. Polythetic classification has been seriously criticized by, e.g. Sutcliffe (1993, 1994, 1996) as logically incoherent.

A monothetic class is defined in terms of characteristics that are both necessary and sufficient in order to identify members of that class. This way of defining a class is termed the Aristotelian definition of a class.

Thus, the DSM categories were conceived by consensus among psychiatrists, and not by nature. It is similar to creating a category by consensus of 'pain on the chest'. All the patients in this category have pain on the chest, but one subject has angina pectoris and the next a simple muscle ache. The optimal treatment and prognosis is diverse for the individual patients in this category and it would not be possible to find one biological substrate in research. Therefore, a polythetic category of 'pain on the chest' would lead to worldwide consistency and reproducibility of diagnosis, but not to validity. It is more useful to use imaging, plasma enzymes, etcetera to narrow down the diagnosis to a point where it does provide information about optimal treatment and prognosis. In many other fields of medicine, categorization is based on biological abnormalities, i.e. determined by nature and not by expert consensus.

In clinical practice, it is not uncommon to do an intake with a patient who has previously received four or more different DSM diagnoses. Unfortunately, the clinician's interpretation of the patient's symptoms with respect to the DSM criteria is the basis for the diagnosis (Stein et al., 2013). No biological test is available to verify the diagnosis, whereas for many physical illnesses (e.g. tuberculosis) there is such a test. Because the patient's symptoms are subject to diverse interpretations of a polythetic classification system by clinicians, the psychiatric diagnosis may appear to be somewhat arbitrary. Also, as the DSM diagnosis is used for treatment allocation, the limitations of this system can have worrisome consequences. For example, children can be diagnosed with ADHD and receive psychotropic medication with possible harmful side-effects, without the certainty that they actually need this medication.

Attention Deficit and Hyperactivity Disorder

In the past decades the number of subjects receiving the DSM diagnosis of ADHD has increased explosively. DSM IV diagnostic criteria for Attention-Deficit/Hyperactivity Disorders are as follows:

A. Either (1) or (2):
(1) inattention: six (or more) of the following symptoms of inattention have persisted for at least 6 months to a degree that is maladaptive and inconsistent with developmental level:
   (a) often fails to give close attention to details or makes careless mistakes in schoolwork, work, or other activities
   (b) often has difficulty sustaining attention in tasks or play activities

(c) often does not seem to listen when spoken to directly
(d) often does not follow through on instructions and fails to finish school work, chores, or duties in the workplace (not due to oppositional behaviour or failure to understand instructions)
(e) often has difficulty organizing tasks and activities
(f) often avoids, dislikes, or is reluctant to engage in tasks that require sustained mental effort (such as schoolwork or homework)
(g) often loses things necessary for tasks or activities (e.g., toys, school assignments, pencils, books, or tools)
(h) is often easily distracted by extraneous stimuli
(i) is often forgetful in daily activities
(2) hyperactivity-impulsivity: six (or more) of the following symptoms of hyperactivity-impulsivity have persisted for at least 6 months to a degree that is maladaptive and inconsistent with developmental level:
Hyperactivity
(a) often fidgets with hands or feet or squirms in seat
(b) often leaves seat in classroom or in other situations in which remaining seated is expected
(c) often runs about or climbs excessively in situations in which it is inappropriate (in adolescents or adults, may be limited to subjective feelings of restlessness)
(d) often has difficulty playing or engaging in leisure activities quietly
(e) is often 'on the go' or often acts as if 'driven by a motor'
(f) often talks excessively
Impulsivity
(g) often blurts out answers before questions have been completed
(h) often has difficulty awaiting turn
(i) often interrupts or intrudes on others (e.g., butts into conversations or games).
B. Some hyperactive-impulsive or inattentive symptoms that caused impairment were present before age 7 years.
C. Some impairment from the symptoms is present in two or more settings (e.g., at school [or work] and at home).
D. There must be clear evidence of clinically significant impairment in social, academic, or occupational functioning.
E. The symptoms do not occur exclusively during the course of a Pervasive Developmental Disorder, Schizophrenia, or other Psychotic Disorder and are not better accounted for by another mental disorder (e.g., Mood Disorder, Anxiety Disorder, Dissociative Disorders, or a Personality Disorder).

Reprinted with permission from the *Diagnostic and Statistical Manual of Mental Disorders*, Fourth Edition, (Copyright ©2000). American Psychiatric Association. All Rights Reserved.

Dalsgaard et al. (2013) reported that the use of ADHD medication such as methylphenidate (e.g. Ritalin) for six months or longer among 852,711 children (aged 6–13 years) increased five-fold from 2003–2010 in Denmark. Similar numbers are found in other countries (Dalsgaard et al., 2013). In the Netherlands, the number of prescriptions for Ritalin increased between 1997 and 1999 by about 160 per cent (65,000 in 1997 to 157,000 in 1999). This steep increase has plateaued in 2000 to about 14 per cent, a total of 178,500 prescriptions. Boys represent 80 per cent of the group. The medication is most used by children of 9 years old and the majority of children take it for one or two years, but there is a trend for longer and longer treatment. The increase in ADHD medication is especially seen in children between 10 and 19 years.

A study of the University of British Columbia (UBC) showed in the medical records of 937,943 Canadian children that the youngest children in the classroom are significantly more likely to be diagnosed with attention deficit hyperactivity disorder – and given medication – than their peers in the same grade (Morrow et al., 2012). Children born in December, close to the cut-off date for entry into school in British Columbia, were 39 per cent more likely to be diagnosed with ADHD than children born 11 months earlier. December-born children also were 48 per cent more likely to be treated with medication than their January-born peers. The gap in ages among students in the same grade creates what researchers call a 'relative age effect', in which younger children within an age cohort are at a disadvantage in academic and athletic activities. Younger students within a grade may be diagnosed with ADHD because they are less mature.

Thus younger, less mature children are inappropriately being labelled and treated. These children are exposed to potential harms from unnecessary diagnosis and use of medications. Medication to treat ADHD, including Ritalin, Dexedrine, Adderall and Strattera, can have negative health effects in children, such as sleep disturbance, increased risk of cardiovascular events, psychosis and slower growth rates (Whiteley, 2014). In addition, younger children who have been labelled with ADHD may be treated differently by teachers and parents, which could lead to negative self-perception and social issues.

The difference between children who act in a certain way and children who don't does not imply that this difference is caused by a disorder (Jacobs and the Youth Affairs Network of Queensland, 2005). We know that people have individual physical differences, but it is dangerous ground to say that those differences are a 'disorder', just because they are in the minority, or because they cause problems with fitting into society-rigid structures (like school). It would be similar to inventing a name for normal short height, e.g. SH and telling people who are shorter than average that they have a disorder (Dehue, 2014). This example is not fiction: a manufacturer of the growth hormone Humanotrope recommends this medicine for the disorder Idiopathic Short Stature (ISS or unexplained shortness). Of course being short has its disadvantages (or in some situations advantages), but it is not a disorder until it is labelled as such. Height is dimensional ranging from very short to very tall. The far end of the dimension may lead to difficulties for which treatment could be considered. The manufacturer of the medication would of course benefit if subjects closer to average height could also be prescribed the medication. A similar problem may have occurred with psychiatric disorders such as ADHD. Severe attention deficit and hyperactivity can lead to stagnant development, and these children may need medication when more benign treatment methods are ineffective. But more and more children who do not fulfil criteria for the far end of the dimension of attention deficit and hyperactivity are prescribed methylphenidate. These children are said to 'have ADHD' but most people do not realize that ADHD is a construct similar to ISS; it is not a medical disorder such as tuberculosis. It was not so long ago that homosexuality was a disorder in the DSM. It is particular that the expert-consensus method of defining disorders in psychiatry determines whether certain preferences, behaviours, feelings are an illness or not.

In clinical practice, it occurs frequently that an adolescent receives a diagnosis of ADHD at some point because he/she failed to give close attention to school/work, had difficulty with planning, avoided tasks that require sustained mental effort, was easily distracted, forgetful and fidgeted with hands or feet. However, in the prodromal phase of several major mental disorders, these symptoms are also prominent. Months to years before a first psychotic episode, subjects experience signs and symptoms very similar to those described in the DSM under the category of ADHD. Unfortunately, medication for ADHD influences the dopamine neurotransmitter system in the brain and administration in the prodromal phase of schizophrenia can have adverse effects.

Methylphenidate is a central nervous system stimulant with a similar mechanism of action as cocaine (Auriel et al., 2009; Abramowicz, 2003) and can lead to psychosis from chronic abuse (Morton et al., 2000; Spensely et al., 1972). The safety profile of methylphenidate has been well established in short-term trials, but the effects of long-term use of methylphenidate remain largely unknown (Ashton et al., 2006; Kimko et al., 1999; Whiteley, 2014).

Dafny and Young (2006) raised concerns that long-term therapy might cause drug dependence, paranoia, schizophrenia and behavioural sensitization in a similar manner to that of other stimulant drugs. It is unpredictable in whom methylphenidate psychosis will occur, as family history of mental illness does not predict the incidence of the condition in children with ADHD. Withdrawal symptoms of methylphenidate can include psychosis and depression (Rosenfeld, 1979). Stimulant withdrawal or rebound reactions can occur, and should be minimized in intensity, i.e. via a gradual tapering off of medication (Schwartz et al., 2004; Garland, 1998; Nolan et al., 1999).

Chakraborty and Grover (2011) describe a case of an 11-year old girl with ADHD and mental retardation, treated with methylphenidate, who developed mania-like symptoms requiring inpatient treatment. Kraemer et al. (2010) stress that careful monitoring of patients with ADHD treated with stimulants is necessary in every single case. Medication with methylphenidate should be avoided in patients with vulnerability to psychotic symptoms and in drug addiction. However, Kraemer et al. (2010) report 3 cases who made the transition to psychosis, without these risk factors, and demonstrate that, even in patients without vulnerability to psychotic symptoms and without drug addiction, a careful and regular psychiatric monitoring is essential.

The key to the marketing success of ADHD is the near universal temporary stimulant effects of dextroamphetamine (e.g. Adderall) and the 'amphetamine-like substance' metylphenidate (e.g. Ritalin). With ADHD medication, these complainant children are regarded as 'biochemically balanced', without them they are considered faulty. When the drugs wear off, however, rebound or withdrawal effects can occur that worsen ADHD-type behaviours. Rebound or withdrawal effects are often worse than the child's original behaviour, even after a single dose (Whiteley, 2014; Breggin, 1998).

The use of the DSM in clinical practice can lead to medication prescription on the basis of psychiatric diagnoses that are subject to individual interpretation by the mental health care professional. For example, 'often' is mentioned 18 times in the DSM IV diagnostic criteria for ADHD, but never specified. One doctor may regard 10 times a day often but another doctor 5 times. Many have noticed the adverse effects of the use of the DSM, leading to people receiving medication that may be harmful for them. In the Netherlands, child and adolescent psychiatrists handed a statement to the secretary of public health and education on April 16, 2015 in which they expressed their concern about the steep increase in ADHD medication that is prescribed to children without thorough diagnostic examination. The trend that students take ADHD medication increasingly to study better is also cause for concern. The psychiatrists emphasize that unwarranted medical treatment of children with the diagnosis ADHD and improper use of ADHD medication is not without danger.

Prescription of methylphenidate, the medicine for ADHD is only allowed after a thorough diagnostic evaluation and in combination with other behavioural interventions. There are alarming signs that that is not always the case according to Professor Dr Robert Vermeiren, president of the division Child and Adolescent Psychiatry of the Dutch Association of Psychiatrists. The side-effects are generally mild, but data about long term use are limited, so little is known, especially in young children. Therefore, it may only be prescribed when hyperactivity or concentration problems have severe consequences and when the problems cannot be solved in another manner.

The division of Child and Adolescent Psychiatry is of the opinion that the increase in unjustified use of ADHD medication is harmful for children and parents for whom this medication is necessary. Parents who give their child medication can be perceived as taking the easy road. Child and adolescent psychiatrists want to work with other professionals on a tightening of the guidelines for prescribing ADHD medication.

In half of the cases, the first prescription for Ritalin is given by a child physician, 20 per cent by a child psychiatrist and 20 per cent by the general practitioner (GP). The rest is prescribed by other specialists (e.g. neurologists, revalidation physicians). The Dutch Health Council finds this division concerning. General practitioners see only a few children with ADHD in a year. How can they get enough experience with diagnosing the disorder? And child physicians have often only 15 minutes for a consultation. It may seem easy and valid to go through the DSM checklist for ADHD, give a diagnosis and prescribe Ritalin but professionals state that 15 minutes is too short, and it is important to withstand the choice for the easiest and quickest 'solution', i.e. Ritalin. Luckily, more and more parents oppose this strategy. It may appear as a good solution for full classrooms, where it is helpful for the teacher if a child sits still in his/her chair and complies with instructions. Seen from a broader perspective, though it is not a good solution, especially as this problem not only holds for methyphenidate, but also for other psychotropic medication, as reported by Karanges et al. (2014).

Karanges et al. (2014) obtained the number of prescriptions dispensed for government-subsidized antidepressant, antipsychotic and ADHD medications from the database maintained by the Department of Human Services in Australia between 2009 and 2012. Over the four-year study period, the dispensing of antidepressants, antipsychotics and ADHD medications showed overall increases of 16.1 per cent, 22.7 per cent and 26.1 per cent respectively. The most rapid percentage increases in antidepressant and antipsychotic dispensing occurred in children aged 10–14 (35.5 per cent and 49.1 per cent respectively), while ADHD medication dispensing rose most rapidly in those aged 20–24 (70.9 per cent). Dispensing to males was more common during childhood for all investigated classes, while two-thirds of adult antidepressant prescribing was to female patients. Most antidepressants and antipsychotics were prescribed by GPs (89.9 per cent and 70.6 per cent respectively), while the majority of ADHD medications were prescribed by paediatricians (59.1 per cent). Thus, dispensing of psychotropic medications increased markedly from 2009 to 2012 in Australia, with notable age-specific trends. General adherence to treatment guidelines is apparent, yet concerns exist about the likely overmedication of persons with mild psychological distress, and the increasing use of powerful psychotropic medications in younger populations despite uncertain risk–benefit profiles.

The New York Times reported on May 16, 2014 that more than 10,000 two and three year olds are being medicated for ADHD outside established paediatric guidelines, according to data presented by the Centers for Disease Control and Prevention in the USA. The American Academy of Pediatrics' standard practice guidelines for ADHD do not even address the diagnosis in children of 3 years and younger, let alone the use of such stimulant medications. Their safety and effectiveness have barely been explored in that age group. This report was the latest to raise concerns about ADHD diagnoses and medications for American children beyond what many experts consider medically justified. In 2013, a nationwide Centers for Disease Control and Prevention survey found that 11 per cent of children aged 4 to 17 have received a diagnosis of the disorder, and that about one in five boys will get one during childhood. A vast majority are put on ADHD medications (Schwartz, 2014).

I am not arguing that psychiatric conditions such as hyperactivity and psychosis do not exist. I am arguing that the DSM diagnostic categories that have been named, e.g. ADHD or schizophrenia are not the specific brain disorders, as is often presented in scientific literature and the media. Sometimes brain scan images, in which certain brain areas 'light up', are shown as evidence that psychiatric disorders are brain disorders. However, a study reported that even a dead salmon can show brain imaging activity, because of the complex statistical procedures necessary to generate the brain scan images (Bennett et al., 2010). This study received the IgNobel Prize, a parody on the Nobel Prize, given each year at Harvard University to 'honor achievements that first make people laugh, and then make them think'.

Weinberger and Radulescu (2016) write in their review in the *American Journal of Psychiatry* that recent technical reports indicate that data from popular brain magnetic resonance imaging (MRI) research are highly sensitive to common artefacts (e.g. head motion and breathing effects) that may dominate the results. Because these and other important confounders of MRI data (e.g. smoking, bodyweight, metabolic variations, medical comorbidities, psychoactive drugs) tend to vary systematically between patient and control groups, the evidence that findings are neurobiologically meaningful is inconclusive, and may represent artefacts or epiphenomena of uncertain value. The authors caution that uncritical acceptance of findings that may represent fallacies of all sorts carries the risk of misinforming practitioners and patients about biological abnormalities underlying psychiatric illness.

The diagnostic categories in psychiatry are different from the diagnostic categories in, e.g. pulmonology or internal medicine, where a biological test can often verify whether you have the disorder or not. There is no such biological test available for the DSM diagnostic categories. This has led to the worrying consequence that subjects can receive a psychiatric diagnosis and medication, based on the subjective interpretation by the clinician of the vague criteria of an invalid, polythetic classification system. Some subjects may need medication, but currently medication prescription sometimes occurs because it is more convenient for the environment, substantiated by the DSM criteria that are multi-interpretable. However, this does not imply that subjects with psychosis, depressive symptoms, hyperactivity are not ill, only that the categorization and the illness threshold needs to be re-examined. Research is necessary to replace the DSM system with another, more valid system that takes into account the prodromal high risk phase (as is done in diabetes and cancer treatment) as well as the dimensional nature of psychiatric symptoms (similar to height).

Furthermore, biological abnormalities across DSM categories need to be investigated for their relationship with prognosis and treatment response (see Chapter 7). In addition, subjective experience has to be taken into account as a separate factor as will be discussed in Chapter 5.

The following case example shows that people can receive multiple diagnoses and subsequent medication that may not be indicated.

> **CASE EXAMPLE: LOWELL**
>
> Lowell came for intake to our Department when he was 22. He had not been to school for two years. His parents were very worried because he was mainly sitting in his room with his curtains closed, playing games. He went to bed around 3 am and woke up at about 1 pm. He quit his study management because he felt depressed and tired and he wanted to take some time off to see if he could find himself again. When he was 15, he was failing his classes because he could not focus or plan, and he was restless. Consequently, he was diagnosed with ADHD and took Ritalin for 5 years. Two years ago, he received the diagnosis with major depressive disorder. Lowell became more and more depressed, because he could not keep up with his peers. The treating psychiatrist prescribed him antidepressants, but the pills did not improve his mood. Lowell told us that he thought he had a gift. He could predict events that he saw in his dreams. He could help other people with this gift. He might even play a leading role in the world if he could develop his gift further. He also heard a voice that told him that he could save the world. It turned out that he had been suffering from psychosis for more than a year.

Following the ADHD checklist in the DSM, the clinician concluded that Lowell suffered from ADHD when he was 15 years and he prescribed Ritalin. However, Lowell's problems with attention and planning were precursor signs of a first psychosis. Research shows that months to years before a first psychosis, subjects often suffer from cognitive deficits that can lead to a decline in psychosocial functioning (Fusar-Poli et al., 2012).

Professionals in mental health care generally do their best to help people. However, they are forced to work with an invalid classification system, and the pharmaceutical industry has spent a lot of money to market their products in psychiatry. Many professionals and non-professionals notice the problems with the DSM and the current overmedication (especially in the USA) of adults and children, but unfortunately this has not yet led to a widespread change. In the next chapter, the roots the problems in contemporary psychiatry are discussed.

References

Abramowicz, M.J., Van Haecke, P., Demedts, M. and Delcroix, M. (2003). Primary pulmonary hypertension after amfepramone (diethylpropion) with BMPR2 mutation. *European Respiratory Journal* 22(3), 560–562.

Ashton, H., Gallagher, P. and Moore, B. (2006). The adult psychiatrist's dilemma: psychostimulant use in attention deficit/hyperactivity disorder. *Journal of Psychopharmacology* 20(5), 602–610.

Auriel, E., Hausdorff, J.M. and Giladi, N. (2009). Methylphenidate for the treatment of Parkinson disease and other neurological disorders. *Clinical Neuropharmacology* 32(2), 75–81.

Bennett, G.M., Baird, A.A., Miller, M.B. and Wolford, G.L. (2010). Neural correlates of interspecies perspective taking in the post-mortem Atlantic Salmon: An argument for multiple comparisons correction. *Journal of Serendipitous and Unexpected Results*. Viewed on 24 October 2015 at https://labs.psych.ucsb.edu/miller/michael/PDF/Bennett-JSUR-2010.pdf

Borsboom, D. and Cramer, A.O. (2013). Network analysis: an integrative approach to the structure of psychopathology. *Annual Review of Clinical Psychology* 9, 91–121.

Bouayed, J., Rammal, H. and Soulimani, R. (2009). Oxidative stress and anxiety: relationship and cellular pathways. *Oxidative Medicine and Cellular Longevity* 2(2), 63–67.

Breggin, P. (1998). *Talking back to Ritalin: What doctors aren't telling you about stimulants for children*. Monroe, ME Common Courage Press.

Chakraborty, K. and Grover, S. (2011). Methylphenidate-induced mania-like symptoms. *Indian Journal of Pharmacology* 43(1), 80.

Chmura Kraemer H., Noda A., and O'Hara R. (2004). Categorical versus dimensional approaches to diagnosis: methodological challenges. *Journal of Psychiatric Research*. 38, 17–25.

Dafny, N. and Yang, P.B. (2006). The role of age, genotype, sex, and route of acute and chronic administration of methylphenidate: a review of its locomotor effects. *Brain Research Bulletin* 68(6), 393–405.

Dalal, P.K. and Sivakumar, T. (2009). Moving towards ICD-11 and DSM-V: Concept and evolution of psychiatric classification. *Indian Journal of Psychiatry* 51(4), 310–319.

Dalsgaard, S., Nielsen, H.S., and Simonsen, M. (2013). Five-fold increase in national prevalence rates of attention-deficit/hyperactivity disorder medications for children and adolescents with autism spectrum disorder, attention-deficit/hyperactivity disorder, and other psychiatric disorders: a Danish register-based study. *Journal of Child Adolescent Psychopharmacology* 23(7), 432–9.

Dean, O., Giorlando, F. and Berk, M. (2011). N-acetylcysteine in psychiatry: current therapeutic evidence and potential mechanisms of action. *Journal of Psychiatry & Neuroscience* 36(2), 78–86.

Dehue, T. (2014). *Betere mensen (Better Humans)*. Amsterdam: Uitgeverij Atlas Contact.

Frances, A. (2013). The new crisis of confidence in psychiatric diagnosis. *Annals of Internal Medicine* 159(3), 221–222.

Fusar-Poli, P., Deste, G., Smieskova, R., Barlati, S., Yung, A.R., Howes, O., Stieglitz, R.D., Vita, A., McGuire, P. and Borgwardt S (2012). Cognitive functioning in prodromal psychosis: a meta-analysis. *Archives of General Psychiatry* 69(6), 562–71.

Garland, E.J. (1998). Reviews: Pharmacotherapy of adolescent attention deficit hyperactivity disorder: challenges, choices and caveats. *Journal of Psychopharmacology* 12(4), 385–395.

Grob, G.N. (1991). Origins of DSM-I: A study in appearance and reality. *American Journal of Psychiatry* 148(4), 421–431.

Helzer, J.E., Kraemer, H.C. and Krueger, R.F. (2006). The feasibility and need for dimensional psychiatric diagnoses. *Psychological Medicine* 36(12), 1671–1680.

Hickie, I.B., Scott, J., Hermens, D.F., Scott, E.M., Naismith, S.L., Guastella, A.J., Glozier, N. and McGorry, P.D. (2013). Clinical classification in mental health at the cross-roads: which direction next? *BMC Medicine* 11, 125–138.

Hyman, S.E. (2010). The diagnosis of mental disorders: the problem of reification. *Annual Review of Clinical Psychology* 6, 155–179.

Jacobs, R. and the Youth Affairs Network of Queensland (2005). *Being an Educated Consumer of 'ADHD' Research*, Viewed on November 8, 2015 at http://www.atca.com.au/wp-content/uploads/2012/09/Bob-Jacobs-being-an-educated-consumer-of-ADHD-research.pdf

Karanges, E.A., Stephenson, C.P. and McGregor, I.S. (2014). Longitudinal trends in the dispensing of psychotropic medications in Australia from 2009–2012: Focus on children, adolescents and prescriber specialty. *Australian and New Zealand Journal of Psychiatry* 48(10), 917–931.

Karsten, J., Hartman, C.A., Ormel, J., Nolen, W.A. and Penninx, B.W.J.H. (2010). Subthreshold depression based on functional impairment better defined by symptom severity than by number of DSM-IV symptoms. *Journal of Affective Disorders* 123(1), 230–237.

Kelleher, I., Keeley, H., Corcoran, P., Lynch, F., Fitzpatrick, C., Devlin, N., Molloy, C., Roddy, S., Clarke, M.C., Harley, M., Arseneault, L., Wasserman, C., Carli, V., Sarchiapone, M., Hoven, C., Wasserman, D. and Cannon, M. (2012). Clinicopathological significance of psychotic experiences in non-psychotic young people: evidence from four population-based studies. *The British Journal of Psychiatry* 201(1), 26–32.

Kessler, R.C., Ormel, J., Petukhova, M., McLaughlin, K.A., Green, J.G., Russo, L.J., Stein, D.J., Zaslavsky, A.M., Aguilar-Gaxiola, S., Alonso, J., Andrade, L., Benjet, C., de Girolamo, G., de Graaf, R., Demyttenaere, K., Fayyad, J., Haro, J.M., Hu, C., Karam, A., Lee, S., Lepine, J.P., Matchsinger, H., Mihaescu-Pintia, C., Posada-Villa, J., Sagar, R. and Üstün, T.B. (2011). Development of lifetime comorbidity in the World Health Organization world mental health surveys. *Archives of General Psychiatry* 68(1), 90–100.

Kim-Cohen, J., Caspi, A., Moffitt, T.E., Harrington, H., Milne, B.J. and Poulton, R. (2003). Prior juvenile diagnoses in adults with mental disorder: developmental follow-back of a prospective-longitudinal cohort. *Archives of General Psychiatry* 60(7), 709–717.

Kimko, H.C., Cross, J.T. and Abernethy, D.R. (1999). Pharmacokinetics and clinical effectiveness of methylphenidate. *Clinical Pharmacokinetics* 37(6), 457–470.

Kraemer, M., Uekermann, J., Wiltfang, J. and Kis, B. (2010). Methylphenidate-induced psychosis in adult attention-deficit/hyperactivity disorder: report of 3 new cases and review of the literature. *Clinical Neuropharmacology* 33(4), 204–206.

Kuloglu, M., Atmaca, M., Tezcan, E., Ustundag, B. and Bulut, S. (2002). Antioxidant enzyme and malondialdehyde levels in patients with panic disorder. *Neuropsychobiology* 46(4), 186–189.

Lahey, B.B., Zald, D.H., Hakes, J.K., Krueger, R.F. and Rathouz, P.J. (2014). Patterns of heterotypic continuity associated with the cross-sectional correlational structure of prevalent mental disorders in adults. *JAMA Psychiatry* 71(9), 989–996.

Lichtenstein, P., Yip, B.H., Björk, C., Pawitan, Y., Cannon, T.D., Sullivan, P.F. and Hultman, C.M. (2009). Common genetic determinants of schizophrenia and bipolar disorder in Swedish families: a population-based study. *The Lancet* 373(9659), 234–239.

McGorry, P.D. (2010). Risk syndromes, clinical staging and DSM V: New diagnostic infrastructure for early intervention in psychiatry. *Schizophrenia Research* 120, 49–53

Maj, M. (2005). 'Psychiatric comorbidity': an artefact of current diagnostic systems? *The British Journal of Psychiatry* 186(3), 182–184.

Merikangas, K.R., Cui, L., Kattan, G., Carlson, G.A., Youngstrom, E.A. and Angst, J. (2012). Mania with and without depression in a community sample of US adolescents. *Archives of general psychiatry* 69(9), 943–951.

Morrow, R.L., Garland, E.J., Wright, J.M., Maclure, M., Taylor, S. and Dormuth, C.R. (2012). Influence of relative age on diagnosis and treatment of attention-deficit/hyperactivity disorder in children. *Canadian Medical Association Journal* 184(7), 755–762.

Morton, W.A. and Stockton, G.G. (2000). Methylphenidate abuse and psychiatric side effects. *Primary Care Companion to the Journal of Clinical Psychiatry* 2(5), 159–164.

Nieman, D.H. and McGorry, P.D. (2015). Detection and treatment of At Risk Mental State for developing a first psychosis: Making up the balance. *The Lancet Psychiatry* 2, 825–34.

Nolan, E.E., Gadow, K.D. and Sprafkin, J. (1999). Stimulant medication withdrawal during long-term therapy in children with comorbid attention-deficit hyperactivity disorder and chronic multiple tic disorder. *Pediatrics* 103(4), 730–737.

Roca, M., Gili, M., Garcia-Garcia, M., Salva, J., Vives, M., Campayo, J.G. and Comas, A. (2009). Prevalence and comorbidity of common mental disorders in primary care. *Journal of Affective Disorders* 119(1), 52–58.

Rosenfeld, A.A. (1979). Depression and psychotic regression following prolonged methylphenidate use and withdrawal: case report. *The American Journal of Psychiatry* 136(2), 226–228.

Schwartz, A. (May 16, 2014). Thousands of toddlers are medicated for A.D.H.D. report finds, raising worries. *New York Times*. Accessed October 21, 2015: http://www.nytimes.com/2014/05/17/us/among-experts-scrutiny-of-attention-disorder-diagnoses-in-2-and-3-year-olds.html?_r=0

Schwartz, R.H. and Rushton, H.G. (2004). Stuttering priapism associated with withdrawal from sustained-release methylphenidate. *The Journal of Pediatrics* 144(5), 675–676.

Shankman, S.A., Lewinsohn, P.M., Klein, D.N., Small, J.W., Seeley, J.R. and Altman, S.E. (2009). Subthreshold conditions as precursors for full syndrome disorders: a 15-year longitudinal study of multiple diagnostic classes. *Journal of Child Psychology and Psychiatry* 50(12), 1485–1494.

Sheehan, D.V., Lecrubier, Y., Sheehan, K.H., Amorim, P., Janavs, J., Weiller, E., Hergueta, T., Baker, R. and Dunbar, G.C. (1998). The Mini-International Neuropsychiatric Interview (MINI): the development and validation of a structured diagnostic psychiatric interview for DSM-IV and ICD-10. *Journal of Clinical Psychiatry* 59(20), 22–33.

Spenseley, J. and Rockwell, D.A. (1972). Psychosis during methylphenidate abuse. *New England Journal of Medicine* 286(16), 880–881.

Stein, D.J., Lund, C. and Nesse, R.M. (2013). Classification systems in psychiatry: diagnosis and global mental health in the era of DSM-5 and ICD-11. *Current Opinion in Psychiatry* 26(5), 493–7.

Sullivan, P.F., Daly, M.J. and O'Donovan, M. (2012). Genetic architectures of psychiatric disorders: the emerging picture and its implications. *Nature Reviews Genetics* 13(8), 537–551.

Sutcliffe, J.P. (1993). Concept, class, and category in the tradition of Aristotle. In: van Mechelen, I., Hampton, J., Michalski, R.S. and Theuns, P. (eds.). *Categories and Concepts: Theoretical Views and Inductive Data Analysis*. London: Academic Press.

Sutcliffe, J.P. (1994). On the logical necessity and priority of a monothetic conception of class, and on the consequent inadequacy of polythetic accounts of category and categorization. In: Diday, E., Lechevallier, Y., Schrader, M., Bertrand, P. and Burtchy, B. (eds.). *New Approaches in Classification and Data Analysis*. Berlin: Springer.

Sutcliffe, J.P. (1996). An Enquiry into Current Understandings of the Notion 'Classification' with Implications for future Directions of Research. *Classification Society of North America Newsletter*: Issue 44, Viewed on November 8, 2015 at: http://www.pitt.edu/~csna/news/csna.news44.html

van Beveren, N.J. and Hoogendijk, W.J. (2011). Clinical utility of serum biomarkers for major Psychiatric disorders. *International Review of Neurobiology* 101, 351–374.

Weinberger, D.R., and Radulescu, E. (2016). Finding the elusive psychiatric 'lesion' with 21st century neuroanatomy: a note of caution. *American Journal of Psychiatry* 173(1), 27–33.

Whiteley, M. (2014). ADHD: How a lie medicated often enough became the truth. In: Speed, E., Moncrieff, J. and Rapley, M (eds.). *De-Medicalizing Misery II: Society, Politics and the Mental Health Industry*. Basingstoke: Palgrave Macmillan.

2

SCIENTIFIC RESEARCH AND ITS OMISSIONS

The way in which research is currently organized limits the possibility to connect knowledge from different disciplines, even though such interdisciplinary connections may play an important role in stimulating progress in psychiatry. To receive a grant, a scientist must publish many papers, preferably in journals with a high impact factor, which implies that it is read by many scientists, and that the paper has an increased chance of being cited. However, the impact factor seems to express status and impact on other researchers, rather than on solving the problems in the field of psychiatry. 'Publish or perish' is a phrase used to describe the pressure in academia to publish academic work rapidly and continuously to sustain or further one's career (Fanelli, 2010; Neill, 2008). Publishing may have become more important than actually solving the problem. Articles that deviate from the current biomedical paradigm are difficult to get published in high impact journals. Valuable scientific research should lead eventually to a reduction in the prevalence and incidence of a disorder. However, neither the prevalence nor the incidence of psychiatric disorders has declined. They have even increased.

Increase in mental illness and psychotropic medication use in the past decennia

In 1955 in the USA, 355,000 adults spent time in state and county mental hospitals because of a psychiatric diagnosis. Between 1955 and 1985, the number of disabled mentally ill rose to 1.25 million. During the subsequent 20 years, the number of disabled mentally ill grew to more than four million adults in 2007. In contrast, for e.g. cardiovascular diseases, mortality has improved drastically from 600 per 100,000 in the Netherlands in 1950 to 190 per 100,000 in 2012 (CBS, 2015). In addition, the prescribing of psychiatric medications to children and adolescents took off between 1987 and 2007 and, as this medical practice took hold, the number of youths in America receiving a government disability check because of a mental illness leapt from 16,200 in 1987 to 561,569 in 2007 (a 35-fold increase). In contrast, between 1987 and 2007 childhood disability rates for all non-psychiatric problems (e.g. Down's syndrome, cancer) declined, suggesting that the USA is making progress with all health conditions except for mental disorders (Whitaker, 2010).

In the USA, more than one in five adults take psychotropic medication (Medco Health Solutions, 2011), which approximates the 12-month prevalence of all mental disorders (Kessler et al., 2005). Most people with a psychiatric diagnosis do not receive adequate treatment, whereas approximately half of the psychotropic medication prescriptions are written for individuals without a psychiatric diagnosis (Kessler et al., 2005).

Antidepressants are a class of drugs most frequently used by adults between the ages of 18 and 44 (Pratt et al., 2011). Antipsychotic medications, traditionally reserved for treating psychotic symptoms experienced by less than 5 per cent of the population (Perälä et al., 2007), have become the fifth highest revenue-generating class of medications with total 2011 sales of $18.2 billion (Deacon, 2013). Particularly among young people, the use of antidepressant, stimulant, mood stabilizing, and antipsychotic medications has increased steeply in recent years (Olfson et al., 2006; Moreno et al., 2007; Medco Health Solutions, 2011). Current psychiatric treatment is characterized by off-label polypharmacy. The majority of patients with psychiatric symptoms take at least two psychotropic medications, and nearly a third receive three or more (Deacon, 2013; Mojtabai and Olfson, 2010). These numbers show that in the USA, the public embraces the biomedical model of psychiatric disorders. Psychiatric disorders are regarded by the majority as neurobiological illnesses – caused by a chemical imbalance in the brain – that requires medication prescription from a psychiatrist or other physician (Pescosolido et al., 2010). However, in many mental health care centres, notably in Europe and Australia, psychosocial interventions play an important role, in addition to medication prescription.

Outcome psychiatric disorders

One could argue that psychiatric disorders have been recognized better in the past decades and that, because of this, the number of diagnoses and subsequent medication prescription has increased. The same may be true for hereditary metabolic disorders. However, hereditary metabolic disorders are assessed by means of an objective biological test, whereas the presence of psychiatric disorders is not (see Chapter 1). Screening for genetic metabolic diseases at birth with the heel prick leads to improved prognosis for patients with some of these metabolic disorders. For example, new-borns with phenylketonuria (PKU) can be treated with a diet, and mental retardation can thus be avoided. PKU is an inborn error of metabolism, involving impaired metabolism of phenylalanine, one of the amino acids. Protein-rich foods or the sweetener aspartame can act as poisons for people with PKU. Untreated PKU can lead to intellectual disability, seizures and other serious medical problems (Filiano, 2006). Before the etiology of PKU became well understood, PKU caused severe disability in most people who inherited the relevant mutations. Many untreated PKU patients, born before widespread new-born screening with the heel prick, are still alive, mainly in dependent living homes/institutions (National Institutes of Health Consensus Development Panel, 2001). Nowadays the prognosis for PKU patients is good; they can live relatively normal lives, because their condition is recognized early in life (due to the heel prick) and they can follow a specific diet.

If the situation in psychiatry was similar to that in internal medicine, then one would expect some progress, less disability caused by psychiatric disorders and a better prognosis. Unfortunately, the opposite is true. Assuming psychotropic medications are safe and effective, why has the rate of mental health disability risen in close temporal association with their increased use? Surely the widespread use of safe and effective psychotropic medications should lead to less severe, chronic and disabling mental disorders, instead of the opposite (Deacon, 2013).

To illustrate this, the prognosis for schizophrenia has not changed substantially since the introduction of antipsychotic medication over 50 years ago and some argue that the prognosis has not shown meaningful improvement since the illness was first described (Kahn and Keefe, 2013; Insel, 2010). Although the first-line treatment of schizophrenia (antipsychotic medication) can suppress delusions and hallucinations, patients still suffer from other schizophrenia (e.g. cognitive) symptoms. They often report adverse side-effects of their medication, including apathy, serious weight gain, restlessness, etcetera. The largest study performed to date showed that 74 per cent of the patients discontinue their medication within 18 months (Lieberman et al., 2005). The rates of medication non-compliance in schizophrenia patients are as high as 40–50 per cent (Lacro et al., 2002).

Schizophrenia outcomes have been compared twice by the World Health Organization between rich (e.g. the USA) and poor countries (e.g. India, Nigeria and Colombia). In both studies, in the poor countries, where psychotropic drug usage was much less, schizophrenia patients had a better outcome at 2 and 5 year follow up (Jablensky et al., 1992; Leff, et al., 1992).

However, it may be easier to have a good outcome in India, Nigeria and Columbia where individuals probably have less difficulty with upholding themselves in society than in the western world. Nevertheless, in the Netherlands, Wunderink et al. (2013) reported that dose reduction or discontinuation of antipsychotics during the early stages of remitted first episode psychosis is associated with superior long-term (7 years) recovery rates (40.4 per cent) compared with the rates achieved with antipsychotic maintenance treatment (17.6 per cent).

Psychiatric medications for mood disorders are also associated with poor long-term outcomes as well. For example, in the USA, the Sequenced Treatment Alternatives to Relieve Depression (STAR*D) study enrolled 4,041 outpatients with non-psychotic depression at 23 psychiatric and 18 primary care sites

(Insel, 2006). All patients began with a 12-week course of the antidepressant serotonin reuptake inhibitor (SSRI) citalopram and, in case of non-response, were allowed to switch from one medication to another up to three times (Rush et al., 2006). The results of this study show that the vast majority of depressed patients did not experience long-term remission with the newer-generation antidepressants (Rush et al., 2006). At the 12 month follow up, only three per cent of the patients who benefited initially from the antidepressant medication maintained their improvement (Pigott, 2011).

Mental disorders are now among the leading causes of disability in the world, and have increased in severity and chronicity (WHO, 2011). Major depression is becoming increasingly treatment-resistant and chronic (El-Mallakh et al., 2011) whereas it used to be regarded as generally self-correcting and transient with the passage of time (Cole, 1964). The disease burden of depression has markedly worsened (Lepine and Briley, 2011) despite a nearly 400 per cent increase in the use of antidepressant medication since 1988 (Pratt et al., 2011). The alarming possibility exists that antidepressants deteriorate the long-term course of the disorder they are intended to remedy (Deacon, 2013; Fava, 2003; Fava and Offidani, 2010).

Similar concerns have been raised with other classes of psychiatric medications (Whitaker, 2010). For example benzodiazepines (anti-anxiety drugs such as temazepam, diazepam, oxazepam) are effective in the short term, although they can have cognitive side-effects and can lead to disinhibition. Taking the medication longer than 2–4 weeks causes dependence in most people. The body needs more of the drugs to have the same effect and it is difficult to stop taking them because of withdrawal effects such as increased tension and anxiety, sweating, confusion, cognitive problems, muscular pain and stiffness, rebound insomnia, and sometimes even hallucinations, psychosis, seizures and suicide. Although the problems with long-term use are known, many subjects were and are prescribed benzodiazepines or benzodiazepine-like drugs (like the sleep medication zoplicone) for years and they struggle with severe side- and withdrawal effects, as shown in recent studies (e.g. Kapil et al., 2014) and discussed on internet forums.

How do these drugs affect the brain? Psychotropic drugs such as antipsychotics, antidepressants and anti-anxiety drugs create perturbations in neurotransmitter functions. In response, the brain goes through a series of compensatory adaptations. For instance, Prozac and other SSRI antidepressants block the reuptake of the neurotransmitters serotonin (and also influence other neurotransmitter systems). As a consequence the brain tones down its whole serotonergic system. Neurons both release less serotonin and down-regulate (or decrease) their number of serotonin receptors. The density of serotonin receptors in the brain may decrease by 50 per cent or more. As part of this adaptation process, there are also changes in gene expression and intracellular signalling pathways. After a few weeks, the patient's brain is functioning in a manner that is both quantitatively and qualitatively different from the normal state (Hyman and

Nestler, 1996). Thus psychotropic drugs may perturb a neurotransmitter system, and the brain undergoes a series of compensatory adaptations. As a result of these changes, the person becomes vulnerable to relapse upon drug withdrawal. That difficulty may, in turn, lead some to take the drugs indefinitely. These patients are likely to become more anxious, more depressed and cognitively impaired.

For a percentage of the patients, antidepressants are helpful but the steep increase in antidepressant medication prescription to a wide range of patients suggests that problems associated with antidepressant use, as summed up in the next paragraphs, are not widely known:

1. SSRIs have been shown to have minimal or non-existent benefit in patients with mild or moderate depression (Fournier et al., 2010; Gøtzsche, 2013, 2014).
2. With respect to the harms of antidepressants, most patients who take these drugs will experience side-effects. The most commonly reported side-effect is sexual dysfunction. In a study (Montejo et al., 2001) designed to assess this side-effect, sexual problems developed in 604 (59 per cent) of 1,022 patients who all reported no problems with sexual function before they started using an antidepressant.
3. The withdrawal effects are very worrying. Even when tapering off them slowly, half the patients have difficulty stopping the drugs because of withdrawal effects, which can be severe (Fava et al., 2007) and long-lasting (Gøtzsche, 2013). Withdrawal symptoms were similar for benzodiazepines and SSRIs for 37 of 42 identified symptoms (Nielsen et al., 2012). However, they were not described as dependence for SSRIs (Nielsen et al., 2012).
4. Some argue that antidepressants protect against suicide. Good observational studies have refuted it (Zahl et al., 2010), and results from randomized trials (Fergusson et al., 2005) have shown that antidepressants are associated with increased risk of suicide attempts (5.6 more suicide attempts per 1,000 patient-years of SSRI exposure compared with placebo). Antidepressants have not only been associated with suicide but also with homicide (Gøtzsche, 2013, 2014; Healy, 2006; Lucire and Crotty, 2001; Moore et al., 2010).
5. SSRIs are particularly harmful for elderly patients. Results from a carefully controlled cohort study (Martin et al., 2004) of people older than 65 years of age with depression showed that SSRIs led to falls more often than did older antidepressants or if the depression was left untreated. For every 28 elderly people treated for 1 year with an SSRI, there was one additional death, compared with no treatment (Coupland et al., 2011)
6. SSRIs have also stimulant effects and might precipitate conversion to bipolar disorder in about 10 per cent of children aged 10–14 years under the care of mental health services (Martin et al., 2004).
7. Le Noury et al. (2015) re-analysed the data of Study 329 (published by Keller and colleagues in 2001) sponsored by the pharmaceutical company SmithKline Beecham. The primary objective of Study 329 was to compare the efficacy and safety of the antidepressants paroxetine and imipramine with placebo in

the treatment of 275 adolescents with major depression. Keller et al. (2001) reported that paroxitine and imipramine are effective in this group. Their paper is influential in the literature supporting the use of antidepressants in adolescents. However, the results of the re-analysis of Le Noury et al. (2015) reveal that neither paroxetine nor high dose imipramine was more efficacious than a placebo for major depression in adolescents, and there was even an increase in harms with both antidepressant drugs. Serious adverse events (defined as an event that 'resulted in hospitalization, was associated with suicidal gestures, or was described by the treating physician as serious') were reported in 11 patients in the paroxetine group (of 93 subjects), five in the imipramine group (n=95), and two in the placebo group (n=87). In clinical practice, psychiatrists also reported that children and adolescents on paroxetine showed increased suicidality. In 2003 all data (also of studies that were not published) were re-analysed and the pharmaceutical company was sued and had to pay 2.5 million dollars compensation because the company had promoted the drug under false pretences. But professionals kept on prescribing these antidepressants to adolescents. For example in the Netherlands, 4 per cent of the depressed children below 18 and 14 per cent of those between 18–24 years still receive paroxetine (*Volkskrant*, October 17, 2015).

There has been heavy marketing and widespread crime committed by drug companies, including fraud and illegal promotion. In the USA, psychiatrists receive more money from the drug industry than any other specialty (Insel, 2010). Enough antidepressants are prescribed every year in Denmark to provide treatment for every person in the country for 6 years of their lives (Gøtzsche, 2013). This situation is not sound, and it also shows that many patients cannot stop these drugs because of intolerable withdrawal symptoms. They should be used sparingly, and always with a clear plan for tapering off them.

Belaise et al. (2012) analysed online self-reported SSRI withdrawal effects. According to the reports, persistent post withdrawal disorders (WD) were often sufficiently severe and disabling to have patients returned to previous drug treatment. When their drug treatment is not restarted, post withdrawal disorders may last several months to years. An example of a report on an internet forum about antidepressant use:

> I was given Seroxat … . I took my last pill, after 5 years use, in September 2004. Since then my life has never been the same, even now 6 years later, I suffer debilitating symptoms daily, I have never had a full day without some symptom of WD. Ongoing problems that were not present prior to taking this drug are: anxiety, panic, depression, headaches, sinus problems, recurring infections, fatigue, heartbeat irregularities … . The list is endless … after 6 years of pure hell and loss of social life, work life and family life that this drug has taken from me, I really just want my life back now … . I'm not kidding myself, I really don't think I will ever be what I once was … .

Many similar stories can be found on this internet forum. There is concordance between SSRI withdrawal symptomatology described in some scientific papers and those reported online by patients (Belaise et al., 2012). However, the withdrawal effects have not changed SSRI prescription policy as can be seen in the rising percentage of people who use the drug. Throughout its history, psychiatry has been slow to admit the negative effects of its drugs, as is well documented in the case of antipsychotic drugs and tardive dyskinesia. With respect to antidepressants, severe adverse reactions are labelled as unexplained medical symptoms and withdrawal-support charities report alarming numbers of people suffering disabling symptoms for multiple years following withdrawal from antidepressants. This issue needs to be properly researched. The future of more humane care depends on our willingness to engage with such uncomfortable realities (Timimi et al., 2014). In addition, patients need to receive all information before starting with the drugs to make an informed decision. The case example of Agnes shows how it is possible that people are prescribed antidepressants and take them for many years with invalidating long-term consequences.

CASE EXAMPLE: AGNES

Agnes was 16 when her GP prescribed her a SSRI because she showed symptoms of obsessive compulsive disorder. She was told that her brain lacked a substance that was supplied by the SSRI. She needed the medication to be balanced, like a diabetic needed insulin. She took the medication for more than 25 years. It was no problem to get a repeat-prescription every once a while. The doctor and she never brought up the topic of stopping. However, the past few years she experienced severe medical problems. One day she woke up and half of her face was paralysed, she sometimes slept for 30 hours, she needed surgery for several problems, she had excruciating tingling sensations throughout her body, her MRI showed an unexplained lesion. The doctors could not find a cause. The last doctor she spoke to told her that the SSRI's she took for so long may be related to her physical symptoms. The medication was slowly tapered off, but she suffered amongst other things from extreme anxiety, rage outbursts, depression and sleeplessness. It was almost unbearable. When she started with the SSRI, she had no idea what she had got herself into. The withdrawal effects lasted for five years while her unexplained medical problems slowly dissolved.

The Dutch poet Rogi Wieg said in a TV interview broadcasted on July 20, 2015 that he used 13/14 different pills: antidepressants, benzodiazepines, morphine, etcetera. Of some pills he took 4 or 5. He requested euthanasia because his life had become unbearable. He could not sleep anymore because he experienced an intense, continuous whizzing or buzzing all through his body. His neurologist told him that his neurotransmitter balance was totally disturbed and that he should stop all medication so he could assess whether the medication was the cause of his symptoms but Rogi said that that was impossible because he could not bear the withdrawal and rebound effects. He started with psychotropic medication when he was 18 and used it for 32 years.

Psychiatric treatments need considerable improvements, including the treatment of psychotic disorders as is shown convincingly by the Schizophrenia Commission in the UK. 'The Abandoned Illness' is a report of the Schizophrenia Commission about mental health care for subjects with psychosis in England (The Schizophrenia Commission, 2012). The independent Commission consisted of 14 experts, who reviewed how outcomes for people with schizophrenia and psychosis can be improved. The Commission spoke with people who have lived with schizophrenia or psychosis, family members and carers, health and social care practitioners and researchers. 2,500 people responded to an online survey, and the Commissioners drew on relevant literature and visited services across England. Their conclusion was that the care for people with psychosis is poor. They find particularly unacceptable that:

- People with severe mental illness such as schizophrenia still die 15–20 years earlier than other citizens.
- Schizophrenia and psychosis cost society £11.8 billion a year, but this could be less if investments in prevention and effective care were made.
- Increasing numbers of people are having compulsory treatment, in part because of the state of many acute care wards. Levels of coercion have increased year on year, and were up by 5 per cent in the last year studied.
- Too much is spent on secure care – £1.2 billion or 19 per cent of the mental health budget last year studied – with many people staying too long in expensive units when they are well enough to start back on the route to the community.
- Only 1 in 10 of those who could benefit get access to Cognitive Behavioural Therapy despite it being recommended by NICE (National Institute of Health and Care Excellence).
- Only 8 per cent of people with schizophrenia are in employment, yet many more could and would like to work.
- Only 14 per cent of people receiving social care services for a primary mental health need are receiving self-directed support (money to commission their own support to meet identified needs) compared with 43 per cent for all people receiving social care services.
- Families who are carers save the public purse £1.24 billion per year, but are not receiving support, and are not treated as partners.
- Service users and family members dare not speak about the condition. 87 per cent of service users report experiences of stigma and discrimination.
- Services for people from African-Caribbean and African backgrounds do not meet their needs well. In 2010 men from these communities spent twice as long in hospital as the average.

Furthermore, the Commission states that we are failing many people who go on to receive a diagnosis of schizophrenia, because not enough is done early on to prevent its development. In addition, the Commission reported that too many doctors believe that people with a psychotic illness, especially if diagnosed with schizophrenia, must be on antipsychotics for life. But in many patients antipsychotic medication could be tapered off after a certain period of stability. Antipsychotic and other psychotropic medication plays a major role in the reduced life expectancy of patients with severe mental illness because of side-effects.

However, many patients need antipsychotic medication, and I am certainly not arguing that psychotropic medication should be avoided. Antipsychotic medication is an important component in the treatment of psychotic symptoms. But the steep increase in medication prescription in the USA shows that psychotropic medication is regarded by many healthcare professionals these days as the main treatment for psychiatric disorders and other conditions, while side-effects, long-term consequences and patient perspectives on medication are secondary. If psychotropic medication is necessary because more benign treatments are ineffective, it should be prescribed in the lowest dose and for the shortest period of time as clinically justifiable, and preferably combined with psychotherapy and other psychosocial treatments.

Stigma

The stigma associated with mental illness is often described by people diagnosed with a psychiatric disorder as more disturbing than the illness itself (Kirby and Keon, 2006). Stigma involves the stereotyping of those with mental illness as having undesirable characteristics or being different. The stigma is associated with discrimination and loss of social status (Link and Phelan, 2006). The biomedical reductionist paradigm was supposed to have a destigmatizing effect on psychiatry, i.e. a psychiatric disorder is a medical condition just like a broken leg, the subject him/herself is not to blame. The disorder is not a consequence of bad character or slackness. However, studies show that the opposite is true: when psychiatric disorders are regarded as more biological, intolerance and need for social distance increases (Read and Law, 1999; Read and Harre, 2001; Angermeyer and Matschinger, 2005; Walker and Read, 2002; Schnittker, 2008).

Various anti-stigma initiatives, such as the National Alliance on Mental Illness in the USA, have advocated for an understanding of mental illness as a biological process: 'a disease like any other' (Pescosolido et al., 2010).

However, although the public has adopted a more biological conception of mental illness as brain disorders in 2006 as compared to 1996, these changes in attitude were not associated with reduced stigma but, rather, with the opposite (Pescosolido et al., 2010). An investigation in Germany came to similar conclusions, finding an increase in the desire for social distance from people with schizophrenia in 2001 as compared to 1990, coincident with increasing public acceptance of the biological causes of mental illness (Angermeyer et al., 2005).

So why aren't mental illnesses diseases like any other? Results show that while the public may assign less blame to individuals for their biologically-determined mental illness (Angermeyer et al., 2005), the idea that their actions may be beyond their conscious control creates fear of their unpredictability, and thus the perception that those with mental illnesses are dangerous (Read and Law, 1999; Read and Harre, 2001; Walker and Read, 2002; Schnittker, 2008; Jorm and Griffiths, 2008) thereby leading to avoidance (Angermeyer et al., 2005; Schnittker, 2008; Lauber et al., 2004; Dietrich et al., 2004; Rüsch et al., 2010). Biological explanations can also lead to an 'us vs. them' attitude, defining individuals with mental illness as being fundamentally different (Phelan, 2002). For example, a 2008 Canadian survey (Canadian Medical Association, 2008) found that:

- 55 per cent wouldn't marry someone who suffered from mental illness;
- 50 per cent would not tell friends or co-workers that a family member was suffering from mental illness;
- 42 per cent would no longer socialize with a friend diagnosed with mental illness;
- 25 per cent were afraid of being around someone who suffers from mental illness.

Similarly, when conceptualized as biological diseases, mental illnesses are seen as less responsive to treatment and more persistent and serious (Phelan, 2005), suggesting that patients with mental illness will never recover, which contributes to stigma (Lam and Salkovskis, 2007).

The current paradigm in psychiatry

Psychiatry is part of the medical sciences. Mental disorders, e.g. schizophrenia, major depressive disorder, ADHD are considered to be brain disorders and thus medical conditions comparable to a broken leg or a heart attack. The biomedical model in psychiatry emphasizes pharmacological treatment to target presumed biological abnormalities. Mental disorders are investigated with similar scientific methods as in other medical sciences. However, an important difference with most other medical sciences is that a classification system has been used in research in the past decennia that is based on expert consensus and not on biological alterations (see Chapter 1). After decades of research, it is not possible to use any biomedical apparatus or method, e.g. magnetic resonance imaging, electroencephalogram, blood markers, etcetera to confirm or refute a DSM diagnosis. The diagnostic categories as defined by the DSM are not valid biological disease entities, but that does not mean that, e.g. psychosis, attention deficit and hyperactivity do not exist as psychiatric conditions.

A second major difference with other medical disciplines is that the main objects of study are aberrant thoughts and emotions which are by nature subjective and impossible to 'catch' with biomedical equipment (see Chapter 5). Perhaps the biomedical paradigm in psychiatry has also hampered progress.

What is a paradigm?

The historian of science Thomas Kuhn (1962) defined a paradigm as the set of practices that define a scientific discipline at any particular period of time. It defines what is to be studied, what kind of questions are to be asked, how an experiment is conducted, and how the results of scientific investigations should be interpreted. It is a framework of interpretation held firmly by the majority. However if there are increasing anomalies that cannot be solved by the current paradigm, a paradigm shift occurs. For example, for a long period in astronomy the earth was considered to be the centre of the universe. However, accumulating evidence pointed to the direction that this model was not accurate. Of course scientists who have spent their life investigating the first paradigm will oppose a change in paradigm. Nobody likes to admit that their life's work was based on false premonitions. According to Kuhn, during a paradigm shift a battle takes place between the followers of the new paradigm and the hold-outs of the old paradigm.

Hopefully science in psychiatry is on the brink of a paradigm shift (Speed et al., 2014). Considering the limitations of the categorical classification system, the biomedical reductionism as discussed in Chapter 1, and the difficulties associated with the scientific production system as discussed in this chapter, the rising number of subjects disabled by psychiatric disorders and the discontents of psychiatric patients and their clinicians, a change in paradigm is necessary.

The biomedical model holds its merits, of course psychiatric disorders have a cause in the brain, but it has become apparent that psychiatric disorders cannot be reduced to the brain, at least not currently and perhaps never. In the field of psychiatry, understanding mental illness is very complex because the pathogenesis not only involves a still largely elusive biological substrate, but the mind also plays an important role. Although the mind probably finds its origin in the brain, unraveling the relationship between mind and brain is not simple. Even if the biomedical paradigm would lead to insight into the biological substrate of the mind, it is unlikely that we could cure psychiatric disorders based on this knowledge alone. Neuroscience, philosophy and art may be needed to fully understand human emotions, thoughts, behaviour and psychiatric symptoms. For example, in the early stage of a psychiatric disorder many people feel as though they are losing themselves (Nelson et al., 2014; Nelson and Sass, 2008; van de Kraats et al., 2012). However, do we know what the self is, how we can lose or find it and can we reduce such a complex concept to the brain? Philosophers have contemplated this topic for centuries and may help us to define the concept (Gallagher, 2000). Furthermore, many writers, filmmakers and other artists have shown their deep insight into the workings of the human mind. The reductionist biomedical paradigm should be exchanged for a paradigm that allows for the inclusion of several disciplines (neuroscience, philosophy, art) in an attempt to better understand mental health and mental illness.

Scientific output

How is it possible that so many researchers all over the world do research into mental disorders and there is so little progress? In many countries, PhD students have to publish a certain number of articles in scientific journals with an impact factor. Since the contribution to improving treatment for patients is not a factor that is taken into consideration, research questions are chosen for articles that can be answered during the period of a PhD thesis and have a high probability to be publishable. Scientists are forced in the rat-race to produce as many articles as possible.

The industry of scientific research is more and more criticized. For example in the Netherlands a group of scientist have formed 'Science in transition' (Dijstelbloem et al., 2014). This movement makes explicit that universities produce a tsunami of publications because PhD students need publications to receive their PhD. However, the societal use of all these articles is often unclear. In addition, the career perspective of those who obtain their PhD is not very good. Only 30 per cent find a job at a university. Education suffers by the scientific output system because professorships are awarded on the basis of number of publications, not excellence in teaching abilities.

In the leading journal *The Lancet*, several articles were published in January 2014 under the title 'Research: increasing value, reducing waste.' One of the articles by Ioannidis et al. (2014) recommend to reduce waste by rewarding replication of previous research results (most studies are never replicated), public availability of protocols, data-sets, analysis plans, etcetera.

Other outcome parameters than number of publications and impact factors need to be formulated. It should be possible to take into consideration whether research is improving treatment for patients, i.e. if the prevalence, incidence and disability numbers are reduced. The goal of scientific research in psychiatry should be to improve treatment of the patients with psychiatric disorders or the prevention of severe psychiatric disorders, not to publish as many papers as possible in journals with a high impact factor.

In current scientific research in psychiatry, several topics are usually not addressed, but they may be important to comprehend psychiatric disorders. The biomedical paradigm discourages inclusion of these topics in scientific research because they cannot be reduced to a (biochemical) imbalance in the brain. Three of these topics are: the nature of social contact, mystic experiences, and the mind-brain problem. These topics and their importance in psychiatry will be discussed in the next three chapters.

References

Angermeyer, M.C. and Matschinger, H. (2005). The stigma of mental illness in Germany: a trend analysis. *International Journal of Social Psychiatry* 51(3), 276–84.

Angermeyer, M.C., Dietrich, S., Pott, D. and Matschinger, H. (2005). Media consumption and desire for social distance towards people with schizophrenia. *European Psychiatry* 20(3), 246–50.

Belaise, C., Gatti, A., Chouinard, V.A. and Chouinard, G. (2012). Patient online report of selective serotonin reuptake inhibitor-induced persistent postwithdrawal anxiety and mood disorders. *Psychotherapy and Psychosomatics* 81(6), 386–388.

Canadian Medical Association. (2008). *Eighth Annual National Report Card on Health Care.* Ontario: Canadian Mental Health Association.

Centraal Bureau voor de Statistiek (CBS) (2015). The Netherlands. Accessed July 6 2015 at http://statline.cbs.nl/Statweb/

Cole, J.O. (1964). Therapeutic efficacy of antidepressant drugs: a review. *Journal of the American Medical Association* 190(5), 448–455.

Coupland, C., Dhiman, P., Morriss, R., Arthur, A., Barton, G. and Hippisley-Cox, J. (2011). Antidepressant use and risk of adverse outcomes in older people: population based cohort study. *British Medical Journal* 343, d4551.

Deacon, B.J. (2013). The biomedical model of mental disorder: A critical analysis of its validity, utility, and effects on psychotherapy research. *Clinical Psychology Review* 33(7), 846–861.

Dietrich, S., Beck, M., Bujantugs, B., Kenzine, D., Matschinger, H. and Angermeyer, M.C. (2004). The relationship between public causal beliefs and social distance toward mentally ill people. *Australian and New Zealand Journal of Psychiatry* 38(5), 348–354.

Dijstelbloem, H., Huisman, F., Miedema, F. and Mijnhardt, W. (2014). *Science in Transition Status Report: Debate, Progress and Recommendations.* Amsterdam. Accessed November 1, 2015 at http://www.scienceintransition.nl/wp-content/uploads/2014/07/Science-in-Transition-Status-Report-June-2014.pdf

El-Mallakh, R.S., Gao, Y. and Roberts, R.J. (2011). Tardive dysphoria: the role of long term antidepressant use in-inducing chronic depression. *Medical Hypotheses* 76(6), 769–773.

Fanelli, D. (2010). Do pressures to publish increase scientists' bias? An empirical support from US States data. *PLoS One* 5(4), e10271.

Fava, G.A. (2003). Can long-term treatment with antidepressant drugs worsen the course of depression? *The Journal of Clinical Psychiatry* 64, 123–133.

Fava, G.A., Bernardi, M., Tomba, E. and Rafanelli, C. (2007). Effects of gradual discontinuation of selective serotonin reuptake inhibitors in panic disorder with agoraphobia. *The International Journal of Neuropsychopharmacology* 10(6), 835–838.

Fava, G.A. and Offidani, E. (2010). The mechanisms of tolerance in antidepressant action. *Progress in Neuro-Psychopharmacology & Biological Psychiatry* 15, 1593–1602.

Fergusson, D., Doucette, S., Glass, K.C., Shapiro, S., Healy, D., Hebert, P. and Hutton, B. (2005). Association between suicide attempts and selective serotonin reuptake inhibitors: systematic review of randomised controlled trials. *British Medical Journal* 330(7488), 396.

Filiano, J.J. (2006). Neurometabolic diseases in the newborn. *Clinics in Perinatology* 33(2), 411–479.

Fournier, J.C., DeRubeis, R.J., Hollon, S.D., Dimidjian, S., Amsterdam, J.D., Shelton, R.C. and Fawcett, J. (2010). Antidepressant drug effects and depression severity: a patient-level meta-analysis. *JAMA* 303(1), 47–53.

Gallagher, S. (2000). Philosophical conceptions of the self: implications for cognitive science. *Trends in Cognitive Sciences* 4(1), 14–21.

Gøtzsche, P.C. (2013). *Deadly Medicines and Organised Crime: How Big Pharma has Corrupted Healthcare.* London: Radcliffe.
Gøtzsche, P.C. (2014). Why I think antidepressants cause more harm than good. *The Lancet Psychiatry* 1, 104–106.
Healy, D. (2006). *Let Them Eat Prozac.* New York: New York University Press.
Hyman, S.E. and Nestler, E.J. (1996). Initiation and adaptation: a paradigm for understanding psychotropic drug action. *American Journal of Psychiatry* 153(2), 151–62.
Insel, T.R. (2006). Beyond efficacy: the STAR*D trial. *American Journal of Psychiatry* 163(1), 5–7.
Insel, T.R. (2010). Psychiatrists relationships with pharmaceutical companies: part of the problem or part of the solution? *JAMA* 303(12), 1192–1193.
Ioannidis, J.P., Greenland, S., Hlatky, M.A., Khoury, M.J., Macleod, M.R., Moher, D., Schulz, K.F. and Tibshirani, R. (2014). Increasing value and reducing waste in research design, conduct, and analysis. *The Lancet* 383(9912), 166–175.
Jablensky, A., Sartorius, N., Ernberg, G., Ansker, M., Korten, A., Cooper J., Day, R. and Bertelsen, A. (1992) Schizophrenia: manifestations, incidence and course in different cultures. A World Health Organization ten-country study. *Psychological Medicine* (Monograph Suppl. 20), 1095.
Jorm, A.F. and Griffiths, K.M. (2008). The public's stigmatizing attitudes towards people with mental disorders: how important are biomedical conceptualizations? *Acta Psychiatrica Scandinavica* 118(4), 315–321.
Kahn, R. S. and Keefe, R. S. (2013). Schizophrenia is a cognitive illness: time for a change in focus. *JAMA Psychiatry* 70(10), 1107–12.
Kapil, V., Green, J.L., Le Lait, C., Wood, D.M. and Dargan, P.I., (2014). Misuse of benzodiazepines and Z-drugs in the UK. *British Journal of Psychiatry* 205(5), 407–8.
Keller, M.B., Ryan, N.D., Strober, M., Klein, R.G., Kutcher, S.P., Birmaher, B., Hagino, O.R., Koplewicz, H., Carlson, G.A., Clarke, G.N., Emslie, G.J., Feinberg, D., Geller, B., Kusumakar, V., Papatheodorou, G., Sack, W.H., Sweeney, M., Wagner, K.D., Weller, E.B., Winters, N.C., Oakes, R. and McCafferty, J.P. (2001). Efficacy of paroxetine in the treatment of adolescent major depression: a randomized, controlled trial. *Journal of the American Academy of Child and Adolescent Psychiatry* 2001, 40:762–72.
Kessler, R.C., Chiu, W.T., Demler, O. and Walters, E.E. (2005). Prevalence, severity, and comorbidity of twelve-month DSM-IV disorders in the National Comorbidity Survey Replication (NCS-R). *Archives of General Psychiatry* 62(6), 617–27.
Kirby, M. and Keon, W. (2006). Out of the shadows at last. Report of the Standing Senate Committee on Social Affairs, Science and Technology. Ottawa, ON: Standing Senate Committee on Social Affairs, Science and Technology.
Kuhn, T.S. (1962). *The Structure of Scientific Revolutions.* Chicago, IL: University of Chicago Press.
Lacro, J. P., Dunn, L. B., Dolder, C. R., Leckband, S. G., and Jeste, D. V. (2002). Prevalence of and risk factors for medication non-adherence in patients with schizophrenia: a comprehensive review of recent literature. *Journal of Clinical Psychiatry* 63, 892–909.
Lam, D.C. and Salkovskis, P.M. (2007). An experimental investigation of the impact of biological and psychological causal explanations on anxious and depressed patients' perception of a person with panic disorder. *Behavior Research & Therapy* 45(2), 405–411.
Lauber, C., Nordt, C., Falcato, L. and Rössler, W. (2004). Factors influencing social distance toward people with mental illness. *Community Mental Health Journal* 40(3), 265–274.
Leff, J., Sartorius, N., Jablensky, A., Korten, A. and Ernberg, G. (1992). The international pilot study of schizophrenia: Five-year follow-up findings . *Psychological Medicine* 22, 131–145.

Le Noury, J., Nardo, J.M., Healy, D., Jureidini, J., Raven, M., Tufanaru, C. and Abi-Jaoude, E. (2015). Restoring Study 329: efficacy and harms of paroxetine and imipramine in treatment of major depression in adolescence. *British Medical Journal* 2015 351:h4320. doi: 10.1136/bmj.h4320.

Lepine, J.P. and Briley, M. (2011). The increasing burden of depression. *Neuropsychiatric Disease and Treatment* 7, 3–7.

Lieberman, J.A., Stroup, T.S., McEvoy, J.P., Swartz, M.S., Rosenheck, R.A., Perkins, D.O., Keefe, R.S., Davis, S.M., Davis, C.E., Lebowitz, B.D., Severe, J., Hsiao, J.K., and the Clinical Antipsychotic Trials of Intervention Effectiveness (CATIE) Investigators. (2005). Effectiveness of antipsychotic drugs in patients with chronic schizophrenia. *New England Journal of Medicine* 353: 1209–23.

Link, B. and Phelan, J. (2006). Stigma and its public health implications. *Lancet*, 367, 528–529.

Lucire, Y. and Crotty, C. (2011). Antidepressant-induced akathisia-related homicides associated with diminishing mutations in metabolizing genes of the CYP450 family. *Pharmgenomics and Personalized Medicine* 4, 65–81.

Martin, A., Young, C., Leckman, J.F., Mukonoweshuro, C., Rosenheck, R. and Leslie, D. (2004). Age effects on antidepressant-induced manic conversion. *Archives of Pediatrics & Adolescent Medicine* 158(8), 773–780.

Medco Health Solutions (2011). *America's State of Mind*. St. Louis, MO: Medco. Accessed November 6, 2015 at http://apps.who.int/medicinedocs/documents/s19032en/s19032en.pdf

Mojtabai, R. and Olfson, M. (2010). National trends in psychotropic medication in office-based psychiatry. *Archives of General Psychiatry* 67, 26–36.

Montejo, A.L., Llorca, G., Izquierdo, J.A. and Rico-Villademoros, F. (2001). Incidence of sexual dysfunction associated with antidepressant agents: a prospective multicenter study of 1022 outpatients. *Journal of Clinical Psychiatry* 62, 10–21.

Moore, T.J., Glenmullen, J. and Furberg, C.D. (2010). Prescription drugs associated with reports of violence towards others. *PLoS One* 5, e15337.

Moreno, C., Laje, G., Blanco, C., Jiang, H., Schmidt, A. B., and Olfson, M. (2007). National trends in the outpatient diagnosis and treatment of bipolar disorder in youth. *Archives of General Psychiatry* 64, 1032–1039.

National Institutes of Health Consensus Development Panel (2001). National Institutes of Health Consensus Development Conference Statement: phenylketonuria: screening and management, October 16–18, 2000. *Pediatrics* 108(4), 972–82.

Neill, U. S. (2008). Publish or perish, but at what cost? *Journal of Clinical Investigation* 118 (7), 2368–2368

Nelson, B., Parnas, J. and Sass, L.A. (2014). Disturbance of minimal self (ipseity) in schizophrenia: clarification and current status. *Schizophrenia Bulletin* 40(3), 479–82.

Nelson, B. and Sass, L.A. (2008). The phenomenology of the psychotic break and Huxley's trip: substance use and the onset of psychosis. *Psychopathology* 41(6), 346–355.

Nielsen, M., Hansen, E.H. and Gøtzsche, P.C. (2012). What is the difference between dependence and withdrawal reactions? A comparison of benzodiazepines and selective serotonin re-uptake inhibitors. *Addiction* 107, 900–908.

Olfson, M., Blanco, C., Liu, L., Moreno, C. and Laje, G. (2006). National trends in the outpatient treatment of children and adolescents with antipsychotic drugs. *Archives of General Psychiatry*, 63, 679–685.

Perälä, J., Suvisaari, J., Saarni, S. I., Kuoppasalmi, K., Isometsä, E., Pirkola, S., Partonen, T., Tuulio-Henriksson, A., Hintikka, J., Kieseppä, T., Härkänen, T., Koskinen, S., and Lönnqvist, J. (2007). Lifetime prevalence of psycotic and bipolar I disorders in a general population. *Archives of General Psychiatry* 64, 19–28.

Pescosolido, B., Martin, J., Long, J.S., Medina, T., Phelan, J. and Link, B. (2010). 'A disease like any other'? A decade of change in public reactions to schizophrenia, depression, and alcohol dependence. *The American Journal of Psychiatry* 167(11), 1321–1330.

Phelan, J.C. (2002). Genetic bases of mental illness – a cure for stigma? *Trends in Neuroscience* 25(8), 430–431.

Phelan, J.C. (2005). Geneticization of deviant behavior and consequences for stigma: the case of mental illness. *Journal of Health and Social Behaviour* 46(4), 307–322.

Pigott, H.E. (2011). STAR*D: A tale and trail of bias. *Ethical Human Psychology and Psychiatry* 13, 6–28.

Pratt, L.A., Brody, D.J. and Gu, Q. (2011). Antidepressant use in persons aged 12 and over: United States, 2005–2008. *Data Brief* 76, Hyattsville, MD: National Center for Health Statistics.

Read, J. and Harre, N. (2001). The role of biological and genetic causal beliefs in the stigmatization of 'mental patients'. *Journal of Mental Health* 10(2), 223–235.

Read, J. and Law, A. (1999). The relationship of causal beliefs and contact with users of mental health services to attitudes to the 'mentally ill'. *International Journal of Social Psychiatry* 45(3), 216–229.

Rüsch, N., Todd, A., Bodenhausen, G. and Corrigan, P. (2010). Biogenetic models of psycho-pathology, implicit guilt, and mental illness stigma. *Psychiatry Research* 179(3), 328–332.

Rush, A.J., Madhukar, H., Trivedi, S.R., Wisniewski, S.R., Nierenberg, A.A., Stewart, J.W., Warden, D., Niederehe, G., Thase, M.E., Lavori, P.W., Lebowitz, B.D., McGrath, P.J., Rosenbaum, J.F., Sackeim, H.A., Kupfer, D.J., Luther, J. and Fava, M. (2006). Acute and longer-term outcomes in depressed outpatients requiring one or several treatment steps: A STAR*D report. *The American Journal of Psychiatry* 163, 1905–1917.

Schnittker, J. (2008). An uncertain revolution: Why the rise of a genetic model of mental illness has not increased tolerance. *Social Science & Medicine* 67(9), 1370–1381.

Speed, E., Moncrieff, J. and Rapley, M. (2014). *De-medicalizing Misery II*. Basingstoke: Palgrave Macmillan.

The Schizophrenia Commission (2012). *The Abandoned Illness: A Report from the Schizophrenia Commission*. London: Rethink Mental Illness. Accessed October 21, 2015 at http://www.rethink.org/media/514093/TSC_main_report_14_nov.pdf

Timimi, S., Thomas, P., Davies, J., and Kinderman, P. (2014). Antipsychiatry and the antidepressants debate. *The Lancet Psychiatry* 1, 174.

van de Kraats, G.B., de Haan, S.E. and Meynen, G. (2012). Self-experience in the early phase of psychosis: a phenomenological approach. *Tijdschrift Psychiatrie* 54(12), 1021–9.

Walker, I. and Read, J. (2002). The differential effectiveness of psychosocial and biogenetic causal explanations in reducing negative attitudes toward 'mental illness'. *Psychiatry* 65(4), 313–325.

Whitaker, R. (2010). *Anatomy of an Epidemic: Magic Bullets, Psychiatric Drugs, and the Astonishing Rise of Mental Illness in America*. New York: Crown.

World Health Organization (2011). *Global Status Report on Non-Communicable Diseases 2010*. Geneva: WHO.

Wunderink, L., Nieboer, R.M., Wiersma, D., Sytema, S. and Nienhuis, F.J. (2013). Recovery in remitted first-episode psychosis at 7 years of follow-up of an early dose reduction/discontinuation or maintenance treatment strategy: long-term follow-up of a 2-year randomized clinical trial. *JAMA Psychiatry* 70(9), 913–20.

Zahl, P.H., De Leo, D., Ekeberg, Ø., Hjelmeland, H. and Dieserud, G. (2010). The relationship between sales of SSRI, TCA and suicide rates in the Nordic countries. *BMC Psychiatry* 10(1), 62.

3
THE NATURE OF SOCIAL CONTACT

Certain aspects of social interactions, described or shown in literature (e.g. *Letters to a Young Poet* by Rainer Maria Rilke) or films (e.g. *La Grande Bellezza* by Paolo Sorrentino and *Breaking the Waves* of Lars von Trier) may be relevant in the development of psychiatric disorders. 'Love is all you need' is a popular phrase in modern Western societies. People put their hope on others to get them through life. Of course, love is important and human beings are capable of altruism and self-sacrifice. However, evolution has endowed living creatures (including humans) with a will to survive, leading to a certain level of egocentricity. This egocentricity can be witnessed daily in society by, e.g. the exclusion of people who deviate from the norm, (underhand) bullying and – in extremity – in war cruelties.

Although people need meaningful connections with others, this is not always as easy as it seems. As the Austrian poet Rainer Maria Rilke (1929) wrote:

> Essentially, and in the deepest and most important things, we are unspeakably alone, and for one person to be able to advise or even help another, a lot must happen, a lot must go well, a whole constellation of events must come right in order once to succeed.

Thus, in social interaction a field of tension exists between one's own goals, desires, feelings, etcetera and those of others, which can make it difficult to form meaningful, deep connections. This seems to be largely suppressed in modern society and in psychiatry, by applying a kind of superficial positivity. The film *La Grande Bellezza* expresses very well how people can become caught up in the attainment of social status, and mainly superficial conversations, which later in life turn out to be less meaningful than may have appeared at the time.

Because of the emphasis in modern western societies on social relationships to obtain happiness, the value of solitude is overlooked. Many people fear solitude, perhaps as a legacy of evolution. However, in solitude one is better able to discover one's true identity (see Chapter 12).

Being alone and trying to find out what one's true feelings, thoughts and ideas are without the constriction and safety of conventions is frightening, as well as liberating. It is easier and safer to go with the majority. The philosopher Heidegger (1962) named the majority 'Das Man' (often translated as the They, People, Anyone). Living life according to what the majority regards as normal, good, desirable leads to high social status, but it can be a threat to authenticity. People are inclined to make choices because 'That is what one does'. Heidegger described the day-to-day talking about topics approved by Das Man as 'idle talk,' because it is often far removed from the core of Being, and conceals the truth.

Heidegger believed there are two fundamental ways of existing in the world: 1) a state of forgetfulness of being or 2) a state of mindfulness of being. Forgetfulness of being is the everyday mode of existence and Heidegger refers to it as inauthentic; one flees in idle talk (das Gerede), curiosity (Neugier), temptation (Versuchung) and comfort (Beruhiging).

In the other state, the state of mindfulness of being, one exists authentically. In this state, one becomes fully aware: of the fragility of life, the freedom of choice, the horrors and wonders of existence – and is anxious in the face of them.

Heidegger is regarded by some as an existentialist. Existentialism is a philosophical movement that came about in Europe in the late nineteenth century and achieved its zenith in the early to mid twentieth century. Existentialism comes from the Latin word 'existere' which means to stand out, to emerge. Authenticity is an important term in the work of many existentialists like Kierkegaard, Nietzsche, Rilke and Sartre.

With other people, there is often a subtle pressure to behave in a certain way that fits with the company and the situation. In addition, it is easier not to confront yourself with frightening truths in company because there is distraction. In solitude, there is no escape from intense emotions and the truths of life (Heidegger, 1962).

Many great minds corroborate that isolation must be experienced before it can be transcended. Camus for example said 'When a man has learned – and not on paper – how to remain alone with his suffering, how to overcome his longing to flee, then he has little left to learn' (quoted in Charlesworth, 1975).

This is also an essence of Rilke's *Briefe an einen jungen Dichter* (1929):

> There is only one solitude, and it is vast and not easy to bear and there will certainly be hours when you would like to exchange it for some form of commonality, be it ever so banal or trivial, for the illusion of some correspondence with whoever one happens to come across, whoever unworthy… But perhaps those are just the hours when solitude grows, for its growth is painful like the growth of boys and sad like the beginning of spring. But that should not mislead you. What is needed is this, and this alone: solitude, great inner solitude. Going into oneself and not meeting anyone for hours - that is what one must arrive at.

A certain degree of solitude can help in existing authentically (Storr, 1988). Many people just follow the majority (Das Man) in their likes and dislikes, or choose goals that were laid out for them by, for example, their parents or peers. Not following your own nature and inclinations may lead to stress, and stress can be the starting point of mental illness. However, it is difficult to follow your own nature, especially if it steers you in a direction that is different from your immediate social environment. For example, in a family of bankers, becoming a banker yourself may be easier than becoming a poet.

Furthermore, people often try to conform to the majority because they do not trust their own judgement, or because they want to avoid the discomfort of standing out. The Asch conformity experiments (or the Asch Paradigm) were a series of laboratory experiments directed by Solomon Asch (1951, 1952, 1955) that demonstrated the degree to which an individual's own opinions are influenced by those of a majority group. In a group of six college students, one is a real subject and the others are confederates who are all instructed to give the wrong answer in a perceptual task. Subsequently, 37 per cent of the real subjects gave the wrong answer.

The first important step in becoming who you really are is facing, experiencing, going through all within, including despair, loneliness, grief, anxiety as well as joy, wonderment. An inner solitude is important in this respect. It is not necessary to live like a hermit, but it is important to have hours of solitude and being able to follow your own path in company. Of course, an important restriction is not to do anything to others that you would not like to have done to yourself.

Rilke (1929) wrote:

> And when we speak of solitude, it becomes ever clearer that fundamentally it is not something that one can choose or not. We *are* solitary. It is possible to deceive ourselves and act as if it were not the case. That is all. How much better is it though, to accept that we are solitary and to even take it as our starting point.

Man's most important task in life may be to have the courage to withstand the pressures of Das Man and to follow his own path. In addition, it is important to come to terms with the harsh truths of life: we are in essence alone, chances that our trust will be betrayed by others are considerable and we will eventually die.

The occasional anxiety and depression associated with existing authentically can easily amount to a psychiatric diagnosis and treatment with medication in contemporary psychiatry. But after the realization and integration of these harsh contingencies of life, a path for personal growth can be found within oneself that can lead to moments of fulfilment and meaningfulness (Jung, 1992; Rilke, 1929). A famous quote from the French existentialist philosopher Jean Paul Sartre reads: 'Life begins on the other side of despair.' The importance of this self-healing path of personal growth should be acknowledged more in contemporary psychiatry and replace the first tendency to prescribe psychotropic drugs, with often detrimental long-term effects as underlined in Chapter 2.

The case example of John shows the coercion that can follow from social interaction and how this can lead to stress and subsequent psychiatric symptoms. Evidently, taking psychotropic drugs to suppress the symptoms is not a good solution in these instances.

CASE EXAMPLE: JOHN

John worked as an oncologist in the academic hospital. Every month he had several meetings in which management issues and scientific output were discussed. He worked very hard to give his patients the best care he could. However, during the meetings, management proclaimed that less time could be spent with individual patients because of production issues. To compensate for federal budget cuts, more patients should be seen in a day. In addition, scientific output should increase because the oncology department would get more money from the board of directors. John protested because he held the opinion that patients should receive the time they needed to ask questions about their diagnosis and treatment options. In addition, John disagreed with the instruction just to produce more articles because it would lead to more money. To him, quality was more important than quantity. Unfortunately, he could not convince the management with his arguments. John had not many colleagues who supported him, probably because there was a reorganization going on and people were afraid of losing their job. John tried to conform to the management instructions, but he became frustrated because he had to cut off patients in his office because the next patient was waiting. He wrote articles about topics he could publish, but his heart was not in it because these papers did not contribute to improved diagnosis or treatment.

John started to sleep poorly at night. He woke up every morning at 3 am and could not sleep anymore. In the evening he needed several beers or stronger drinks to relax. He became very tired and dragged himself to work every day. He did not look forward to anything anymore. He went to his GP who told him that he suffered from a depression, a treatable brain disorder, and prescribed him antidepressants. His intuition told John that the antidepressants were not the solution. He sometimes felt a flare of longing for a place where he could find himself again away from his social environment that would not acknowledge his concerns and arguments.

He told his management that he wanted to take 2 months off. This decision scared him because he might lose his job, his health, his financial security

> and his future. Family and friends thought that his decision was irresponsible, strange and foolish. They said that everybody had to cope with frustrating management decisions. Nevertheless, he booked a trip to Tibet and hiked alone in the Himalayas. He slept in monasteries that overlooked massive, snow covered mountains. He realized that the truth was the truth despite what other people said and did. He started sleeping better and when he woke up, there was a lightness in his mind about the things to come that day. He decided not to return to his job and stayed in the Himalayas for over a year. Then he returned to the west and took a job in another regional hospital where he was granted the time that he needed for his patients.

In conclusion, everybody needs relationships in their life, and they can provide meaning and happiness. But the other side of relationships (the pressure to conform, the often concealed inherent egocentricity of man, etcetera) also needs to be acknowledged to come to a truthful estimation of the value of human relationships in life. Relationships are not the only road to mental health, and placing too much value on them conceals the importance of solitude. During mental illness, patients may need a certain degree of solitude to live through their grief, anxiety, psychotic mystic experiences. Solitude is not a state that needs to be avoided at any cost, but it should even be stimulated in psychotherapy to live through emotions and find one's authentic self, leading to personal growth (Yalom, 1980). Becoming yourself, existing authentically, is an important step in being able to relate to others in a meaningful way (Rilke, 1929; Heidegger, 1962).

Furthermore, solitude has often been described as a facilitating condition for mystic experiences which can provide life with a profound meaning (Storr, 1988).

References

Asch, S.E. (1951). Effects of group pressure on the modification and distortion of judgments. In: Guetzkow, H. (Ed.). *Groups, Leadership and Men,* pp. 177–190. Pittsburgh, PA: Carnegie Press.
Asch, S.E. (1952). *Social Psychology*. Englewood Cliffs, NJ: Prentice Hall.
Asch, S.E. (1955). Opinions and social pressure. *Scientific American* 193, 31–35.
Charlesworth, M. (1975). *The Existentialists and Jean-Paul Sartre*. Brisbane: University of Queensland Press.
Heidegger, H. (1962). *Being and Time*, Macquarrie, J. and Robinson, E. trans. New York: Harper & Row.
Jung, C.G. (1992). *Two Essays on Analytical Psychology*, second edition, Collected Works of C.G. Jung, London: Routledge.
Rilke, R.M. (1929). *Briefe an einen jungen Dichter.* Leipzig: Insel-Verlag.
Storr A. (1988). *Solitude: A Return to the Self.* New York: Ballantine Books.
Yalom, I.D. (1980). *Existential Psychotherapy*. New York: Basic Books.

4
MYSTIC EXPERIENCES

During a psychosis, individuals often describe mystic experiences (Nelson and Sass, 2008; Podvoll, 1990). The Oxford psychologist and philosopher William James (1902) commented on the similarities between mystic experiences and mental illness, which he calls lower mysticisms:

> It is evident that from the point of view of their psychological mechanism, the classic mysticism and these lower mysticisms spring from the same mental level, from that great subliminal or transmarginal region of which science is beginning to admit the existence, but of which so little is really known. That region contains every kind of matter: 'seraph and snake' abide there side by side. To come from thence is no infallible credential. What comes must be sifted and tested, and run the gauntlet of confrontation with the total context of experience, just like what comes from the outer world of sense. Its value must be ascertained by empirical methods, so long as we are not mystics ourselves.

Many artists, scientists and philosophers (including Carl Jung, John Perry, Albert Einstein, Paolo Coelho) have written about this 'subliminal or transmarginal region' of which James states in 1902 '... science is just beginning to admit its existence.' Since then, science has made little progress in exploring this region (that may also be related to the creation of art). In our aim to understand mental health and mental illness, we cannot ignore the tendency of man to have experiences that transcend daily life and the individual. These experiences can probably be traced back to a primordial region in the human psyche (which can be investigated), rather than to a supernatural being that created the world and determines the course of events. The phenomenology of psychiatric symptoms may be a part of the puzzle that is just as important as the underlying biological

44 Limitations in current psychiatric practice and research

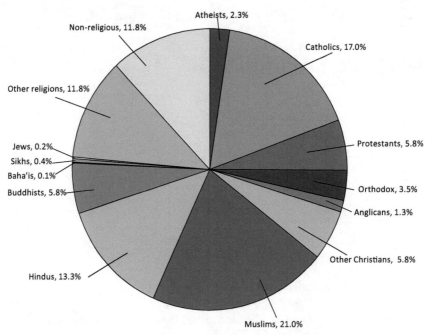

FIGURE 4.1 Religious adherence as a percentage of the world population in 2007

mechanisms. Certainly not at this point in time – and perhaps never – can the experience of mental illness be reduced entirely to a biological substrate. More insight into both the phenomenology and the biology of psychiatric symptoms is needed to improve understanding and treatment of mental illness.

The existence of God can be disputed. Scientists justly question whether it is possible that God created the world, that He determines what happens and can cause plagues, etcetera. However, it is evident that humans are inclined to have mystic experiences (Ziegelaar, 2015), and to believe in some sort of God (Armstrong, 1993). Scientists cannot question that. Even after secularisation, a small percentage of the world-population is non-religious or atheist (see Figure 4.1). Man can be considered as essentially religious.

Some argue that religion has been 'invented' to reduce anxiety. Religion can reduce (as well as invoke) anxiety but it is unlikely that religion was just made up. Would it be so important to so many people then? Furthermore, God, religion in general, is a topic in the work of many philosophers. And why would there be so many similarities in religions? As Joseph Campbell (1972) has described in his comparison of myths and religions all over the world, there are certain core elements that tend to occur, even in very secluded tribes. That may be the case because the myths, religions and eastern philosophies come from the same source: an ancient part of the human mind that transcends the ego and unifies people because of its collective nature.

The Perennial Philosophy, also referred to as Perennialism, is a perspective in the philosophy of religion which views each of the world's religious traditions as sharing a single, universal truth on which foundation all religious knowledge and doctrine has grown.

Aldous Huxley (1894–1963) was an English writer and philosopher and he wrote a book about this topic (Huxley, 1946). In this book, he describes people who have gone on a spiritual path:

> Finding the eternal Self in the depth of particular, individualized selves, and identical with, or at least akin to, the divine Ground. Based upon the direct experience of those who have fulfilled the necessary conditions of such knowledge, this teaching is expressed most succinctly in the Sanskrit formula, tat tvam asi (That art thou); the Ātman, or immanent eternal Self, is one with Brahman, the Absolute Principle of all existence; and the last end of every human being is to discover the fact for himself, to find out Who he really is.

According to Hinduism, to attain liberation a human being must acquire self-knowledge (atma jnana), which is to realize that one's true self (Ātman) is identical with the transcendent self (Brahman). Thus, by becoming who you really are you can coincide with the divine Ground in the human mind (Huxley, 1946). God can be found 'in the deepest and most central part of the soul' (William Law, 1828). The same wisdom is found in Zen Buddhism and even Christianity: 'To gauge the soul we must gauge it with God, for the Ground of God and the Ground of the Soul are one and the same' (Meister Eckhart, 1293–1328 [2010]).

Huxley (1946) writes that the hermitage, monastery and academies used to give the religious, philosophical, artistic or scientific contemplative protection from the ordinary strains and stresses of social life:

> The born contemplative has to face the struggle for existence and social predominance without protection. The result, in most cases, is that he either dies young or is too desperately busy merely keeping alive to be able to devote his attention to anything else. When this happens the prevailing philosophy will be that of the hardy, extraverted man of action.

Furthermore, he describes that the child tends to grow out of his direct awareness of the one Ground of things. The mode of analytical thought is fatal to the intuitions of integral experience. Daily hassles in order to survive are a major obstacle in the way of genuine spirituality.

The ancient domain

The ancient domain, indicated with the Ground in the text above, may consist of the collective experience of human kind. Intense, relevant experiences of people living before us may have been sieved from daily life to constitute a reservoir of essences of humanity. Rilke describes it beautifully (1929):

> Like the bees collect honey, we fetch the sweetness out of everything and build *Him*. We begin with the very slightest things, with that what is barely noticeable (as long as it is done out of love), with our work and the rest that comes after, with a moment of silence or with a small solitary joy, with all that we do alone without helpers and followers, we begin him whom we shall never know, just as our ancestors could not live to know us. And yet they are in us, these people long gone, as a disposition, as a load weighing on our destinies, as a murmur in the blood and as a gesture that rises up out of the depths of time

Coming in to contact with the ancient domain can be a healing experience but can also be frightening. It helps to conceptualize life as more than daily routine and the person you are in the eyes of others.

Intuition comes from this region and it often hints at a direction that can be taken to heal yourself. These intuitions should be taken seriously. It is possible not to listen to these intuitions and inclinations. Many adults are bound by obligations, and decide to live their lives according to Das Man, what they are supposed to do. It is possible to live a life disconnected from the ancient domain. However, most people stumble upon it during their life in intense situations. During psychosis, people seem to be immersed in it.

The Dutch writer and philosopher Wouter Kusters (2014), who experienced psychosis himself, has written a fascinating book about the frequent occurrence of mystic experiences during psychosis. He calls antipsychotic medications 'antimystics' because they dampen the psychosis and therewith the mystic experiences. The work of the Greek philosopher Plotinus (c. AD 205–266) plays an important role in Kusters' book. Plotinus describes 'The One' that can be conceived as Plato's light outside the cave. During experience of 'The One' contradictions are resolved, and this can be overwhelming. Another writer who experienced psychosis, Custance (1952), describes in the analyses of his psychosis the work of Carl Jung. In the psychosis of the clinical psychologist David Lukoff (2000), shamanistic themes occur, and in retrospect he interprets his madness with shamanistic literature. The psychosis of a well-known American psychologist Mary Newton occurred after intensive study of Joseph Campell's work about myths, and many years afterwards she uses this work to interpret her psychosis. The connection between the work of all these individuals who went through a psychosis, is that they refer to authors who have written about the ancient domain.

This part of the human mind can be characterized by its intensity. As James (1902) wrote: 'That region contains every kind of matter: "seraph and snake" abide there side by side'. Perhaps the state most exemplary of the ancient domain is the rhythmic trance of a tribe dancing around a fire at night. It is not good, it is not bad but it follows a natural rhythm and it is intense. Artist and children usually live close to it.

Because it is so relevant for psychosis, but also for treatment in psychiatry, it should be taken seriously and studied so it can play a role in understanding psychiatric symptoms. It can be studied by giving phenomenology the prominent place that it deserves in psychiatry. The dominant biomedical paradigm in psychiatry that attributes psychosis, depression, anxiety, etcetera to disturbed neurotransmitters should be expanded with research that investigates the phenomenology of mystic experiences. There is already a lot of knowledge about the ancient domain (the origin of these experiences) that is discussed in Chapter 12. This knowledge could be a basis from which to understand psychiatric symptoms and subsequent new ways of treatment.

The case example of Marc illustrates the relationship between mystic experiences and psychiatric symptoms.

CASE EXAMPLE: MARC

Marc was a sophomore English literature student. He had always been an honours student as well as a gentle and kind soul. He was very impressed with J.D. Salinger's book The *Catcher in the Rye*. He profoundly understood what Salinger meant with saving children from the phoney adult life. When he travelled on the subway to the University he saw the weary faces of forensics going to their demanding jobs. He imagined that there would be more to life than joining the forensics stream in the morning and evening after his studies. He was curious what extreme experiences would do to him. He wanted to explore the borders of his mind. He planned a trip to Australia, where it is possible to hike for days alone. He walked a trail of 5 days through the desert to Ayers rock. He was overwhelmed by the sky with stars at night that looked so different from what he had seen all his life in the northern hemisphere. The framework of his life that kept everything in place was loosened because of jet lag, extreme weather conditions, beautiful landscapes, wildlife and vegetation he had never seen before. The soil was very hard, red-brown and old. The ancient aboriginal art seemed to take him back thousands of years and he felt connected to an ancient past of human kind. At moments, he felt merged with the universe. One day when he rested to drink some water, a moth landed on his arm. Somehow, the experience was intense and beautiful.

A few months later, he was in a museum back home and he saw a moth on a painting. It immediately took him back to the desert in Australia. He was convinced that this was not a coincidence but a sign that he was Jesus Christ. His mother's name was Maria, which fuelled his conviction. He used his savings to buy food for wanderers. He gave away all his possessions, and wanted to live in a monastery. His family was very concerned that he would

> throw away his bright future. He was admitted involuntarily to a psychiatric ward. He was told in the hospital that his intense experiences of the past year had just been a sign of a deregulated neurotransmitter system, and that he needed to take antipsychotic medication to correct the imbalance. His intense experiences were replaced by a feeling of numbness. He was kept on antipsychotic medication for 3 years, during which he gained 8 kilos and was unable to finish his studies. When he stopped his medication, he started thinking that his family conspired against him to have him locked up again. He heard them talking behind his back even when they were not around. He was admitted to hospital again, where he stayed for 5 months. Then he returned to the city but was unable to provide for himself. He had lost contact with his family and friends, and he slept under the bridge with the same wanderers he gave his possessions to years before. The next years he was in and out of the hospital. All sorts of psychotropic medications and their combinations were tried during the following years: Lithium, SSRIs antipsychotics, anxiolytics. He died at age 50 of liver failure probably caused by prolonged lithium use.

Considering this case example, the life of a monk that Marc wanted to choose was incongruent with what his parents expected from him, but he may have found there what he was looking for during his psychosis. The antipsychotic medication dampened his religious delusion but replaced it with a numbness that is worse for Marc.

In conclusion, religions, eastern philosophies, ancient myths are so alike because they are an expression of something very important and valuable in the human psyche (the ancient domain). Finding the path of personal growth, becoming yourself and therewith gaining access to the ancient domain (Ātman = Brahman), can have amazing effects like a realization of what is valuable in life and what is not, a sense of unity with other people and the world, access to deep truths, etcetera. The risks are not being able to control the experiences (as James wrote: 'To come from thence is no infallible credential,') and being regarded as peculiar, or even mad by the majority, as illustrated by the case example of Marc.

I do not want to argue that psychosis is not an illness. However, reducing it solely to a chemical imbalance in the brain denies the complexity of the problem and this has not led to improved understanding of psychotic illness and better treatments. Many psychiatric patients speak of mystic experiences, or are in search of meaning and truth in their life. Ignoring the essential religious nature of man in psychiatric research and practice precludes options for more natural, benign treatments than psychotropic medication. Patients suffering from psychiatric symptoms deserve a holistic approach that sometimes includes psychotropic medication.

References

Armstrong, K. (1993). *A History of God.* New York: Ballantine Books.
Campbell, J. (1972). *Myths to Live By.* New York: Penguin Compass.
Custance, J. (1952). *Wisdom, Madness and Folly: The Philosophy of a Lunatic.* New York: Pellgrini & Cudahy.
Huxley, A. (1946). *The Perennial Philosophy.* London: Chatto and Windus.
James, W. (1902). The *Varieties of Religious Experience: A Study in Human Nature.* Gifford lectures. New York: Random House.
Kusters, W. (2014). *Filosofie van de waanzin (Philosophy of Madness).* Rotterdam: Lemniscaat.
Law, W. (1828). *Extracts from the Letters and Writings from William Law,* Ashby, M. (ed.) London: Harvey and Darton.
Lukoff, D. (2000). The importance of spirituality in mental health. Interview by Bonnie Horrigan. *Alternative Therapies in Health and Medicine* 6(6), 80–7.
Meister Eckhart (1293–1328 [2010]). *The Complete Mystical Works of Meister Eckhart.* Walshe, M. O'C. trans. Spring Valley, NY: The Crossroad Publishing Company.
Nelson, B. and Sass, L.A. (2008). The phenomenology of the psychotic break and Huxley's trip: substance use and the onset of psychosis. *Psychopathology* 41(6), 346–55.
Plotinus (c. AD 205–266 [1966–1988]). *Enneads,* Armstrong, A.H. trans. Loeb Classical Library. Cambridge, MA: Harvard University Press and London: Heinemann.
Podvoll, E.M. (1990). *The Seduction of Madness: Revolutionary Insights into the World of Psychosis and a Compassionate Approach to Recovery at Home.* New York: Harper Collins.
Rilke, R.M. (1929). *Briefe an einen jungen Dichter.* Leipzig: Insel-Verlag.
Ziegelaar, A. (2015). *Aardse Mystiek (Earthly Mysticism).* Leusden: ISVW uitgevers.

5

THE MIND–BRAIN PROBLEM

The mind–brain problem in philosophy examines the relationship between mind and matter, in particular between the brain and consciousness. In the seventeenth century, the philosopher Descartes proposed that mind and matter were essentially different, i.e. Cartesian dualism. Monism maintains that there is only one unifying substance, in terms of which everything can be explained. A variety of theories have been proposed, most are either dualist or monist. The extensive literature will not be summarized here. I will confine myself to aspects of the problem that are relevant for contemporary psychiatry. The mind is according to the dictionary 'the element of a person that enables them to be aware of the world and their experiences, to think, and to feel; the faculty of consciousness and thought.'

It is a popular stance these days to say that we are our brains (Swaab, 2012). The mind is marginalized to an epiphenomenon. Our brains determine who we are; our brains have already determined for us what we are going to do before we have decided for ourselves.

The mind is probably produced by the brain, but reducing the mind to the brain is not possible and has the undesirable consequence that people think that their choices are irrelevant. If depression is the consequence of a dysfunctioning brain, one treats it with medication and one does not have to dig into one's life or mind for what the cause of the depression is. In some cases, depression may have a purely biological cause but there are also many cases in which choices in life had a major influence on the onset and persistence of depression.

For 30 years, neuroscience has held the promise to unravel the mysteries of the brain with more and more advanced scanning devices. Unravelling the brain's mysteries would lead to a true understanding of psychiatric symptoms. Indeed, scanning devices are becoming more and more advanced, but how the brain produces the mind remains unclear. We can only investigate correlations, not causal relationships of brain structure and function with subjective experience. We cannot find the subjective experience itself in the brain and it is very doubtful if this would ever be possible.

It is similar to looking at the individual words of a book when you try to understand the content of the book or investigating the individual instruments of an orchestra when you want to understand the experience of music. The words and the instruments are part of the whole, but the whole cannot be reduced to its constituting components. The mind may be an emergent process. When you investigate the constituent components in the brain, the higher order emergent process is lost (Alexander, 1920).

It is probably true that all thoughts, feelings, myths, etcetera are the result of brain activity, but for understanding mental illness both biology and phenomenology are necessary, because currently we are unable to map subjective experience onto a delineated biological substrate. 100 years of psychiatric research has led to many reports of biological abnormalities found in psychiatric patients, but this has not resulted in a comprehensive theory of the origin and course of mental illness. The problem is linking subjective experience to biological abnormalities. Extreme subjective experience is the main symptom of psychiatric disorders. We are missing an important part of the puzzle: how the brain produces the mind. We do not know the exact mechanism by which thoughts are produced by the brain. It is even very difficult to define a thought in physical terms. It is unknown of what matter a thought is composed. Consequently, it is not possible to see a thought in a scanner or 'catch' it with another apparatus. Thus, in psychiatry, the object of study (aberrant thoughts) is ill-defined. We should acknowledge this problem, and focus on ways to move forward in the direction of increased insight into relevant mechanisms underlying psychiatric symptoms. It should be kept in mind that by investigating the brain, we are looking at correlations with subjective experience, not at the subjective experience itself. Therefore, increased insight into brain functioning is an important part of improved understanding of the nature of psychiatric symptoms, but in most patients, the symptoms cannot be reduced to aberrant brain functioning. Other factors, like past experiences, the structure of the human mind, relationships with the immediate and wider social environment etcetera also need to be considered.

The current state of science with respect to the mind–brain problem is not much different from the period in which Karl Jaspers published his classic handbook Allgemeine Psychopathologie (1913). Jaspers suggested to employ scientific methods to discover the biology associated with psychiatric disorders (Erklären) as well as to employ an individual phenomenological approach to understand the subjective experience of the patient (Verstehen). Because the mind–brain problem is not (yet) solved, psychiatry should focus on linking both approaches, e.g. through neurophenomenology (see the next Chapters). Although proponents of the biomedical paradigm would like us to believe that we can reduce psychiatric symptoms to the brain, there is not much clinical evidence to sustain this claim (Deacon, 2013). Kingdon and Young (2007) wrote: 'Research into biological mechanisms of mental and behavioural responses has failed to deliver anything of value to clinical psychiatrists and is very unlikely to do so in the future.' Similarly, Kleinman (2012) predicted that the current biology-based model of academic psychiatry will be ruinous to the profession due to its consistent failure to deliver.

The rising disability numbers in psychiatry suggest that trying to treat problems of the mind solely with medication as first line intervention is not adequate. Suggesting that psychiatry should disregard the mind because 'The idea of a medicine for something lacking in substance (the mind) might seem a priori implausible, irrational, and undesirable' (Nutt et al., 2014) is throwing out the baby with the bathwater.

In the previous chapters, the major problems in contemporary psychiatry have been highlighted as well as possible causes of these problems such as the scientific research system and its omissions. In the next chapters, recent research results are summarized with respect to prevention in psychiatry and the biological component in psychiatric symptoms. Although no differential biological substrate has been found of the specific DSM diagnostic categories such as major depressive disorder and schizophrenia, a biological component often plays a role in psychiatric symptoms to a bigger or lesser extent. In the last chapters, research results and insights from philosophers and artists are joined in a new model of mental health care.

References

Alexander, S. (1920). *Space, Time, and Deity*. London: Macmillan & Co Ltd.
Deacon, B.J. (2013). The biomedical model of mental disorder: A critical analysis of its validity, utility, and effects on psychotherapy research. *Clinical Psychology Review* 33, 846–86.
Jaspers, K. (1947). *General Psychopathology*. Vols 1 & 2. Hoenig, J. and Hamilton, M.W. trans. Baltimore, MD: Johns Hopkins University Press; 1997. First published as: Jaspers, K (1913). *Allgemeine Psychopathologie*. Berlin, Germany: Springer.
Kingdon, D. and Young, A. (2007). Research into putative biological mechanisms of mental disorders has been of no value to clinical psychiatry. *British Journal of Psychiatry* 191, 285–90.
Kleinman, A. (2012). Rebalancing academic psychiatry: why it needs to happen – and soon. *British Journal of Psychiatry* 201, 421–22.
Nutt, D.J., Goodwin, G.M., Bhugra, D., Fazel, S. and Lawrie, S. (2014). Attacks on antidepressants: signs of deep-seated stigma? *Lancet Psychiatry* 1, 103–04.
Swaab, D.F. (2012). *Wij zijn ons brein (We are Our Brains)*. Amsterdam: Atlas Contact.

PART II
Possibilities and opportunities for change in psychiatry

6

TRANSDIAGNOSTIC PHENOMENOLOGICAL SYMPTOM DIMENSIONS

Much research efforts have been invested in finding the biological substrate of the DSM diagnostic categories, e.g. schizophrenia, anxiety disorders, mood disorders. Scientists meet at conferences like the International Congress of Schizophrenia Research or the International Anxiety Disorders Symposium. Often anxiety disorder researchers are not acquainted with schizophrenia researchers. In the field of anxiety disorders, schizophrenia and depression, etcetera researchers have come to the same conclusion independently, for example that the patients suffer from a deficit in executive functioning or selective attention. It is not surprising that no specific biological substrates have been found to aid the diagnostic process like a test for tuberculosis. Many biological abnormalities have been reported in psychiatric disorders, e.g. in the field of neuroimaging, cognition and neurophysiology but these deficits are not specific to the DSM categories. In an excellent review article of Millan et al. (2012), cognitive deficits were summarized across psychiatric disorders, showing the large overlap.

The National Institute of Mental Health in the USA also promotes new ways of classifying psychopathology based on dimensions of observable behaviour and neurobiological measures. The Research Domain Criteria project has been launched by the National Institute of Mental Health to implement this strategy. In brief, the effort is to define basic dimensions of functioning (such as fear circuitry or working memory) to be studied across multiple units of analysis, from genes to neural circuits to behaviours, cutting across disorders as traditionally defined (Cuthbert and Insel, 2010; Insel et al., 2010). The intent is to translate rapid progress in basic neurobiological and behavioural research to an improved integrative understanding of psychopathology and the development of new and/or optimally matched treatments for mental disorders.

Having a psychiatric illness is extremely anxiety provoking because it often leads to loss of control over one's life. Furthermore, not being able to reach vocational and social goals because of a psychiatric illness induces depression. Thus, a majority of the psychiatric patients experience anxiety and depression on top of more specific psychiatric symptoms such as psychosis. It is difficult to find the biological basis of a diagnostic category when patients fall into several diagnostic categories at the same time. In addition, the DSM categories are broad, including heterogeneous symptoms and therefore it is unlikely that one biological substrate can be found. For example, a subject who receives the diagnosis of major depressive disorder can show agitation or psychomotor retardation, insomnia or sleeping too much, weight loss or weight gain, etcetera. A reason that the biological cause of major depressive disorder has not been found yet may be that the symptoms in this category are just too diverse. Likewise, the DSM diagnostic category of schizophrenia that encompasses negative symptoms (e.g. anedonia, flat affect), positive symptoms (hallucinations and delusions) and disorganization symptoms is too broad to find a biological substrate.

To overcome the problem of psychiatric comorbidity and heterogeneity of the DSM diagnostic categories, research should focus on narrowly defined symptom dimensions that cut across the traditional DSM boundaries. There is no clear cut-off point where the threshold from mental health to morbidity is passed, just as there is no clear threshold for day to become night. There is a twilight period where it is neither day nor night. In this twilight period patients would not fulfil criteria for a disorder but it is an excellent period for intervention with benign treatments because in this early phase biological and psychosocial damage is less extensive than when subjects have severe psychiatric symptoms.

Biological mechanisms are important in psychiatry but subjective experience is as least as important and we have not yet been able and probably will not be in the near future to understand subjective experience by investigating the brain with neuroscience methods. A way forward in psychiatry may be neurophenomenology. This approach combines neuroscience with phenomenology (subjective experience) in order to explore experience, mind and consciousness, with an emphasis on the embodied condition of the human mind (Varela, 1996). We should investigate the relationship between narrowly defined symptom dimensions and biological parameters. One such symptom dimension may be 'level of energy' that crosses the borders of the DSM categories. For example, depression is associated with severely reduced energy and mania with increased energy. In anxiety and psychotic disorders, this symptom dimension is also important. This symptom dimension could be related to markers in the blood and other biological variables. For example, think about having the flu which is also often is accompanied by lack of energy but also depression and changes in blood markers. Symptom dimensions should be defined by listening to the phenomenological reports of patients. Another example of a symptom dimension is hallucinations. Psychosis would not be a good symptom dimension because it compasses hallucinations and delusions and is therefore too broad. Hallucinations and delusions are phenomenologically very different and may also have different neurobiological substrates.

A comprehensive project using this dimensional approach is currently being performed at the Academic Medical Center, University of Amsterdam, the Netherlands: the Biobank Cognition study. All patients coming for intake to our Department irrespective of their DSM diagnosis are asked if they want to participate in a biobank study in which data is collected concerning cognitive, neurophysiological, genetic, blood marker and brain imaging abnormalities. In addition, patients are assessed with dimensional psychopathology questionnaires to capture all aspects of subjective experience. We can investigate if certain biological abnormalities are related to certain aspects of subjective experience.

In the following case example of Liam, the biological component predominates in the aetiology of his illness. His depressive symptoms started during the flu, a state in which blood biomarkers, such as cytokines, are often disturbed (Van Reeth, 2000). During the period thereafter, Liam seems unable to recuperate. Biological assessments have abnormal outcomes. Similar results can be found in patients with for example, psychotic illness.

CASE EXAMPLE: LIAM

Liam had a severe flu a year ago. He had just turned 50 and he always worked very hard as a bank manager but now he had to stay in bed for a week. After this week, it seemed as if he just could not get his health back. When he woke up, he was extremely tired; he could hardly get out of bed. He had a knot in his stomach and it felt as if he could not face up to his obligations that day. He also could not get excited about anything anymore. Previously he always looked forward to something, e.g. the weekend, or the holidays. Now it all seemed grey and meaningless. He also had no appetite, and lost 10 kilos in a year. Even though he was exhausted, he could not sleep anymore. He lay awake at night with his eyes wide open, staring into the cold darkness. His wife could not help him and he felt only irritation with respect to his children of 16 and 18 years whereas he used to be a family man. He was unable to read or look at the TV because he could not comprehend what he read or could not keep his concentration when watching a film. He was unable to work for 6 months and the world had become a hell for Liam. At the physical examination, Liam had a very high pulse and high blood pressure. In addition, cytokines in his blood were elevated. At the neuropsychological examination he performed a lot worse than the norm group on tests of attention and memory.

References

Cuthbert, B.N. and Insel, T.R. (2010). Toward new approaches to psychotic disorders: the NIMH research domain criteria project. *Schizophrenia Bulletin* 36, 1061–2.

Insel, T., Cuthbert, B., Garvey, M., Heinssen R., Pine D.S., Quinn K., Sanislow C., Wang P. (2010). Research domain criteria (RDoC): toward a new classification framework for research on mental disorders. *American Journal of Psychiatry* 167, 748–51.

Millan, M.J., Agid, Y., Brüne, M., Bullmore, E.T., Carter, C.S., Clayton, N.S. Connor, R., Davis, S., Deakin, B., DeRubeis, R.J., Dubois, B., Geyer, M.A., Goodwin, G.M., Gorwood, P., Jay, T.M., Joëls, M., Mansuy, I.M., Meyer-Lindenberg, A., Murphy, D., Rolls, E., Saletu, B., Spedding, M., Sweeney, J., Whittington, M., and Young, L.J. (2012). Cognitive dysfunction in psychiatric disorders: characteristics, causes and the quest for improved therapy. *Nature Reviews Drug Discovery* 11(2),141–68.

Van Reeth, K. (2000). Cytokines in the pathogenesis of influenza. *Veterinary Microbiology* 74(1–2), 109–16.

Varela, F. (1996). Neurophenomenology: A methodological remedy for the hard problem. *Journal of Consciousness Studies* 3, 330–49.

7
BIOLOGICAL MARKERS IN PSYCHIATRIC DISORDERS

Some people doubt if psychiatric diseases are real because it is not possible to do a biological test to confirm that someone is suffering from a DSM psychiatric disorder. The main reason that there are no biological tests is not that there are no biological abnormalities in psychiatric disorders, but that the DSM categories are not valid biological entities. Furthermore, if one tries to reduce a DSM psychiatric disorder to a biological substrate in the brain, one ends up empty handed, because a psychiatric disorder is partly a disorder of the mind. There is a biological component in many psychiatric disorders, but other components concern social relationships, the environment, etcetera. But this does not imply that psychiatric diseases are less real than, for example, pulmonary diseases. It is important to gain more insight into the transdiagnostic biological mechanisms that play a role in the origin and maintenance of psychiatric symptoms in relationship to other components.

The DSM has been leading in research and treatment in the past decennia, which may have hampered research into biological abnormalities or biomarkers that are assessed transdiagnostically, cutting across the borders of the DSM diagnostic categories. The term 'biomarker', or 'biological marker', refers to an objective indication of physical functioning observed from outside the patient which can be measured accurately and reproducibly (Strimbu and Tavel, 2010). It may be possible that trandiagnostic biomarkers correlate with narrowly defined subjective symptom dimensions.

In a recent paper, McGorry et al. (2014) give an overview of transdiagnostic biomarkers in psychiatry. Cognitive, brain structural, neurophysiological, sleep/chronobiological, stress and fatty acids parameters are promising candidate markers with emerging data in support. A large body of data already exists that may offer predictive and early diagnostic indicators of pathophysiological processes that may vary across the stages of the evolution of major psychiatric disorders. McGorry

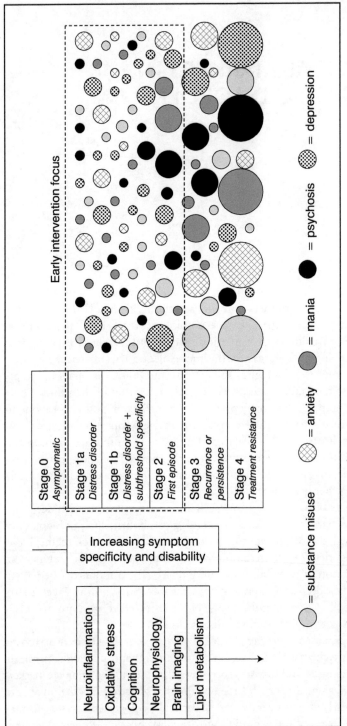

FIGURE 7.1 Biomarkers and clinical staging in psychiatry

et al. (2014) bring together evidence from several lines of neurobiological work to address problems of the complex overlaps, and heterogeneity of course and outcome across psychiatric disorders. A key obstacle is the continuing tendency to conduct studies within the confining DSM silos of current diagnostic orthodoxy. A neurobiologically-informed staging approach that crosses current diagnostic silos may bring clarity to contemporary confusion and complexity (see Figure 7.1).

Figure 7.1 shows that subjects often present with a multitude of symptoms, especially in the early stages (1a, 1b and 2). In the later illness stages, symptoms can grow into a clinical picture that is dominated by certain symptoms like psychosis or substance misuse, but often mixed with other symptoms. In the later stages (3 and 4), biological processes like extreme stress are more difficult to turn back to normal than in the earlier stages. It seems as if certain routes become ingrained in the brain, like a river can create a path in a mountain. Biomarkers can be helpful in defining the different stages of illness and finding new treatments for the biological component. The clinical stages in Figure 7.1 are specified in Panel 7.1. Interrater reliability of the model in Panel 7.1 is good with 90 per cent concordance between experienced raters.

Research should focus on novel and more benign treatments (probably not specific for any DSM diagnostic category) which influence these biomarkers in the early stages and may result in benefit via specific mechanisms of this kind: so called 'target engagement'. Perhaps objective biomarkers combined with clinical symptoms and psychosocial functioning could be used in the future in a combined profiling and clinical staging model to assess a patients' individual risk and need for particular types of care instead of the current crude and general characterisation of the patients' symptoms with respect to the broad DSM criteria by the clinician. Hopefully, in the future the DSM could be replaced by a more biologically and personally valid, clinical staging and profiling model (see Chapter 8).

PANEL 7.1 CLINICAL STAGING IN PSYCHIATRY

Stage 0   Asymptomatic individuals at risk of a disorder who have not yet presented for care

Stage 1a   Help-seeking individuals with mild symptoms and mild functional impacts

Stage 1b   Those with attenuated syndromes with partial specificity, often with mixed or ambiguous symptomatology and moderate functional impacts

Stage 2   Subjects with discrete disorders: clear episodes of psychotic, manic, or severe depressive symptoms

Stage 3   Those with a recurrent or persistent disorder

Stage 4   Patients with severe, treatment resistant, and unremitting illness

Adapted from Hickie et al (2013).

To create a valid nosology of mental illness, a bottom-up rather than top-down approach is also necessary. The scientific literature on psychiatry reveals that, although there are biological (cognitive, genetic, neurophysiological, neuroimaging, blood marker, etcetera) dysfunctions underlying psychiatric disorders, these are not specific for the DSM diagnostic categories, which have been defined top-down (by expert consensus). The biological dysfunctions should be studied transdiagnostically, across psychiatric disorders, without taking the DSM diagnosis into consideration (McGorry et al., 2014; Nieman and McGorry, 2015). For example, cognitive dysfunctions (such as problems with attention, memory and planning) can be found – to a greater or lesser extent – among psychiatric patients covering the complete range of DSM diagnoses. The challenge for the future is linking these deficits to specific aberrant subjective experience.

Cognitive impairment

In psychiatry research and clinical practice, changes in emotion are universally recognized as being inherent to psychiatric disorders, whereas cognitive impairment – which has an equally or even more disabling effect on patients – has been comparatively neglected (Millan et al., 2012). Cognitive dysfunctions are more predictive than affective symptoms of functional outcome. Unfortunately, there are no effective treatments for cognitive dysfunctions. Most psychiatric medications target the affective symptoms (Millan et al., 2012).

Millan et al. (2012) define cognition as:

> A suite of interrelated conscious (and unconscious) mental activities, including: pre-attentional sensory gating; attention; learning and memory; problem solving, planning, reasoning and judgment; understanding, knowing and representing; creativity, intuition and insight; 'spontaneous' thought; introspection; self-awareness and meta-cognition (thinking and knowledge about cognition).

Figure 7.2 shows an example of a neuropsychological test that assesses visuospatial memory: the Complex Figure of Rey. In this test, the example figure has to be copied. Both the control subject and the schizophrenia patient do quite well copying the figure. The figure is then removed, and people have to draw the figure from memory. As can be seen in the second row of the Figure, the schizophrenia patient has much more difficulty with drawing the figure from memory than the control subject. The lower part shows the figure drawn after 20 minutes, when the age- and intelligence- matched healthy control subject still outperforms the schizophrenia patient. This is also found in larger groups of healthy controls compared to schizophrenia subjects (Nieman et al., 2002). Reduced performance on the Complex Figure of Rey has been reported in patients with schizophrenia, but also in patients with obsessive compulsive (Penadés et al., 2005) and major depressive disorder (Behnken et al., 2010; Hammar and Schmid, 2013).

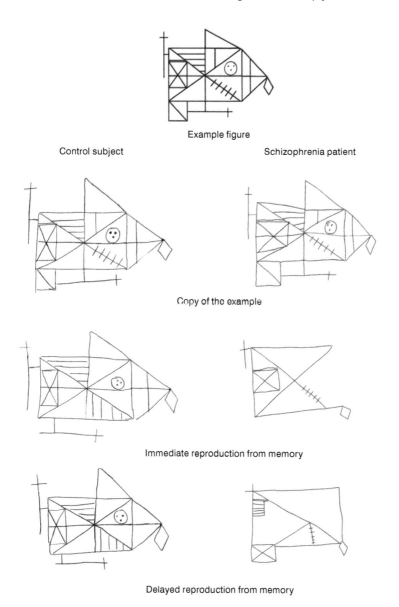

FIGURE 7.2 The Complex Figure of Rey

A study by the Dutch Trimbos institute (Hendriksen-Favier et al., 2012) showed that patients with schizophrenia especially want treatment for their cognitive deficits. Antipsychotic medication, usually prescribed to schizophrenia patients, does not improve and sometimes worsens cognitive ompairment (Husa et al., 2014). Professionals may think that schizophrenia patients want to be cured of their psychotic experiences (delusions and hallucinations), but if you ask the patients, they say that they want a job and a girlfriend. Especially for the first, it helps if you can focus and plan. Patients want to function and to have a meaningful life like other people, and cognitive functions are very important to reach this goal (Hendriksen-Favier et al., 2012).

Cognitive dysfunction is, therefore, a poorly controlled and highly relevant dimension of psychiatric disorders that cuts across traditional diagnostic boundaries. Improved treatment should be a major goal in efforts to enhance quality of life for patients (Millan et al., 2012).

Millan et al. (2012) reviewed transdiagnostic neuropsychological deficits in psychiatric patients. Most studies have investigated cognitive deficits in schizophrenia, major depressive disorder or obsessive compulsive disorder. But if you combine all these studies, it becomes apparent that cognitive dysfunctioning in DSM disorders shows much overlap, and within the categories there is much interpatient heterogeneity. In all DSM categories, cognitive deficits are found, but they vary between patients with the same diagnosis.

Table 7.1. shows cognitive deficits found in psychiatric and neurological disorders. For example, the DSM IV diagnoses of major depressive disorder, bipolar disorder, schizophrenia, autism spectrum disorder (ASD), ADHD, obsessive compulsive disorder (OCD), post traumatic stress disorder (PTSD), panic disorder, generalized anxiety disorder (GAD) disease all show a decrease or increase in attention and/or vigilance. The following video about selective attention shows that you only notice certain aspects of the environment: https://www.youtube.com/watch?v=ubNF9QNEQLA

Selective attention can both be a healthy as well as a pathological cognitive bias. Prolonged and extreme selective attention to certain aspects of the environment characterizes most psychiatric disorders. Depressed patients mainly notice sad faces and misfortune (de Raedt et al., 2010; Peckham et al., 2010; Everaert et al., 2014). People with an anxiety disorder are focused on the object of their anxiety (Bar-Haim et al., 2007; Cisler and Koster, 2010), as are alcohol dependent people on alcohol related cues (Sharbanee et al., 2013), and paranoid patients can perceive threat in many situations (Bentall et al., 2001; Warman and Martin, 2006).

Another cognitive deficit that is seen in the majority of psychiatric disorders is a deficit in executive functioning which encompasses purposeful, goal-directed operations such as planning, decision making, problem solving, reasoning, concept formation, self-monitoring or cognitive flexibility (Table 7.1, Millan et al., 2012). To summarize, executive functions are important for self-control that includes the suppression of inappropriate responses and the initiation of appropriate ones, as illustrated by the antisaccade test (Nieman et al., 2000; Nieman et al., 2007). In this task, subjects have to inhibit the reflexive reaction to look at a suddenly appearing dot, and then look in the other direction. A feedback signal indicates if the subject looked in the correct direction. Figure 7.3 shows the registration of eye movements of a control subject and a schizophrenia patient during the antisaccade task.

The control subject is quite good at inhibiting the reflexive reaction and looking in the other direction, but the patient first looks at the dot and then in

TABLE 7.1 Cognitive deficits in psychiatric and neurological disorders

	Attention and/or vigilance	Working memory	Executive functioning	Episodic memory	Semantic memory	Visual memory	Verbal memory	Fear extinction	Processing speed	Procedural memory	Social cognition (theory of mind)	Language
Major depression	+(+)	++	++	++	+	+	+(+)	0/+?	++(+)	+	+	+
Bipolar disorder	++(+)	++	++	++	+	+	++	+?	++	0	++	++
Schizophrenia	+++M	+++M	+++M	+++	++	+(+)M	+++M	++	++M	+	++++M	+++
ASD	+++	++	+++	++	+	+	+(+)	+(+)	+++	0/+	+++	+++
ADHD	+++	++	++	0/+	+	++	++	+	++	+	+	0/+
OCD	+++(↑)	+(+)	++	+	0/+	0/+	0/+	++	++	++	+	0/+
PTSD	+++(↑)	+(+)	+(+)	++	0/+	+	++(+)	+++	+	0	0/+	0
Panic disorder	+++(↑)	+	0/+	+	+		+	++	++	0	0	0
GAD	+	+	0	0				+	0	0	0/+	0
Parkinson's disease	+(+)	++	+(+)	+	0/+	+++	+	0?	+++	+++	+(+)	+(+)
Alzheimer's disease	+(+)	++(+)	++	+++	+++	+++	++(+)	0?	+++	+	+	++

0, essentially absent; 0/+, poorly documented, ambiguous, mild and/or variable; +, consistently present but not pronounced: ++, a common, marked characteristic; +++, a core, severe and virtually universal characteristic of the disorder. ?, not clearly evaluated: ↑, increase; AD, Alzheimer's disease; ADHD, attention deficit hyperactivity disorder; ASD, autism spectrum disorder; GAD, generalized anxiety disorder; OCD, obsessive compulsive disorder; PD, Parkinsons disease: PTSD, post-traumatic stress disorder. Social cognition encompasses theory of mind. In rare cases (such as Savant syndrome), autistic individuals display a remarkable increase in declarative memory and processing speed for selected domains of interest. ADHD observations refer to the young; similar symptoms usually persist into adulthood. Individuals with OCD, PTSD and panic disorders show hypervigilance to threatening (intrusive) stimuli, which can disrupt performance of goal-directed tasks. For AD, observations are for a modest degree of progression. Brackets around '+' symbols indicate an intermediate magnitude of deficit: for example. "+(+)' indicates between '+' and '++'.

Reprinted by permission from Macmillan Publishers Ltd, copyright 2012. Millan, M.J., et al. Cognitive dysfunction in psychiatric disorders: characteristics, causes and the quest for improved therapy. *Nature Reviews Drug Discovery* 11(2), 141-68.

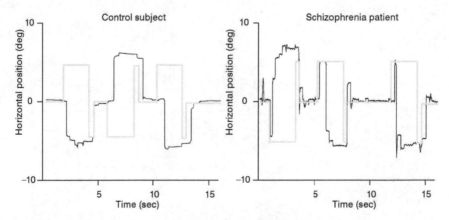

FIGURE 7.3 Antisaccade task performance in a control subject and a patient (Nieman et al, 2000). The grey lines represent the laser target (fixation, appearance, feedback) and the black lines represent the eye movements. The patient looks at the visual target in each trial, whereas the control inhibits this reflexive response. deg=degrees

the other direction. People often do not notice it themselves, and therefore you need to make a registration to detect it. Deficits in antisaccade test performance can be found in schizophrenia patients, but also in patients with depression (Malsert et al., 2012) or obsessive compulsive disorder (Lennertz et al., 2012).

Brodmann area 46 in the prefrontal cortex has often been found as an important biological substrate of executive functioning (see Figure 7.4).

Executive function reciprocally interacts with attention (Millan et al., 2012). Deficits in both cognitive functions may be underlying the phenomenological inability to change thoughts and/or emotions during a severe psychiatric disorder. It is not fruitful to reason with a severely depressed patient about the sunny side of life, or with a floridly psychotic patient about the scientific improbability of telepathy, or with an obsessive compulsive patient about the harmlessness of touching a doorknob. During severe mental illness, subjects are often not able to use executive function and selective attention to get themselves out of their agonizing situation. Results show that it is possible in the early stages of psychiatric disorders, when self-reflection and cognitive functions are less impaired (Fusar-Poli et al., 2012; van der Gaag et al., 2012, 2013).

Operationalized criteria, giving rise to ultra high risk (Miller et al., 2003), clinical high risk (Cornblatt et al., 2003) or At Risk Mental State (ARMS) (Yung et al., 1996) status, have been developed to identify the early stages of psychiatric disorders in young individuals (14–35 years) seeking help for their mental health problems. These criteria require one or more of three presentations: attenuated psychotic symptoms, full-blown psychotic symptoms that are brief (less than a week) and self-limiting, and/or a significant decrease in functioning in the context of a schizotypal personality disorder or a first-degree relative with psychosis. The ARMS criteria as assessed by the most recent versions of the Comprehensive

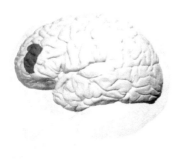

FIGURE 7.4 Brodmann area 46

Source: this image was made from content published in a BodyParts3D/Anatomography website. The content of the website is published under the Creative Commons Attribution 2.1 Japan license. The author and licenser of the contents is BodyParts3D, © The Database Center for Life Science licensed under CC Attribution-Share Alike 2.1 Japan

Assessment of At Risk Mental States (CAARMS) (Yung et al., 2008) require a sustained low psychosocial functioning or a recent drop in functioning in all of the above mentioned groups. Belonging to one of these 'putative prodromal' groups (hereafter: ARMS) is associated with an enhanced risk to develop a first psychosis.

Metacognitive training, in which subjects learn to correct the effects of their cognitive biases, decreased the severity of symptoms and the chance of transition to psychosis in ARMS subjects (van der Gaag et al., 2012, 2013), whereas in schizophrenia patients metacognitive training did not improve outcome (van Oosterhout et al., 2014). This example illustrates clinical staging in psychiatry, implying that at earlier stages of a disorder less harmful treatments can be more effective than later in the illness course (Nieman and McGorry, 2015; McGorry et al., 2006, 2007, 2013, 2014).

Intervention in the ARMS phase may be more effective than intervention after psychotic onset, because subjects are in a more treatment responsive stage of illness in which neurobiological and psychosocial damage is less extensive. We found that in ARMS subjects, antisaccade task performance was intermediate between control subjects and schizophrenia patients (Nieman et al., 2007, see Figure 7.5).

Thus, it may be possible to influence cognitive processes in the early phases of mental disorders. The ARMS phase that precedes most psychiatric disorders is discussed in more detail in the next chapter.

ARMS patients often say that their problems started with cognitive dysfunction (like not being able to focus in class, not being able to extract the essence of what the teacher is saying). Years before the start of a florid psychotic episode, you often see a drop in school level. Could cognitive deficits be the cause of psychiatric symptoms? This is an important question, and the answer is still unclear. One

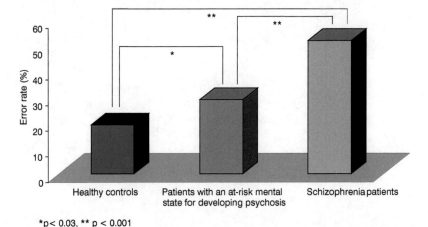

FIGURE 7.5 Mean antisaccade error rate in schizophrenia patients, healthy control subjects and patients with an at risk mental state (ARMS) for developing a first psychosis

could imagine that poor memory results in confusion. Alzheimer's disease starts with reduced cognitive performance and results in anxiety, confusion, psychosis, depression, etcetera. Recently, more insight has been gained into the longitudinal development of cognitive deficits and the emergence of psychiatric symptoms. In their review, Kahn and Keefe (2013) report that cognitive decline precedes the diagnosis of schizophrenia by years. Furthermore, Vorstman et al. (2015) show that, in subjects with 22q11 deletion syndrome, early cognitive decline is a robust indicator of the risk of developing a psychotic illness, but also other psychiatric symptoms such as depression and anxiety. 22q11 deletion syndrome is a disorder caused by the deletion of a small piece of chromosome 22. These patients have an elevated (25%) risk of developing schizophrenia. A subgroup of children with 22q11 deletion syndrome display a substantial decline in cognitive abilities starting at a young age.

Cognitive deficits have frequently been reported in ARMS subjects (Fusar-Poli et al., 2012). These results are consistent with the subjective reports of patients, who often have problems with attention and concentration long before the first affective symptoms show. Of course, these results do not prove that cognition causes psychosis, that is still unclear, but the results do indicate that cognitive deficits are not just the result of psychosis, as was sometimes presumed in the past. More research is needed to determine the exact relationship between cognition and psychiatric symptoms.

To develop new cognitive treatments, we need to gain insight into why psychiatric patients have cognitive deficits. As can be seen in Figure 7.6, the problem is very complex. It encompasses the most basic cellular processes, as well as higher neural networks. Dysfunction underlying cognitive impairment is hierarchically and spatially diverse, and enacted over a temporal scale running from milliseconds (for example, cellular firing) to hours (for example, protein

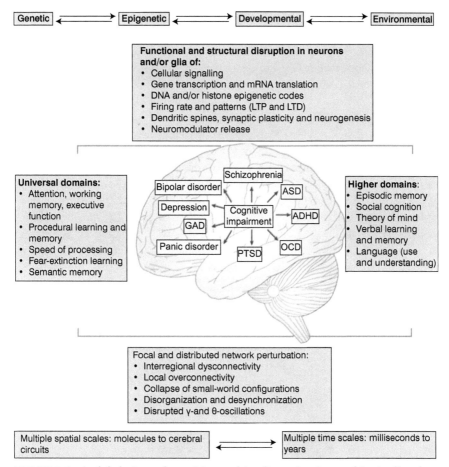

FIGURE 7.6 A global view of cognition and its disruption in psychiatric disorders (Millan et al, 2012). *LTD, long-term depression; LPD, long-term potentiation*

Source: reprinted by permission from Macmillan Publishers Ltd, copyright 2012. M.J. Millan, et al. (2012) 'Cognitive dysfunction in psychiatric disorders: characteristics, causes and the quest for improved therapy'. *Nature Reviews Drug Discovery* 11(2), 141–168.

synthesis) to years (for example, synaptic architecture). Some susceptibility factors, can be passed on to offspring. Certain causes of cognitive impairment can be rectified or compensated, but network shifts at the molecular to systems level are not necessarily reversible so prevention and early treatment is crucial.

As mentioned previously, if we want to gain more insight into the biological basis of cognitive deficits, the DSM will not be of much help. Increased insight into these deficits will be only one part of the puzzle. A psychiatric disorder can probably not be reduced in most instances to a biological deficit, but treatment of this deficit with specific therapies could ameliorate the clinical picture in certain patients. Furthermore, cognitive remediation before subjects start experiencing psychiatric symptoms could lead to prevention or improved prognosis. It may be possible to find clusters of biological deficits that have prognostic value. It may be that the evidence will lead to a nature-based clustering that shows overlap with the current DSM categories but perhaps it will not.

Wessman et al. (2009) report on the results of a study that illustrates the bottom-up approach as discussed in the first paragraphs of this chapter. A large group of subjects was selected from families in which psychotic disorders occurred. The subjects were assessed with a cognitive test battery, genetics and symptomatology questionnaires. Then a cluster analysis was performed, and three clusters were found. Cluster 1 encompassed a mood disorder component, and showed an association with the DISC 1 gene. The second cluster consisted of mainly subjects with neurocognitive deficits and negative symptoms such as apathy, and an association was found with the DTNBP1 gene (see Figure 7.7). The third cluster consisted of relatively well subjects. This study shows that there may be different subtypes with a distinct neurobiological substrate within the DSM category of 'Schizophrenia and Other Psychotic Disorders', as most clinicians suspected.

In the previously mentioned transdiagnostic Biobank Cognition study, patients who come for intake to our Psychiatry Department are assessed, when they want to participate, with a cognitive testbattery as well as (self-report) questionnaires about symptom dimensions like level of energy, ability to reassure oneself, anhedonia, hallucinations, medication and drug use at inclusion and 1 year follow up. We

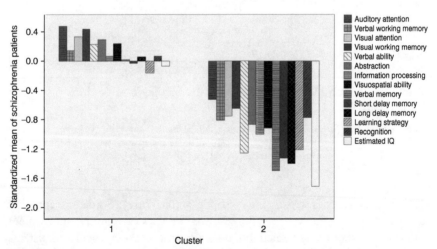

FIGURE 7.7 Average neuropsychological performance of the clusters (Wessman et al., 2010). Cluster 1: psychotic disorder with mood symptoms, association with DISC1 gene. Cluster 2: schizophrenia with negative symptoms, cognitive deficits and early onset, association with DTNBP1 gene

Source: reprinted from J. Wessman et al. (2010) 'Mixture model clustering of phenotype features reveals evidence for association of DTNBP1 to a specific subtype of schizophrenia', *Biological Psychiatry* 66(11) 990–996 Copyright 2010 with permission from Elsevier.

collect data about information processing deficits with an electroencephalogram (EEG), blood markers like cytokines, genetics and hair cortisol, which gives an indication of stress. Already more than 550 patients with various DSM diagnoses have participated. Deficits in the different cognitive domains (memory, attention, executive functioning, etcetera) will be investigated for their relationships with symptom dimensions and biological parameters such as indicators of stress, markers in the blood, firing of neurons with EEG. Stress probably plays a major role in cognitive dysfunctioning, as has been reported often (Millan et al., 2012). Markers in the blood, for example inflammatory cytokines (regulators produced throughout the body that help in cell signalling) have shown a relationship with reduced cognitive functioning in several studies (Marin and Kipnis, 2013).

In the Biobank Cognition study, we may learn more about biological mechanisms associated with cognitive deficits, their improvement or worsening. We may find new clusters with better prognostic value than the DSM categories (which is not very difficult since the DSM categories have hardly any prognostic validity). Because of the repeated assessment after a year, we can investigate when cognitive deficits arise, and the relationship with symptom dimensions and biological parameters. Increased insight into the relationship among cognitive deficits, biological parameters and narrowly defined symptom dimensions can lead to new treatment possibilities.

Treatment of cognitive impairment

Research into new treatment options of cognitive dysfunction is currently being performed at the Academic Medical Center in Amsterdam. An example is a transdiagnostic Randomized Controlled Trial for improving cognition with a serious online game and cognitve assessment tool (Nieman et al., 2015). The game is dynamic, adjusting itself to the performance level of the patient. Patients are trained holistically, in all domains, but with greater intensity where their need is highest. Since cognitive dysfunction is prominent in many psychiatric disorders, its treatment may lead to reduced symptoms and increased ability to function socially and occupationally. To remediate cognitive dysfunctions, cognitive remediation test batteries have been employed. Cognitive remediation is the systematic use of methods aimed at improving cognitive functioning through computer-based or paper and pencil cognitive exercises, teaching more effective strategies for addressing cognitive challenges, and teaching coping or compensatory skills to reduce the effects of cognitive impairment on psychosocial functioning.

While cognitive remediation approaches are promising, several caveats remain. Effects of cognitive remediation exercise batteries often do not generalize to improvement in real life cognitive and occupational functioning as assessed with the General Assessment of Functioning scale. One of the reasons for this may be that psychiatric patients often stop with the cognitive remediation battery, because the exercises are not very challenging or appealing.

Furthermore, cognitive remediation batteries often do not adjust the difficulty level to the cognitive abilities of the patient.

Cognitive remediation with an individualized cognitive applied game and assessment tool has not yet been fully investigated in a scientifically valid and clinically relevant, randomized controlled trial design. If cognitive improvement occurs, it is still unclear what the neurobiological substrate is of this improvement. Therefore, subjects participate in the Biobank Cognition study at baseline and after 12 weeks.

Patients with schizophrenia, obsessive compulsive disorder, and major depressive disorder are randomized to treatment as usual, or treatment as usual plus an online link so they can play the game and do the cognitive assessment at home. They are required to play at least 3 times a week for half an hour for 12 weeks. Data collection takes place online. In a study investigating the cognitive game in elementary school children, the group that played the game improved significantly more in cognitive functioning than the control group. Results of a pilot study into the feasibility of the project, efficacy of the game and validity of the online assessment tool are promising (Nieman et al., 2015; Domen et al., 2015). If the game turns out to be effective in a comprehensive Randomized Controlled Trial that is currently underway, psychiatry will have a new, patient-friendly treatment option, with few side-effects, that can lead to health care cost reduction. It could be that cognitive decline could be stopped or even turned around before psychiatric symptoms emerge.

Sahakian and Morein-Zamir (2015) argue that cognitive deficits are common in psychiatric disorders, and that cognitive enhancement before the psychiatric disorder is full blown could be beneficial. However, using drugs such as methylphenidate for such purposes may carry the risk of changing neurotransmitter systems in the brain in an unnatural way, and lead to withdrawal effects. Research efforts should focus on natural ways to enhance cognitive function, for example with a cognitive game or other natural evidence-based cognitive enhancing strategies.

The case example of Steven shows that a typical course of a first psychotic episode with cognitive dysfunction starting long before the affective symptoms occur.

CASE EXAMPLE: STEVEN

Steven is a 20 year old philosophy student who is skipping a lot of classes lately. In the classroom, he hears his name whispered by fellow students in the front row, although the distance is too far to be able to hear them. During the breaks he hears other students talk and laugh about him. Sometimes he thinks they are conspiring to kill him, especially since he hears them talking when he is alone in his room about how they are going to get him. He is unable to concentrate on what the professor says in the classroom. It is as if he cannot extract the meaning of what is being said. He has had that problem for several years. His grades have decreased during this period, and he will probably drop out of college now. He feels like he cannot structure his life, his thoughts, his experiences. It is very frightening because it means losing control. When he thinks back, the inability to plan and structure came first, and when this got progressively worse, he became anxious and withdrawn. He felt inferior because he could not keep up with his peers and started to sleep poorly. Subsequently the paranoia and hallucinations started.

References

Bar-Haim, Y., Lamy, D., Pergamin, L., Bakermans-Kranenburg, M.J. and van IJzendoorn, M.H. (2007). Threat-related attentional bias in anxious and nonanxious individuals: a meta-analytic study. *Psychological Bulletin* 133(1), 1–24.

Behnken, A., Schöning, S., Gerss, J., Konrad, C., de Jong-Meyer, R., Zwanzger, P. and Arolt, V. (2010). Persistent non-verbal memory impairment in remitted major depression – caused by encoding deficits? *Journal of Affective Disorders* 122(1), 144–148.

Bentall, R.P., Corcoran, R., Howard, R., Blackwood, N. and Kinderman, P. (2001). Persecutory delusions: A review and theoretical integration. *Clinical Psychology Review* 21, 1143–1192.

Cisler, J.M. and Koster, E.H.W. (2010). Mechanisms of attentional bias towards threat in anxiety disorders: An integrative review. *Clinical Psychology Review* 30, 203–216.

Cornblatt, B.A., Lencz, T., Smith, C.W., Correll, C.U., Auther, A.M. and Nakayama, E. (2003). The schizophrenia prodrome revisited: a neurodevelopmental perspective. *Schizophrenia Bulletin* 29, 633–651.

de Raedt, R. and Koster, E.H.W. (2010). Understanding vulnerability for depression from a cognitive neuroscience perspective: A reappraisal of attentional factors and a new conceptual framework. *Cognitive, Affective & Behavioral Neuroscience* 10(1), 50–70.

Domen, A.C., Kumar R, Harrison, J., de Haan, L., Denys, D. and Nieman, D.H. (2015) The validation of a new online cognitive assessment tool: the MyCognition Quotient (MyCQ). *European Neuropsychopharmacology* 25, S344.

Everaert, J., Duyck, W. and Koster, E.H.W. (2014). Attention, interpretation, and memory biases in subclinical depression: a proof-of-principle test of the combined cognitive biases hypothesis. *Emotion* 14(2), 331–40.

Fusar-Poli,P. Deste, G., Smieskova, R., Barlati, S., Yung, A.R., Howes, O., Stieglitz, R.D., Vita, A., McGuire, P. and Borgwardt, S. (2012). Cognitive functioning in prodromal psychosis: a meta-analysis. *Archives of General Psychiatry* 69(6), 562–71.

Hammar, Å. and Schmid, M. (2013). Visual memory performance in patients with major depression: a 9-month follow-up. *Applied Neuropsychology: Adult* 20(3), 192–196.

Hendriksen-Favier, A., van Rooijen, S., Vink, L., Rijkaart, A. and Kroon, A. (2012). *Bridging the Gap*. Utrecht: Trimbos Instituut.

Hickie, I.B., Scott, E.M., Hermens, D.F., Naismith, S.L., Guastella, A.J., Kaur, M., Sidis, A., Whitwell, B., Glozier, N., Davenport, T., Pantelis, C., Wood, S.J. and McGorry, P.D. (2013). Applying clinical staging to young people who present for mental healthcare. *Early Intervention Psychiatry* 7, 31–43.

Husa, A.P., Rannikko, I., Moilanen, J., Haapea, M., Murray, G.K., Barnett, J., Jones, P.B., Isohanni, M., Koponen, H., Miettunen, J. and Jääskeläinen, E. (2014). Lifetime use of antipsychotic medication and its relation to change of learning and memory in midlife schizophrenia – An observational 9-year follow-up study. *Schizophrenia Research* 158(1–3), 134–41.

Kahn, R.S. and Keefe, R.S. (2013). Schizophrenia is a cognitive illness: time for a change in focus. *JAMA Psychiatry* 70(10), 1107–12.

Lennertz, L., Rampacher, F., Vogeley, A., Schulze-Rauschenbach, S., Pukrop, R., Ruhrmann, S., Klosterkötter, J., Maier, W., Falkai, P. and Wagner, M. (2012). Antisaccade performance in patients with obsessive-compulsive disorder and unaffected relatives: further evidence for impaired response inhibition as a candidate endophenotype. *European Archives of Psychiatry and Clinical Neuroscience* 262(7), 625–34.

Malsert, J., Guyader, N., Chauvin, A., Polosan, M., Poulet, E., Szekely, D., Bougerol, T. and Marendaz, C. (2012). Antisaccades as a follow-up tool in major depressive disorder therapies: a pilot study. *Psychiatry Research* 200(2), 1051–3.

Marin, I. and Kipnis, J. (2013). Learning and memory ... and the immune system. *Learning & Memory* 20(10), 601–6.

McGorry, P.D. (2007). Issues for DSM-V: clinical staging: a heuristic pathway to valid nosology and safer, more effective treatment in psychiatry. *American Journal of Psychiatry* 164, 859–60.

McGorry, P.D. (2013). Early clinical phenotypes, clinical staging, and strategic biomarker research: building blocks for personalised psychiatry. *Biological Psychiatry* 74, 394–395.

McGorry, P.D., Hickie, I.B., Yung, A.R., Pantelis, C. and Jackson, H.J. (2006). Clinical staging of psychiatric disorders: a heuristic framework for choosing earlier, safer and more effective interventions. *Australian and New Zealand Journal of Psychiatry* 40, 616–22.

McGorry, P.D., Keshavan, M., Goldstone, S., Amminger, P., Allott, K., Berk, M., Lavoie, S., Pantelis, C., Yung, A., Wood, S. and Hickie, I. (2014). Biomarkers and clinical staging in psychiatry. *World Psychiatry* 13(3), 211–23.

Millan, M.J., Agid, Y., Brüne, M., Bullmore, E.T., Carter, C.S., Clayton, N.S., Connor, R., Davis, S., Deakin, B., DeRubeis, R.J., Dubois, B., Geyer, M.A., Goodwin, G.M., Gorwood, P., Jay, T.M., Joëls, M., Mansuy, I.M., Meyer-Lindenberg, A., Murphy, D., Rolls, E., Saletu, B., Spedding, M., Sweeney, J., Whittington, M. and Young, L.J. (2012). Cognitive dysfunction in psychiatric disorders: characteristics, causes and the quest for improved therapy. *Nature Reviews Drug Discovery* 11(2), 141–68.

Miller, T.J., McGlashan, T.H., Rosen, J.L., Cadenhead, K., Cannon, T., Ventura, J., McFarlane, W., Perkins, D.O., Pearlson, G.D. and Woods, S.W. (2003). Prodromal assessment with the structured interview for prodromal syndromes and the scale of prodromal symptoms: predictive validity, interrater reliability, and training to reliability. *Schizophrenia Bulletin* 29(4), 703–15.

Nieman, D.H., and McGorry, P.D. (2015). Detection and treatment of 'At Risk Mental State' for developing a first psychosis: Making up the balance. *The Lancet Psychiatry* 2, 825–34.

Nieman, D.H., Bour, L.J., Linszen, D.H., Goede, J., Koelman, J.H.T.M., Gersons, B.P.R. and Ongerboer de Visser, B.W. (2000). Neuropsychological and clinical correlates of antisaccade task performance in schizophrenia. *Neurology* 54(4), 866–71.

Nieman, D.H., Koelman, J.H., Linszen, D.H., Bour, L.J., Dingemans, P.M. and Ongerboer de Visser, B.W. (2002). Clinical and neuropsychological correlates of the P300 in schizophrenia. *Schizophrenia Research* 55, 105–113.

Nieman, D.H., Becker, H., van de Fliert, R., Plat, N., Koelman, H., Klaassen, M., Dingemans, P., Niessen, M. and Linszen, D. (2007). Antisaccade task performance in patients at ultra high risk for developing psychosis. *Schizophrenia Research* 95, 54–60.

Nieman, D.H., Domen A., Kumar R., Harrison, J., de Haan, L. and Denys, D. (2015). Cognitive remediation with an online cognitive game and assessment tool. *European Neuropsychopharmacology* 25, S344–S345.

Peckham, A.D., McHugh, R.K. and Otto M.W. (2010). A meta-analysis of the magnitude of biased attention in depression. *Depression and Anxiety* 27, 1135–1142.

Penadés, R., Catalán, R., Andrés, S., Salamero, M. and Gastó, C. (2005). Executive function and nonverbal memory in obsessive-compulsive disorder. *Psychiatry Research* 133(1), 81–90.

Sahakian, B.J. and Morein-Zamir, S. (2015) Pharmacological cognitive enhancement: treatment of neuropsychiatric disorders and lifestyle use by healthy people. *Lancet Psychiatry* 2, 357–62.

Sharbanee, J.M., Stritzke, W.G., Wiers, R.W. and MacLeod, C. (2013). Alcohol-related biases in selective attention and action tendency make distinct contributions to dysregulated drinking behaviour. *Addiction* 108(10), 1758–66.

Strimbu, K. and Tavel, J.A. (2010). What are biomarkers? *Current Opinion in HIV and AIDS* 5(6), 463–466.

van der Gaag, M., Nieman, D.H., Rietdijk, J., Dragt, S., Ising, H.K., Klaassen, R.M., Koeter, M., Cuijpers, P., Wunderink, L. and Linszen, D.H. (2012). Cognitive behavioral therapy for subjects at ultra high risk for developing psychosis: a randomized controlled clinical trial. *Schizophrenia Bulletin* 38, 1180–8.

van der Gaag, M., Nieman, D.H. and van den Berg, D. (2013). *CBT for Those At Risk for a First Episode Psychosis: Evidence Based Psychotherapy for People with an 'At Risk Mental State'*. Oxford: Routledge.

van Oosterhout, B., Krabbendam, L., de Boer, K., Ferwerda, J., van der Helm, M., Stant, D. and van der Gaag, M. (2014). Metacognitive group training for schizophrenia spectrum patients with delusions: a randomized controlled trial. *Psychological Medicine* 44(14), 3025–35.

Vorstman, J.A., Breetvelt, E.J., Duijff, S.N., Eliez, S., Schneider, M., Jalbrzikowski, M., Armando, M., Vicari, S., Shashi, V., Hooper, S.R., Chow, E.W., Fung, W.L., Butcher, N.J., Young, D.A., McDonald-McGinn, D.M., Vogels, A., van Amelsvoort, T., Gothelf, D., Weinberger, R., Weizman, A., Klaassen, P.W., Koops, S., Kates, W.R., Antshel, K.M., Simon, T.J., Ousley, O.Y., Swillen, A., Gur, R.E., Bearden, C.E., Kahn, R.S. and Bassett, A.S. (2015). International Consortium on Brain and Behavior in 22q11.2 Deletion Syndrome. Cognitive decline preceding the onset of psychosis in patients with 22q11.2 deletion syndrome. *JAMA Psychiatry* 72(4), 377–85.

Warman, D.M. and Martin, J.M. (2006). Cognitive insight and delusion proneness: An investigation using the Beck cognitive insight scale. *Schizophrenia Research* 84, 297–304.

Wessman, J., Paunio, T., Tuulio-Henriksson, A., Koivisto, M., Partonen, T., Suvisaari, J., Turunen, J.A., Wedenoja, J., Hennah, W., Pietiläinen, O.P., Lönnqvist, J., Mannila, H. and Peltonen, L. (2009). Mixture model clustering of phenotype features reveals evidence for association of DTNBP1 to a specific subtype of schizophrenia. *Biological Psychiatry* 66(11), 990–6.

Yung, A.R., McGorry, P.D., McFarlane, C.A., Jackson, H.J., Patton, G.C. and Rakkar, A. (1996). Monitoring and care of young people at incipient risk of psychosis. *Schizophrenia Bulletin* 22, 283–303.

Yung, A.R., Nelson, B., Stanford, C., Simmons, M.B., Cosgrave, E.M., Killackey, E., Phillips, L.J., Bechdolf, A., Buckby, J. and McGorry, P.D. (2008). Validation of 'prodromal' criteria to detect individuals at ultra high risk of psychosis: 2 year follow-up. *Schizophrenia Research* 105(1), 10–17.

8
FROM CLINICAL STAGING AND PROFILING TO PREVENTION IN PSYCHIATRY

In many serious illnesses (e.g. cancer, cardiovascular disease), early detection and optimal and sustained treatment has led to greatly improved prognosis. In light of limited treatment possibilities in late stages of major mental disorders, early detection and treatment in psychiatry has generated a great deal of indicative, if not yet conclusive, evidence of its value. We know that the need for care emerges well before traditional diagnoses such as schizophrenia and bipolar disorder can be applied (McGorry et al., 2006; McGorry and van Os, 2013). Early clinical phenotypes (i.e. the clinical presentation) are often subthreshold forms of these late phenotypes blended with prominent comorbid features of nonspecific distress, including anxiety and depressive symptoms, substance use and functional disturbance. Clinical experience and research has revealed that it is easier to engage a patient in treatment when distress is prominent while symptoms are not yet so severe that illness-insight is lost. With accurate public education and pathways to access to care in novel stigma-free settings, the fear and confusion that people feel may be overcome (Nieman and McGorry, 2015; Johannessen et al., 2005; Joa et al., 2008).

Because of the limited treatment possibilities in the late stages of severe mental disorders such as schizophrenia, there is a pressing need for indicated prevention, i.e. identifying individuals who are experiencing early signs of a severe mental disorder and treating them with evidence-based, non-invasive therapies (McGorry et al., 2006; McGorry, 2007, 2013; van Os, 2013; Nieman and McGorry, 2015).

Clinical staging and profiling

Clinical staging and profiling are promising in psychiatry. Clinical staging has been developed because in an earlier phase of a disorder treatments are usually more effective than later in the illness course (Hickie et al., 2013; McGorry et al., 2007; Scott, 2011; Scott et al., 2006). Profiling entails using variables in the diagnosis that have shown a prognostic value, or can predict treatment response in patients with specific characteristics (Kapczinski et al., 2009; Beekman et al., 2012). Optimal prediction and early treatment of mental illness with benign interventions may therefore lead to considerable gains in both the patient's quality of life and health care costs. Another advantage of implementation of a clinical staging model would be that in the earliest stages, symptoms would not have to be labelled as a specific disease, with a formal diagnosis or even as an at-risk stage – more like a mild to moderate mental ill-health situation. Furthermore, research on profiling could make clinical care more personalized, leading to optimal treatment selection.

A first psychotic episode in the context of schizophrenia, bipolar disorder, major depression, or other severe mental illness, rarely starts out of the blue and in retrospect, is usually preceded by a period of initially subtle, yet evolving, symptom burden and psychosocial impairment (McGorry, 2007). Subjects can, for example, describe that they sometimes think that they are being followed, but they know that it is not true, and they are often afraid that they are developing a mental illness. In the early 1990s, criteria for an at-risk mental state (ARMS) (McGorry et al., 2003; Yung et al., 2005; Yung et al., 2008) were developed, which proved to be strongly predictive of transition to psychosis (see Chapter 7). This led to an exponential increase in research into the prodromal or ARMS stage of psychosis, focusing on the neurobiology of this stage of illness and interventions to alleviate the symptoms, restore functioning, reduce the risk and ultimately delay or prevent the transition to psychosis (McGorry, 2007). Transition to psychosis is defined as a psychotic episode of a week or longer. Most ARMS patients already have a psychiatric diagnosis. In our previous study (van der Gaag et al., 2012), ARMS patients were diagnosed with anxiety disorders (n=53), depression (52), mixed anxiety and depression (10), personality disorders (15), attention deficit hyperactivity disorder (13), addiction (12), eating disorders (11), post traumatic stress disorder (10), oppositional defiant disorder (6) and Asperger syndrome (5).

In a recent meta-analysis, transition to psychosis in ARMS subjects was 22 per cent after 1 year, accumulating to 29 per cent at 2 year and 36 per cent at 3 year follow up (Fusar-Poli et al., 2013). Even with significant exposure to care, 36 per cent become psychotic within 2 years. Of those who do not make the transition, the majority manifest persistent subthreshold psychotic symptoms and/or mood and anxiety disorders (Fusar-Poli et al., 2013). Furthermore, a significant percentage of ARMS subjects who do not make the transition to psychosis show impaired psychosocial functioning at the follow up (Addington et al., 2011). Because of these findings, clinical symptoms and psychosocial functioning are regarded as an important outcome in addition to transition to psychosis.

There have been many studies trying to enhance the prediction of the transition to psychosis, with a variety of candidate biomarkers. The goal is to define a biosignature that could not only accurately define the level of risk for a particular outcome but also guide treatment selection (profiling followed by specific treatment allocation) (McGorry, 2007).

In the Dutch Prediction of Psychosis Study, we combined the best predictors reported in separate studies in a Cox regression analysis (Nieman et al., 2014). Two risk factors for psychosis turned out to be independent predictors with a high prognostic (predictive) value: the P300 event-related potential (ERP) amplitude and the social personal adjustment item of the Premorbid Adjustment Scale (Cannon-Spoor et al.,1982). The P300 is derived from the electro-encephalogram (EEG). The EEG is assessed with electrodes on the scalp, and gives an indication of the firing of neurons (which is the basis of cognition). With derivatives of the EEG, so called event-related potentials, it is possible to get an indication of information-processing deficits. An event-related potential is the measured brain response to a specific stimulus, for example, a tone. In the P300 event-related potential task, subjects have to count high tones among low tones. The high tones generate a large positive wave after 300 msec. It is similar to seeing a familiar face in a crowd, this generates a P300. The shape and the latency of the P300 wave reflect to what extent you direct your attention to this face and update your memory that you saw that person there.

As can be seen in Figure 8.1, subjects who later make the transition to psychosis have a smaller P300 wave compared to those who do not make the transition as well as compared to healthy control subjects. Furthermore, the topographic map shows that P300 amplitude is especially reduced on the back of the head, at the parietal (Pz) electrode site in ARMS subjects who later make the transition to psychosis compared to ARMS subjects who do not and healthy controls.

Thus, the P300 is a cognition related wave, closely associated with attention and memory and a reduced P300 amplitude is one of the most promising biomarkers in psychiatry (Bramon et al., 2004; Turetsky et al., 2015).

Many papers showed P300 amplitude reduction in ARMS subjects (Atkinson et al., 2012; Bramon et al., 2008; Frommann et al., 2008; Jahshan et al., 2012; Jeon and Polich, 2003; Nieman et al., 2014; Ozgurdal et al., 2008; Patel and Azzam, 2005; van der Stelt et al., 2005; van Tricht et al., 2010). These findings are consistent with the attention and memory deficits reported by and found in ARMS subjects (Becker et al., 2010a; Becker et al., 2010b; Korver et al., 2010) that make it difficult to keep up with school and work, leading to psychosocial dysfunction.

A risk stratification approach considers risk not only at an 'all-or-nothing' level but at individually different levels with regard to severity and time to transition to the full blown disorder (Ruhrman et al., 2014). The prognostic index is a well-established and widespread risk modelling procedure used for multivariate clinical staging and profiling in somatic medicine, e.g. oncology (Briggs et al., 2008; Sperduto et al., 2008). In such a prognostic index, an algorithm encompassing predictors of outcome is used for calculating an

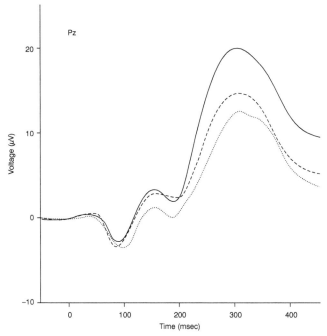

FIGURE 8.1 Grand average target waveforms for each group at Pz. ARMS subjects with transition to psychosis = dotted lower line; ARMS subjects without transition = dashed middle line; and control group= solid upper line. Pz, midline parietal

Source: reprinted by permission of Oxford University Press. D.H. Nieman et al. (2014). 'Psychosis prediction: stratification of risk estimation with information-processing and premorbid functioning variables'. Schizophrenia Bulletin 40(6), 1482–90.

individual prognostic score. In oncology, the algorithm may include, for example, size of the tumour, metastases, age of the patient, etcetera. Subjects with a worse prognostic score usually need more aggressive treatment with more serious side-effects (e.g. chemotherapy) than subjects with a better prognostic score (e.g. outpatient surgical procedure to remove the tumour).

The prognostic index was first introduced into psychiatry in 2010 by the European Prediction of Psychosis Study (Ruhrmann et al., 2010). In a prognostic index, individual prognostic scores are stratified in different risk classes for clinical usability (Ruhrmann et al., 2010). An example of a prognostic index in ARMS subjects is an algorithm that includes the P300 event-related potential amplitude and premorbid adjustment. In the Dutch Prediction of Psychosis Study, these two risk factors turned out to be most predictive for transition to psychosis of all risk factors that were investigated. Premorbid adjustment refers to the state of functionality (social and school-functioning) prior to the onset of the symptoms. The indices of the predictive model (in bold) were used in a predictive algorithm: {**.76** × Premorbid adjustment score} + {**−.23** × Pz P300 amplitude}.

The individual prognostic scores resulting from this algorithm could be stratified in 3 statistically different prognostic index risk classes, with a transition rate to a first psychosis of 4 per cent in risk class I, 25 per cent in risk class II and 74 per cent in risk class III (Nieman et al., 2014). Thus, compared to the overall transition rate of 29 per cent predicted by the inclusion criteria as assessed with the Comprehensive Assessment of At Risk Mental States (CAARMS), application of the prognostic index improved individual risk estimation significantly. The prognostic index also enabled adequate prediction of the time to transition, which differed markedly between class III and the other classes; the mean difference from the lowest class was more than 17 months (see Figure 8.2). As in somatic medicine, the individualized information about magnitude of risk and time to transition should allow tailoring preventive measures to individual needs.

Other promising candidates for additional predictors are currently electroencephalographic (EEG) paradigms, i.e. mismatch negativity (Bodatsch et al., 2011; Perez et al., 2014), and quantitative EEG (Zimmermann et al., 2010; van Tricht et al., 2014), abnormalities in structural magnetic resonance imaging (Koutsouleris et al., 2015), neurocognitive deficits (Riecher-Rossler et al., 2009), inflammation and oxidative stress blood biomarkers (McGorry et al., 2014). However, these results need replication in independent ARMS samples and beyond. The inclusion of biomarkers in prediction and clinical staging

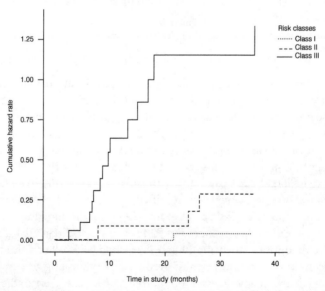

FIGURE 8.2 Kaplan-Meier survival analysis of risk classes of the prognostic index. Transition rate in risk class I = 4% in risk class II = 25% and risk class III = 74%. With regard to the survival curves, class I differed significantly from class II (χ^2 = 4.03, P < .045) and class III (χ^2 = 29.28, P < .0001). Furthermore, class II differed significantly from class III (χ^2 = 7.44, P < .006)

models could also provide insight into progression or remission of underlying transdiagnostic illness processes (McGorry et al., 2007).

Treatment and underlying neurobiological mechanisms

Meta-analyses (Stafford et al., 2013; van der Gaag et al., 2013), including our own research (van der Gaag, Nieman and van den Berg, 2013; van der Gaag et al., 2012), has shown that cognitive behavioural therapy can reduce the risk of transition to psychosis by about 50 per cent and improve symptoms in those with an ARMS. However, cognitive behavioural therapy alone is insufficient to treat information processing deficits that lead to psychosocial impairment. Psychosocial impairment is an essential ARMS inclusion criterion, because the predictive value of mild psychotic symptoms without psychosocial impairment for transition to a first psychosis is not very high (Yung et al., 2008). Therefore, ameliorating information processing disturbances that lead to psychosocial impairment with a neurobiological intervention could significantly improve prognosis in ARMS subjects. The neurobiological processes underlying development of severe mental illness are not fully known, but several studies show that alterations in immune function, possibly caused by stress may play a role (Kahn and Sommer, 2015; Perkins et al., 2015; Schizophrenia Working Group of the Psychiatric Genomics Consortium, 2014). Exposure to a stressor often results in pro-inflammatory responses in the brain and periphery. These responses are mediated by a variety of inflammatory molecules including neuropeptides, cytokines and stress hormones among others (Grippo and Scotti, 2013).

In the Dutch Prediction of Psychosis Study, about one fifth of the ARMS patients had already received antipsychotic medication when they were referred for a second opinion to our department, despite international clinical practice guidelines for ARMS subjects (International Early Psychosis Association Writing Group, 2005; Nieman et al., 2009). However, antipsychotic medication is not indicated for ARMS subjects because of the serious side-effects, the risk of triggering psychosis after cessation of antipsychotics (Moncrieff, 2006) and the lack of scientific evidence for the efficacy of antipsychotics to prevent a first psychotic episode (International Early Psychosis Association Writing Group, 2005).

In contrast, N-acetylcysteine is a promising and safe medication/nutritional supplement for the prevention and treatment of a multitude of psychiatric disorders, for example, schizophrenia, bipolar disorder, trichotillomania, skin picking, autism, obsessive-compulsive disorder, drug (including nicotine, cannabis, methamphetamine, cocaine, etcetera) and gambling addiction (Bavarsad et al., 2014; Berk et al., 2013; Dean et al., 2011; Molina et al., 2011).

N-acetylcysteine has been hypothesized to exert beneficial effects through its modulation of inflammatory processes (Dean et al., 2011). Increased neuroinflammation is associated with cognitive, information-processing deficits (Najjar et al., 2013). Several studies have shown that N-acetylcysteine can reduce information processing abnormalities (as assessed with EEG) found in humans. N-acetylcysteine significantly increased P300 amplitude in healthy volunteers who were given ketamine (a drug that can induce schizophrenia symptoms) (Gunduz-Bruce et al., 2012). In addition, Lavoie et al. (2008) reported that N-acetylcysteine normalized mismatch negativity EEG abnormalities in patients with schizophrenia. Carmeli et al. (2012) administered N-acetylcysteine and studied its effects on resting state EEGs in schizophrenia patients. They found that N-acetylcysteine significantly decreased EEG abnormalities (Carmeli et al., 2012).

Importantly, N-acetylcysteine is safe and well tolerated when administered orally, even in long treatments with high doses (Dean et al., 2011). As such, N-acetylcysteine holds great promise for the treatment of prodromal states and the prevention of serious psychiatric disorders (see Chapter 9).

Thus, the P300 biomarker has been shown to be very useful in the individualized prediction of psychosis in ARMS patients, and it may also be a valuable technique to monitor the effect of pharmacological interventions such as N-acetylcysteine in the prevention of psychosis in ARMS patients.

References

Addington, J., Cornblatt, B.A., Cadenhead, K.S., Cannon, T.D., McGlashan, T.H., Perkins, D.O., Seidman, L.J., Tsuang, M.T., Walker, E.F., Woods, S.W. and Heinssen, R. (2011). At clinical high risk for psychosis: outcome for nonconverters. *American Journal of Psychiatry* 168(8), 800–5.

Atkinson, R.J., Michie, P.T. and Schall, U. (2012). Duration mismatch negativity and P3a in first-episode psychosis and individuals at ultra-high risk of psychosis. *Biological Psychiatry* 71, 98–104.

Bavarsad Shahripour, R., Harrigan, M.R. and Alexandrov, A.V. (2014). N-acetylcysteine (NAC) in neurological disorders: Mechanisms of action and therapeutic opportunities. *Brain and Behavior* 4(2), 108–122.

Becker, H.E., Nieman, D.H., Dingemans, P.M., van de Fliert, J.R., De Haan, L. and Linszen, D.H. (2010a). Verbal fluency as a possible predictor for psychosis. *European Psychiatry* 25(2), 105–10.

Becker, H.E., Nieman, D.H., Wiltink, S., Dingemans, P.M., van de Fliert, J.R., De Haan, L., van Amelsvoort, T.A. and Linszen, D.H. (2010b). Neurocognitive functioning before and after the first psychotic episode: Does psychosis result in cognitive deterioration? *Psychological Medicine* 5, 1–8.

Beekman, A.T., van Os, J., van Marle, H.J. and van Harten, P.N. (2012). Staging and profiling in psychiatry. *Tijdschrift Psychiatrie* 54(11), 915–20.

Berk, M., Malhi, G.S., Gray, L.J. and Dean, O.M. (2013). The promise of N-acetylcysteine in neuropsychiatry. *Trends in Pharmacological Sciences* 34(3), 167–77.

Bodatsch, M., Ruhrmann, S., Wagner, M., Müller, R., Schultze-Lutter, F., Frommann, I., Brinkmeyer, J., Gaebel, W., Maier, W., Klosterkötter, J. and Brockhaus-Dumke, A. (2011). Prediction of psychosis by mismatch negativity. *Biological Psychiatry* 69, 959–66.

Bramon, E., Rabe-Hesketh, S., Sham, P., Murray, R.M., and Frangou, S. (2004). Meta-analysis of the P300 and P50 waveforms in schizophrenia. *Schizophrenia Research* 70, 315–329.

Bramon, E., Shaikh, M., Broome, M., Lappin, J., Bergé, D., Day, F., Woolley, J., Tabraham, P., Madre, M., Johns, L., Howes, O., Valmaggia, L., Pérez, V., Sham, P., Murray, R.M. and McGuire, P. (2008). Abnormal P300 in people with high risk of developing psychosis. *Neuroimage* 41, 553–560.

Briggs, A., Spencer, M., Wang, H., Mannino, D. and Sin, D.D. (2008). Development and validation of a prognostic index for health outcomes in chronic obstructive pulmonary disease. *Archives of International Medicine* 168: 71–79.

Cannon-Spoor, H.E., Potkin, S.G. and Wyatt, R.J. (1982). Measurement of premorbid adjustment in chronic schizophrenia. *Schizophrenia Bulletin* 8, 470–484.

Carmeli, C., Knyazeva, M.G., Cuénod, M. and Do, K.Q. (2012). Glutathione precursor N-acetyl-cysteine modulates EEG synchronization in schizophrenia patients: a double-blind, randomized, placebo-controlled trial. *PLoS One* 7(2), e29341.

Dean, O., Giorlando, F. and Berk, M. (2011). N-acetylcysteine in psychiatry: current therapeutic evidence and potential mechanisms of action. *Journal of Psychiatry & Neuroscience* 36(2), 78–86.

Frommann, I., Brinkmeyer, J., Ruhrmann, S., Hack, E., Brockhaus-Dumke, A., Bechdolf, A., Wölwer, W., Klosterkötter, J., Maier, W. and Wagner, M. (2008). Auditory P300 in individuals clinically at risk for psychosis. *International Journal of Psychophysiology* 70(3), 192–205.

Fusar-Poli, P., Borgwardt, S., Bechdolf, A., Addington, J., Riecher-Rössler, A., Schultze-Lutter, F., Keshavan, M., Wood, S., Ruhrmann, S., Seidman, L.J., Valmaggia, L., Cannon, T., Velthorst, E., De Haan, L., Cornblatt, B., Bonoldi, I., Birchwood, M., McGlashan, T., Carpenter, W., McGorry, P., Klosterkötter, J., McGuire, P. and Yung, A. (2013). The psychosis high-risk state: a comprehensive state-of-the-art review. *JAMA Psychiatry* 70(1), 107–20.

Grippo, A.J. and Scotti, M.A. (2013). Stress and neuroinflammation. *Modern Trends Pharmacopsychiatriatry* 28, 20–32.

Gunduz-Bruce, H., Reinhart, R.M., Roach, B.J., Gueorguieva, R., Oliver, S., D'Souza, D.C., Ford, J.M., Krystal, J.H. and Mathalon, D.H. (2012). Glutamatergic modulation of auditory information processing in the human brain. *Biological Psychiatry* 71(11), 969–77.

Hickie, I.B., Scott, E.M., Hermens, D.F., Naismith, S.L., Guastella, A.J., Kaur, M., Sidis, A., Whitwell, B., Glozier, N., Davenport, T., Pantelis, C., Wood, S.J. and McGorry, P.D. (2013). Applying clinical staging to young people who present for mental health care. *Early Intervention Psychiatry* 7, 31–43.

International Early Psychosis Association Writing Group (2005). International clinical practice guidelines for early psychosis. *British Journal of Psychiatry* 187, S120-S124.

Jahshan, C., Cadenhead, K.S., Rissling, A.J., Kirihara, K., Braff, D.L. and Light, G.A. (2012). Automatic sensory information processing abnormalities across the illness course of schizophrenia. *Psychological Medicine* 42, 85–97.

Jeon, Y.W. and Polich, J. (2003). Meta-analysis of P300 and schizophrenia: patients, paradigms, and practical implications. *Psychophysiology* 40, 684–701.

Joa, I., Johannessen, J.O., Auestad, B., Friis, S., McGlashan, T., Melle, I., Opjordsmoen, S., Simonsen, E., Vaglum, P. and Larsen, T.K. (2008). The key to reducing duration of untreated first psychosis: information campaigns. *Schizophrenia Bulletin* 34(3), 466–72.

Johannessen, J.O., Larsen, T.K., Joa, I., Melle, I., Friis, S., Opjordsmoen, S., Rund, B.R., Simonsen, E., Vaglum, P. and McGlashan, T.H. (2005). Pathways to care for first-episode psychosis in an early detection healthcare sector: part of the Scandinavian TIPS study. *British Journal of Psychiatry Supplement* 48, s24–8.

Kahn, R.S. and Sommer, I.E. (2015). The neurobiology and treatment of first-episode schizophrenia. *Molecular Psychiatry* (20)1, 84–97.

Kapczinski, F., Dias, V.V., Kauer-Sant'Anna, M., Brietzke, E., Vázquez, G.H., Vieta, E. and Berk, M. (2009). The potential use of biomarkers as an adjunctive tool for staging bipolar disorder. *Biological Psychiatry* 33, 1366–7.

Korver, N., Nieman, D.H., Becker, H.E., van de Fliert, J.R., Dingemans, P.M., De Haan, L., Spiering, M., Schmitz, N. and Linszen, D.H. (2010). Symptomatology and neuropsychological functioning in cannabis using subjects at ultra high risk for developing psychosis and healthy controls. *Australian and New Zealand Journal of Psychiatry* 44(3), 230–6.

Koutsouleris N., Riecher-Rössler, A., Meisenzahl, E.M., Smieskova, R., Studerus, E., Kambeitz-Ilankovic, L., von Saldern, S., Cabral, C., Reiser, M., Falkai, P. and Borgwardt, S. (2015). Detecting the psychosis prodrome across high-risk populations using neuroanatomical biomarkers. *Schizophrenia Bulletin* 41, 471–82.

Lavoie, S., Murray, M.M., Deppen, P., Knyazeva, M.G., Berk, M., Boulat, O., Bovet, P., Bush, A.I., Conus, P., Copolov, D., Fornari, E., Meuli, R., Solida, A., Vianin, P., Cuénod, M., Buclin, T. and Do, K.Q. (2008). Glutathione precursor, N-acetyl-cysteine, improves mismatch negativity in schizophrenia patients. *Neuropsychopharmacology* 33(9), 2187–99.

McGorry, P.D. (2007). Issues for DSM-V: clinical staging: a heuristic pathway to valid nosology and safer, more effective treatment in psychiatry. *American Journal of Psychiatry* 164, 859–60.

McGorry, P.D. (2013). Early clinical phenotypes, clinical staging, and strategic biomarker research: building blocks for personalised psychiatry. *Bioological Psychiatry* 74, 394–395.

McGorry, P.D. and van Os, J. (2013). Redeeming diagnosis in psychiatry: timing versus specificity. *Lancet* 381(9863), 343–5.

McGorry, P.D., Yung, A.R. and Phillips, L.J. (2003). The 'close-in' or ultra high-risk model: a safe and effective strategy for research and clinical intervention in prepsychotic mental disorder. *Schizophrenia Bulletin* 29, 771–790.

McGorry, P.D., Hickie, I.B., Yung, A.R., Pantelis, C. and Jackson, H.J. (2006). Clinical staging of psychiatric disorders: a heuristic framework for choosing earlier, safer and more effective interventions. *Australian New Zealand Journal of Psychiatry* 40, 616–22.

McGorry, P.D., Purcell, R., Hickie, I.B., Yung, A.R., Pantelis, C. and Jackson, H.J. (2007). Clinical staging: a heuristic model for psychiatry and youth mental health. *Medical Journal of Australia* 187, S40–42.

McGorry, P.D., Keshavan, M., Goldstone, S., Amminger, P., Allott, K., Berk, M., Lavoie, S., Pantelis, C., Yung, A., Wood, S. and Hickie, I. (2014). Biomarkers and clinical staging in psychiatry. *World Psychiatry* 13(3), 211–23.

Molina, V., Papiol, S., Sanz, J., Rosa, A., Arias, B., Fatjó-Vilas, M., Calama, J., Hernández, A.I., Bécker, J. and Fañanás, L. (2011). Convergent evidence of the contribution of TP53 genetic variation (Pro72Arg) to metabolic activity and white matter volume in the frontal lobe in schizophrenia patients. *Neuroimage* 56(1), 45–51.

Moncrieff, J. (2006). Does antipsychotic withdrawal provoke psychosis? Review of the literature on rapid onset psychosis (supersensitivity psychosis) and withdrawal-related relapse. *Acta Psychiatrica Scandinavica* 114(1), 3–13.

Najjar, S., Pearlman, D.M., Alper, K., Najjar, A. and Devinsky, O. (2013). Neuroinflammation and psychiatric illness. *Journal of Neuroinflammation* 10, 43–66.

Nieman D.H. and McGorry P.D. (2015). Detection and treatment of At Risk Mental State for developing a first psychosis: Making up the balance. *The Lancet Psychiatry* 2(9), 825–834.

Nieman, D.H., Koelman, J.H., Linszen, D.H., Bour, L.J., Dingemans, P.M. and Ongerboer de Visser, B.W. (2002). Clinical and neuropsychological correlates of the P300 in schizophrenia. *Schizophrenia Research* 55, 105–113.

Nieman, D.H., Rike, W., Becker, H.E., Dingemans, P.M., Amelsvoort, T., De Haan, L., van der Gaag, M., Denys, D.A.J.P. and Linszen, D.H. (2009). The prescription of antipsychotic medication to patients at ultra high risk for developing psychosis. *International Clinical Psychopharmacology* 24, 223–228.

Nieman, D.H., Ruhrmann, S., Dragt, S., Soen, F., van Tricht, M.J., Koelman, J.H., Bour, L.J., Velthorst, E., Becker, H.E., Weiser, M., Linszen, D.H., and de Haan, L. (2014). Psychosis prediction: Stratification of risk estimation with information-processing and premorbid functioning variables. *Schizophrenia Bulletin* 40(6), 1482–90.

Ozgurdal, S., Gudlowski, Y., Witthaus, H., Kawohl, W., Uhl, I., Hauser, M., Gorynia, I., Gallinat, J., Heinze, M. and Juckel, G. (2008). Reduction of auditory event-related P300 amplitude in subjects with at-risk mental state for schizophrenia. *Schizophrenia Research* 105, 272–278.

Patel, S.H. and Azzam, P.N. (2005). Characterization of N200 and P300: Selected Studies of the event-related potential. *International Journal of Medical Science* 2(4), 147–154.

Perez V.B., Woods S.W., Roach B.J., Ford, J.M., McGlashan, T.H., Srihari, V.H. and Mathalon, D.H. (2014). Automatic auditory processing deficits in schizophrenia and clinical high-risk patients: forecasting psychosis risk with mismatch negativity. *Biological Psychiatry* 75, 459–69.

Perkins, D.O., Jeffries, C.D., Addington, J., Bearden, C.E., Cadenhead, K.S., Cannon, T.D., Cornblatt, B.A., Mathalon, D.H., McGlashan, T.H., Seidman, L.J., Tsuang, M.T., Walker, E.F., Woods, S.W. and Heinssen, R. (2015). Towards a psychosis risk blood diagnostic for persons experiencing high-risk symptoms: preliminary results from the NAPLS Project. *Schizophrenia Bulletin* 41(2), 419–28.

Riecher-Rössler, A., Pflueger, M.O., Aston, J., Borgwardt, S.J., Brewer, W.J., Gschwandtner, U. and Stieglitz, R.D. (2009). Efficacy of using cognitive status in predicting psychosis: a 7-year follow-up. *Biological Psychiatry* 66, 1023–30.

Ruhrmann, S., Schultze-Lutter, F., Salokangas, R.K., Heinimaa, M., Linszen, D., Dingemans, P., Birchwood, M., Patterson, P., Juckel, G., Heinz, A., Morrison, A., Lewis, S., von Reventlow, H.G. and Klosterkötter, J. (2010). Prediction of psychosis in adolescents and young adults at high risk: results from the prospective European prediction of psychosis study. *Archives of General Psychiatry* 67(3), 241–51

Ruhrmann, S., Schultze-Lutter, F., Schmidt, S.J., Kaiser, N. and Klosterkötter, J. (2014). Prediction and prevention of psychosis: current progress and future tasks. *European Archive of Psychiatry and Clinical Neuroscience* 264 (suppl 1), S9–16.

Schizophrenia Working Group of the Psychiatric Genomics Consortium (2014). Biological insights from 108 schizophrenia-associated genetic loci. *Nature* 511(7510), 421–427.

Scott, J. (2011). Bipolar disorder: from early identification to personalized treatment. *Early Intervention Psychiatry* 5, 89–90.

Scott, J.A.N., Paykel, E., Morriss, R., Bentall, R., Kinderman, P., Johnson, T., Abbott, R. and Hayhurst, H. (2006). Cognitive-behavioural therapy for severe and recurrent bipolar disorders. *British Journal of Psychiatry* 188, 313–320.

Sperduto, P.W., Berkey, B., Gaspar, L.E., Mehta, M. and Curran, W. (2008). A new prognostic index and comparison to three other indices for patients with brain metastases: an analysis of 1960 patients in the RTOG database. *International Journal of Radiation Oncology Biology Physics* 70, 510–14.

Stafford, M.R., Jackson, H., Mayo-Wilson, E., Morrison, A.P. and Kendall, T. (2013). Early interventions to prevent psychosis: systematic review and meta-analysis. *British Medical Journal* 346, 185.

Turetsky, B.I., Dress, E.M., Braff, D.L., Calkins, M.E., Green, M.F., Greenwood, T.A., Gur, R.E., Gur, R.C., Lazzeroni, L.C., Nuechterlein, K.H., Radant, A.D.,

Seidman, L.J., Siever, L.J, Silverman, J.M., Sprock, J., Stone, W.S., Sugar, C.A., Swerdlow, N.R., Tsuang, D.W., Tsuang, M.T. and Light, G. (2015). The utility of P300 as a schizophrenia endophenotype and predictive biomarker: clinical and sociodemographic modulators in the COGS-2 Study. *Schizophrenia Research* 163, 53–62.

van der Gaag, M., Nieman, D.H., Rietdijk, J., Dragt, S., Ising, H.K., Klaassen, R.M., Koeter, M., Cuijpers, P., Wunderink, L. and Linszen, D.H. (2012). Cognitive behavioral therapy for subjects at ultra high risk for developing psychosis: a randomized controlled clinical trial. *Schizophrenia Bulletin* 38, 1180–1188.

van der Gaag, M., Nieman, D.H. and van den Berg, D. (2013). *CBT for Those At Risk for a First Episode Psychosis: Evidence Based Psychotherapy for People with an 'At Risk Mental State'*. Oxford: Routledge.

van der Gaag, M., Smit, F., Bechdolf, A., French, P., Linszen, D.H., Yung, A.R., McGorry, P. and Cuijpers, P. (2013). Preventing a first episode of psychosis: meta-analysis of randomized controlled prevention trials of 12 month and longer-term follow-ups. *Schizophrenia Research* 149(1–3), 56–62.

van der Stelt, O., Lieberman, J.A. and Belger, A. (2005). Auditory P300 in high-risk, recent-onset and chronic schizophrenia. *Schizophrenia Research* 77, 309–320.

van Os, J. (2013). The dynamics of subthreshold psychopathology: implications for diagnosis and treatment. *American Journal of Psychiatry* 170(7), 695–8.

van Tricht, M.J., Nieman, D.H., Koelman, J.H., van der Meer, J.N., Bour, L.J., de Haan, L. and Linszen, D.H. (2010). Reduced parietal P300 amplitude is associated with an increased risk for a first psychotic episode. *Biological Psychiatry* 68, 642–648.

van Tricht, M.J., Ruhrmann, S., Arns, M., Müller, R., Bodatsch, M., Velthorst, E., Koelman, J.H., Bour, L.J., Zurek, K., Schultze-Lutter, F., Klosterkötter, J., Linszen, D.H., de Haan,L. and Nieman, D.H. (2014). Can quantative EEG measures predict clinical outcome in subjects at ultra high risk for psychosis? A prospective mulicentre study. *Schizophrenia Research* 153, 42–47.

Yung, A.R., Yuen, H.P., McGorry, P.D., Philips, L.J., Kelly, D., Dell'Olio, M., Francey, S.M., Cosgrave, E.M., Killackey, E., Stanford, C., Godfrey, K. and Buckby, J. (2005). Mapping the onset of psychosis: the comprehensive assessment of at-risk mental states. *Australian and New Zealand Journal of Psychiatry* 39(11–12), 964–71.

Yung, A.R., Nelson, B., Stanford, C., Simmons, M.B., Cosgrave, E.M., Killackey, E., Phillips, L.J., Bechdolf, A., Buckby, J. and McGorry, P.D. (2008). Validation of 'prodromal' criteria to detect individuals at ultra high risk of psychosis: 2 year follow-up. *Schizophrenia Research* 105(1–3), 10–7.

Zimmermann, R., Gschwandtner, U., Wilhelm, F.H., Pflueger, M.O., Riecher-Rössler, A. and Fuhr, P. (2010). EEG spectral power and negative symptoms in at-risk individuals predict transition to psychosis. *Schizophrenia Research* 123, 208–16.

9

EVIDENCE FOR PREVENTIVE TREATMENT IN PSYCHIATRY

In specialties like oncology and cardiology, the biggest successes have been accomplished in the arena of prevention. In the case of cancer, you preferably do not wait until patients have metastases because prognosis is worse then. For example, breast cancer at stage 1 can be treated with a breast saving operation with 100 per cent survival rate after 5 years, but for breast cancer stage 4 (metastases) chemotherapy is often necessary, leading to a long recovery period with only a 20 per cent chance of survival. In cases of diabetes 2, if you treat the high risk phase with benign interventions, prognosis is much better than after diagnosis of the full blown disorder. Why would this be so much different in psychiatry? In the ARMS phase, people often seek help themselves, while after onset of the full blown disorder, patients can be convinced they are the victim of a conspiracy, and that they do not need psychiatric help, but assistance of the police, rendering it difficult to engage patients in psychiatric treatment.

The WHO report *Prevention of Mental Disorders* (2004) stated that prevention of these disorders is obviously one of the most effective ways to reduce the disease burden. Effective preventive interventions have been developed for, amongst others, depression (Cuijpers et al., 2008), anxiety disorders (Higgins and Hacker, 2008) and psychosis.

Evidence-based ARMS treatment options have been developed. Opponents argued that ARMS detection and treatment would lead to overtreatment with antipsychotic medication. However, research shows that ARMS subjects (even when not recognized or labelled as such) are already overmedicated, since they are distressed and impaired when seen by primary care and other physicians (Broome et al., 2005; Fusar-Poli et al., 2012; Nieman et al., 2009). For example, in a naturalistic study, 21 per cent of the ARMS subjects had been prescribed antipsychotics by the health professional who referred them for ARMS intake (Nieman et al., 2009). In generic clinical practice, it is often assumed that subjects with mild psychotic symptoms need a low dose of antipsychotics, while this is clearly advized against in the international treatment guidelines, which are better adhered to in specialized 'prodromal' clinics (International Early Psychosis Association Writing Group, 2005).

Hence rather than the implementation of ARMS detection and treatment leading to overtreatment with medication that is not indicated, it is actually the lack of implementation of ARMS detection and treatment that may have such an effect (Nieman and McGorry, 2015). In clinical practice, many clinicians are not yet acquainted with the ARMS concept. Because ARMS patients are help-seeking, and the DSM criteria are subject to diverse interpretations by clinicians, many ARMS subjects are prescribed medication such as antipsychotics. If professionals were familiar with the ARMS concept, they would recognize it and hopefully would treat it according to evidence-based guidelines. The first treatment option should be psychosocial interventions, notably cognitive behavioural therapy, because there is cumulative evidence that cognitive behavioural therapy is effective without serious side-effects (Hutton and Taylor, 2014; van der Gaag et al., 2012). Available data do not support antipsychotic medications as a first-line treatment for ARMS patients (Heinssen and Insel, 2015; McGorry et al., 2013).

Six meta-analyses and reviews have been published that corroborate the effect of interventions on transition rate after 12 months (Hutton and Taylor, 2014; Marshall and Lockwood, 2004; Preti and Cella, 2010; Fusar-Poli et al., 2012; Stafford et al., 2013; van der Gaag et al., 2013). The largest meta-analysis to date was published by Stafford et al. (2013), and included 11 studies, totalling 1246 ARMS subjects. van der Gaag et al. (2013) reported an average 12-month risk reduction of 54 per cent for a first psychosis in 10 studies (totalling 1,112 ARMS patients) reporting 12 month follow up data and 5 studies with follow ups varying from 24 to 48 months. The number needed to treat was 9. The number needed to treat is the average number of patients who need to be treated to prevent one additional bad outcome (i.e. psychosis). For comparison, the number needed to treat for standard stroke prophylaxis in atrial fibrillation with acetylsalicylic acid is 24–87 (Lip and Edwards, 2006; Ruhrmann et al., 2014).

With respect to the assertion that most ARMS subjects recover without treatment, recent reports indicate that those who do not make the transition to psychosis are at significant risk for continued attenuated psychotic symptoms, and recurrent or persistent disorders. They are therefore likely to benefit from early intervention (Carrión et al., 2013; Cornblatt et al., 2002; Lin et al., 2015; Nelson et al., 2013). Furthermore, without treatment, many ARMS subjects function poorly, even in the absence of a psychotic episode (Carrión et al., 2013) and a certain percentage of ARMS subjects will develop psychosis years later (Nelson et al., 2013). In addition, ARMS treatment is cost effective because a time limited, low cost treatment such as cognitive behavioural therapy can prevent in some patients the extensive health care costs of hospital admission, as well as economic costs of psychosocial drop-out and government disability funding (Ising et al., 2015).

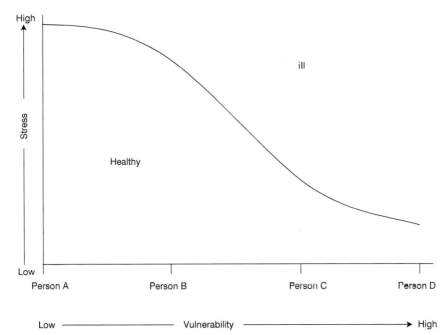

FIGURE 9.1 The stress–vulnerability model

Subjects who later develop a severe psychiatric disorder, can have a certain (neurobiological or other) vulnerability, for example, in information processing. Stress has usually a negative influence (see Figure 9.1). Subjects with increased vulnerability for example, because of preexistent information processing difficulties, have a bigger chance to become ill under stress.

When someone hears a voice or thinks he is being followed, this person becomes anxious. This often results in withdrawal from social situations, sleep difficulties and sick leave from work or school. They can become trapped in a vicious circle that can lead to psychosis. Research and clinical practice shows that it is reassuring for people to receive psycho-education about their symptoms, including scientific evidence that, for example, hearing a voice does not inevitably results in going mad. 10 per cent of the population sometimes hears a voice, and these people are not necessarily diagnosed with a mental disorder. Furthermore, in metacognitive training, ARMS subjects can learn to recognize the effect of cognitive biases, like selective attention, and subsequently to correct the effects of the biases.

We wrote a book about a newly developed psychotherapy based on these principles (van der Gaag et al., 2013). This book encompasses a review of the literature on cognitive biases and a comprehensive therapy manual, illustrated by numerous clinical examples. A multicentre randomized controlled trial involving 200 ARMS patients showed that this new preventive psychotherapy can reduce the chance of a first psychosis by about 50 per cent (van der Gaag et al., 2012). At the moment this therapy is implemented in clinical routine care in the Netherlands and other countries, which is very hopeful. In the 13 years I have been working with

ARMS subjects, it has been disturbing to see that it is difficult for these subjects to find adequate care once they are finally ready to take the step to ask for professional help because there is still limited knowledge about ARMS in clinical practice.

In the following paragraphs, a brief overview of the contents of the therapy is given, illustrated with a case example. Goals of the therapy are:

- prevention of catastrophic and delusional interpretation of extraordinary experiences (such as hearing a voice) by means of psycho-education;
- learning to recognize the effects of cognitive biases and correct these secondarily;
- prevention of psychosocial dropout;
- intervention in drug use.

The preventive psychotherapy encompasses psycho-education about the neurotransmitter dopamine and cognitive biases (van der Gaag et al. 2013). Reality testing is usually largely intact, so ARMS subjects often know that something is going wrong. Psycho-education has a normalizing effect, leading to a reduction of the fear of 'going crazy'. In the media, especially in movies and television series, subjects who are violent and out of control are sometimes called psychotic. Out of fear and shame, these young people often keep their symptoms to themselves, and do not discuss these experiences with family and friends. For adolescents without symptoms, life can be difficult, but for subjects with developing psychotic symptoms it is even more so. An early detection team from Cornwall made a movieclip that shows how frightening it is to become psychotic and how important it is to intervene early: http://eff.org.uk/howlong/.

As discussed in Chapter 7, cognitive biases play an important role in the pathogenesis of psychiatric symptoms. For example:

- *Jumping to conclusions:* the tendency to draw a conclusion without having all the facts, thus to reach unwarranted conclusions. For example, Mike (from the next case example) notices lately that people are looking at him on the street in an unfriendly way. He jumps to the conclusion that these people are against him. However, it is of course also possible that these people look angrily at him, because they have had an argument with their wife or because they missed the bus.
- *Covariation bias:* This is the tendency to see a causal connection between two events that occur simultaneously. For example, a young woman has experienced a few times that someone in her surroundings became sick when she thought about that person. She doubts if she can influence events with her thoughts. When someone becomes convinced of such an idea, it can evolve into a delusion.
- *Selective attention:* as discussed in Chapter 7.

In the metacognitive training, patients learn to recognize the effects of cognitive biases within themselves, and to subsequently correct these effects by

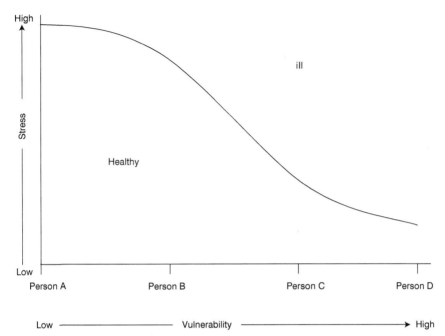

FIGURE 9.1 The stress–vulnerability model

Subjects who later develop a severe psychiatric disorder, can have a certain (neurobiological or other) vulnerability, for example, in information processing. Stress has usually a negative influence (see Figure 9.1). Subjects with increased vulnerability for example, because of preexistent information processing difficulties, have a bigger chance to become ill under stress.

When someone hears a voice or thinks he is being followed, this person becomes anxious. This often results in withdrawal from social situations, sleep difficulties and sick leave from work or school. They can become trapped in a vicious circle that can lead to psychosis. Research and clinical practice shows that it is reassuring for people to receive psycho-education about their symptoms, including scientific evidence that, for example, hearing a voice does not inevitably results in going mad. 10 per cent of the population sometimes hears a voice, and these people are not necessarily diagnosed with a mental disorder. Furthermore, in metacognitive training, ARMS subjects can learn to recognize the effect of cognitive biases, like selective attention, and subsequently to correct the effects of the biases.

We wrote a book about a newly developed psychotherapy based on these principles (van der Gaag et al., 2013). This book encompasses a review of the literature on cognitive biases and a comprehensive therapy manual, illustrated by numerous clinical examples. A multicentre randomized controlled trial involving 200 ARMS patients showed that this new preventive psychotherapy can reduce the chance of a first psychosis by about 50 per cent (van der Gaag et al., 2012). At the moment this therapy is implemented in clinical routine care in the Netherlands and other countries, which is very hopeful. In the 13 years I have been working with

ARMS subjects, it has been disturbing to see that it is difficult for these subjects to find adequate care once they are finally ready to take the step to ask for professional help because there is still limited knowledge about ARMS in clinical practice.

In the following paragraphs, a brief overview of the contents of the therapy is given, illustrated with a case example. Goals of the therapy are:

- prevention of catastrophic and delusional interpretation of extraordinary experiences (such as hearing a voice) by means of psycho-education;
- learning to recognize the effects of cognitive biases and correct these secondarily;
- prevention of psychosocial dropout;
- intervention in drug use.

The preventive psychotherapy encompasses psycho-education about the neurotransmitter dopamine and cognitive biases (van der Gaag et al. 2013). Reality testing is usually largely intact, so ARMS subjects often know that something is going wrong. Psycho-education has a normalizing effect, leading to a reduction of the fear of 'going crazy'. In the media, especially in movies and television series, subjects who are violent and out of control are sometimes called psychotic. Out of fear and shame, these young people often keep their symptoms to themselves, and do not discuss these experiences with family and friends. For adolescents without symptoms, life can be difficult, but for subjects with developing psychotic symptoms it is even more so. An early detection team from Cornwall made a movieclip that shows how frightening it is to become psychotic and how important it is to intervene early: http://eff.org.uk/howlong/.

As discussed in Chapter 7, cognitive biases play an important role in the pathogenesis of psychiatric symptoms. For example:

- *Jumping to conclusions:* the tendency to draw a conclusion without having all the facts, thus to reach unwarranted conclusions. For example, Mike (from the next case example) notices lately that people are looking at him on the street in an unfriendly way. He jumps to the conclusion that these people are against him. However, it is of course also possible that these people look angrily at him, because they have had an argument with their wife or because they missed the bus.
- *Covariation bias:* This is the tendency to see a causal connection between two events that occur simultaneously. For example, a young woman has experienced a few times that someone in her surroundings became sick when she thought about that person. She doubts if she can influence events with her thoughts. When someone becomes convinced of such an idea, it can evolve into a delusion.
- *Selective attention:* as discussed in Chapter 7.

In the metacognitive training, patients learn to recognize the effects of cognitive biases within themselves, and to subsequently correct these effects by doing real life exercises. Furthermore, patients are given individual cognitive behavioural therapy in which they learn to distinguish the activating event, belief and consequences in their experiences. Challenging dysfunctional beliefs that cause negative emotions like fear can give the control back to the patient. Finally, attention is given to consolidation and relapse prevention. It is advisable to arrange some booster sessions over a period of months to check how the patient is doing, and if he still practises what he learned in therapy.

The ARMS cognitive behavioural therapy (van der Gaag et al., 2013) is illustrated with the next case example of Mike.

CASE EXAMPLE: MIKE

Mike is a 17 year old high school pupil who had to repeat his class. He tries to avoid going out alone, because he feels unsafe. He spends a lot of time alone in his room with his curtains closed. He thinks often that his classmates are talking and laughing about him. He frequently hears his name, or sees something moving in the corner of his eye, while there is nobody there. He is afraid that he is going crazy.

Psycho-education about dopamine and cognitive biases has a normalizing effect. He reads the information and realizes that too much dopamine highlights certain harmless events, like his classmates talking and laughing, causing him to pay too much attention to these events. He also realizes that the continuous scanning of his environment for suspicious looking people (and he found almost everybody above the age of 12 suspicious looking) makes him anxious.

In metacognitive training, with the selective attention exercise, Mike learns that he becomes less anxious if he looks at other aspects of his environment like the trees or children. And he learns to come up with alternative explanations instead of jumping to conclusions.

In cognitive behavioural therapy, with a case formulation, Mike gains insight into factors that played a role in the pathogenesis and maintenance of his symptoms. In the past he was severely bullied (see Figure 9.2).

Exposure is an effective intervention in psychotherapy in which patients confront themselves with the feared situation instead of avoiding it. Because patients have difficulty with confronting their fears, a fear hierarchy can be made. Patients expose themselves to the situation lowest in the fear hierarchy first. Mike hardly dares to go outside alone because he is afraid of being attacked. He reasons that this has not yet happened because he stays mostly at home. We make a fear hierarchy. He agrees to take the first step in his fear hierarchy; to sit on a bench on Sunday morning in the park, and avoid scanning his environment all the time for suspicious looking people. Mike experiences that the feared outcomes do not occur, and he is able to confront himself with more difficult situations in the fear hierarchy, like taking the subway. After 12 sessions, Mike is less afraid in several situations. He is able to go out alone, and has some more social contacts. We make an appointment for a booster session after 2 months. He passes to the next class. He is still a bit less socially active than his peers, but he is not as socially isolated as he was. He still sometimes hears his name, but he does not pay much attention to it. At 2 year follow up, Mike is a freshman at college, he lives in a student residence and has a girlfriend.

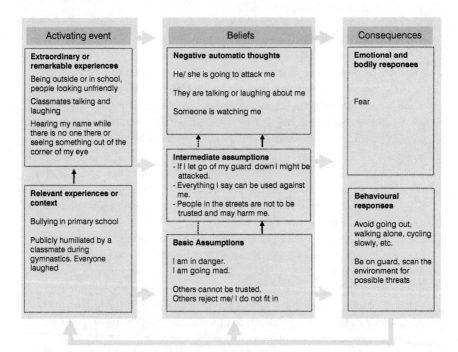

FIGURE 9.2 Case conceptualization – Mike

Source: reprinted from M. van der Gaag, D.H. Nieman, D. van den Berg (2013). *CBT for Those at Risk for a First Episode Psychosis: Evidence based Psychotherapy for People with an 'At Risk Mental State'*. London: Routledge.

It is very encouraging that there is often a good recovery in ARMS subjects with a short, benign intervention while this is much more rare after a first psychotic episode. Then people often have lost their employment and social network. In the ARMS phase, people are starting to drop out, but with some interventions much can be restored. Some critics are of the opinion that treating subjects early in the course of mental illness may lead to stigmatization. I do not agree with this standpoint from either a clinical or research perspective. In our institute we treat help-seeking subjects. These individuals and their families are already very concerned about the symptoms, otherwise they would not have sought help.

The literature on stigma in ARMS is small, and actual data even more scarce. Two papers about the subject analyse the theoretical and empirical stigma literature to evaluate the potential effects of stigma associated with the psychosis risk syndrome (Warner, 2001; Yang et al., 2010). Stigma can be divided into self-stigmatization, that is felt irrespective of help-seeking in mental health care, and stigma which can be due to the diagnostic and treatment process. Self-stigmatization may occur before help-seeking in ARMS subjects, when they start experiencing symptoms like hearing a voice and become afraid of 'going mad' (Morrison et al., 2013; van der Gaag et al., 2013). In the media madness and psychosis are often depicted as being criminal and violent. In the first research paper on stigma in ARMS, cognitive therapy decreased negative appraisals of unusual experiences in young people at risk of psychosis and could thus be regarded as non-stigmatizing intervention (Morrison et al., 2013). ARMS subjects in treatment do not report that they feel stigmatized by receiving normalizing psycho-education and individually tailored, adequate help for their symptoms (Morrison et al., 2013; van der Gaag et al., 2013).

Two other recent papers investigated stigma in ARMS subjects (Rüsch et al., 2014a; Rüsch et al., 2014b). Self-labelling and perceived public stigma was associated with reduced wellbeing and increased stigma stress among young people at risk of psychosis (Rüsch et al., 2014b). A longitudinal analysis in the same patient group showed that an increase in self-labelling predicted heightened stigma stress one year later, controlling for socio-demographic variables and symptoms. The authors conclude that strategies are needed to reduce the public stigma associated with at-risk status in addition to early intervention programmes, and to help young people at risk to better cope with self-labelling (Rüsch et al., 2014a).

In conclusion, there is increasing evidence for the health care cost and misery saving potential of preventive treatment with benign interventions such as cognitive behavioural therapy in the early stages of psychiatric disorders. Possibilities for clinical implementation are described in the last chapter of this book.

References

Broome, M.R., Woolley, J.B., Johns, L.C., Valmaggia, L.R., Tabraham, P., Gafoor, R., Bramon, E. and McGuire, P.K. (2005). Outreach and support in south London (OASIS): implementation of a clinical service for prodromal psychosis and the at risk mental state. *European Psychiatry* 20, 372–8.

Carrión, R.E., McLaughlin, D., Goldberg, T.E., Auther, A.M., Olsen, R.H., Olvet, D.M., Correll, C.U. and Cornblatt, B.A. (2013). Prediction of functional outcome in individuals at clinical high risk for psychosis. *JAMA Psychiatry* 70, 1133–42.

Cornblatt, B., Lencz, T. and Obuchowski, M. (2002). The schizophrenia prodrome: treatment and high-risk perspectives. *Schizophrenia Research* 54, 177–86.

Cuijpers, P., van Straten, A., Smit, F., Mihalopoulos,, C. and Beekman, A. (2008). Preventing the onset of depressive disorders: a meta-analytic review of psychological interventions. *American Journal of Psychiatry* 165(10), 1272–80.

Fusar-Poli, P., Byrne, M., Badger, S., Valmaggia, L.R. and McGuire, P.K. (2012). Outreach and support in South London (OASIS), 2001–2011: ten years of early diagnosis and treatment for young individuals at high clinical risk for psychosis. *European Psychiatry* 28(5), 315–26.

Heinssen, R.K. and Insel, T.R. (2015). Preventing the onset of psychosis: not quite there yet. *Schizophrenia Bulletin* 41(1), 28–9.

Higgins, D.M. and Hacker, J.E. (2008). A randomized trial of brief cognitive-behavioral therapy for prevention of generalized anxiety disorder. *The Journal of Clinical Psychiatry* 69(8), 1336.

Hutton, P. and Taylor, P.J. (2014). Cognitive behavioural therapy for psychosis prevention: a systematic review and meta-analysis. *Psychological Medicine* 44, 449–68.

International Early Psychosis Association Writing Group (2005). International clinical practice guidelines for early psychosis. *Brititish Journal of Psychiatry* 187, S120–S124.

Ising, H.K., Veling, W., Rietdijk, J., Dragt, S., Klaassen, R., Savelsberg, N., Boonstra, N., Nieman, D., Wunderink, L., Linszen, D., Smit, F. and van der Gaag, M (2015). Cost-utility and cost-effectiveness of the prevention of a first episode psychosis in ultra high risk subjects. *Psychological Medicine* 45, 1435–46.

Lin, A., Wood, S., Nelson, B., Beavon, A., McGorry, P. and Yung, A.R. (2015). Outcomes of nontransitioned cases in a sample at ultra high risk. *American Journal of Psychiatry* 172(15), 249–58.

Lip, G.Y. and Edwards, S.J. (2006). Stroke prevention with aspirin, warfarin and ximelagatran in patients with non-valvular atrial fibrillation: a systematic review and meta-analysis. *Thrombosis Research* 118, 321–33.

Marshall, M. and Lockwood, A. (2004). Early intervention for psychosis. *Cochrane Database of Systematic Reviews* 4, CD004718.

McGorry, P.D., Nelson, B., Phillips, L.J., Yuen, H.P., Francey, S.M., Thampi, A., Berger, G.E., Amminger, G.P., Simmons, M.B., Kelly, D., Dip, G., Thompson, A.D. and Yung, A.R. (2013). Randomized controlled trial of interventions for young people at ultra-high risk of psychosis: twelve-month outcome. *Journal of Clinical Psychiatry* 74, 349–56.

Morrison, A.P., Birchwood, M., Pyle, M., Flach, C., Stewart, S.L., Byrne, R., Patterson, P., Jones, P.B., Fowler, D., Gumley, A.I. and French, P. (2013). Impact of cognitive therapy on internalised stigma in people with at-risk mental states. *British Journal of Psychiatry* 3(2), 140–5.

Nelson, B., Yuen, H.P., Wood, S.J., Lin, A., Spiliotacopoulos, D., Bruxner, A., Broussard, C., Simmons, M., Foley, D.L., Brewer, W.J., Francey, S.M., Amminger, G.P., Thompson, A., McGorry, P.D. and Yung, A.R. (2013). Long-term follow-up of a group at ultra high risk ('prodromal') for psychosis: the PACE 400 study. *JAMA Psychiatry* 70, 793–802.

Nieman, D.H., Rike, W.H., Becker, H.E., Dingemans, P.M., van Amelsvoort, T.A., De Haan, L., van der Gaag, M., Denys, D.A. and Linszen, D.H. (2009). The prescription of antipsychotic medication to patients at ultra high risk for developing psychosis. *International Clinical Psychopharmacology* 24, 223–8.

Nieman, D.H. and McGorry, P.D. (2015). Detection and treatment of at risk mental state for developing a first psychosis: making up the balance. *The Lancet Psychiatry* 2, 825–34.

Preti, A. and Cella, M. (2010). Randomized-controlled trials in people at ultra high risk of psychosis: a review of treatment effectiveness. *Schizophrenia Research* 123, 30–36.

Ruhrmann, S., Schultze-Lutter, F., Schmidt, S.J., Kaiser, N. and Klosterkötter, J. (2014). Prediction and prevention of psychosis: current progress and future tasks. *European Archives of Psychiatry and Clinical Neuroscience* 264(Suppl 1), 9–16.

Rüsch, N., Corrigan, P.W., Heekeren, K., Theodoridou. A., Dvorsky, D., Metzler, S., Müller, M., Walitza, S. and Rössler, W. (2014a). Well-being among persons at risk of psychosis: the role of self-labeling, shame, and stigma stress. *Psychiatric Services* 65(4), 483–9.

Rüsch, N., Müller, M., Heekeren, K., Theodoridou, A., Metzler, S., Dvorsky, D., Corrigan, P.W., Walitza, S. and Rössler, W. (2014b). Longitudinal course of self-labeling, stigma stress and well-being among young people at risk of psychosis. *Schizophrenia Research* 158(1–3), 82–4.

Stafford, M.R., Jackson, H., Mayo-Wilson, E., Morrison, A.P. and Kendall, T. (2013). Early interventions to prevent psychosis: systematic review and meta-analysis. *British Medical Journal* 346, 185.

van der Gaag, M., Nieman, D.H., Rietdijk, J., Dragt, S., Ising, H.K., Klaassen, R.M., Koeter, M., Cuijpers, P., Wunderink, L. and Linszen, D.H. (2012). Cognitive behavioral therapy for subjects at ultra high risk for developing psychosis: a randomized controlled clinical trial. *Schizophrenia Bulletin* 38, 1180–8.

van der Gaag, M., Nieman, D.H., and van den Berg, D. (2013a). *CBT for Those at Risk for a First Episode Psychosis: Evidence Based Psychotherapy for People with an 'At Risk Mental State'*. London: Routledge.

van der Gaag, M., Smit, F., Bechdolf, A., French, P., Linszen, D.H., Yung, A.R., McGorry, P.D. and Cuijpers, P. (2013b). Preventing a first episode of psychosis: meta-analysis of randomized controlled prevention trials of 12 month and longer-term follow ups. *Schizophrenia Research* 149, 56–62.

Warner, R. (2001). The prevention of schizophrenia: what interventions are safe and effective? *Schizophrenia Bulletin* 27, 551–62.

World Health Organization (2004). *Prevention of Mental Disorders: Effective Interventions and Policy Options*. Geneva: World Health Organization. Accessed on November 6, 2015 at http://www.who.int/mental_health/evidence/en/prevention_of_mental_disorders_sr.pdf

Yang, L.H., Wonpat-Borja, A.J., Opler, M.G. and Corcoran, C.M. (2010). Potential stigma associated with inclusion of the psychosis risk syndrome in the DSM-V: an empirical question. *Schizophrenia Research* 120, 42–8.

10

THE STRESS–RELAXATION CONTINUUM

Mental and physical states are intertwined in a complex manner. High levels of stress are often related to anxiety, insomnia and depression (Walker et al., 2014), whereas relaxation is usually associated with increased positive affect (Fritz et al., 2010). The stress–relaxation continuum provides a link between mind and brain, and plays an important role in psychiatric symptoms, from onset to remission. In Eastern philosophies, techniques like yoga and meditation are employed to influence the stress–relaxation continuum. Relaxation can be a natural antidote to anxiety, depression and psychosis.

The physiological stress–relaxation continuum plays an important role in the etiology and pathophysiology of mental illness. Anxiety is related to stress, and the core of many psychiatric disorders is anxiety. In the stress–relaxation continuum, at the one end a person is extremely stressed and in a state of hyperarousal. On the other end, a person is completely relaxed. In most daily life situations, people are somewhere in between both extremes. Mental illness is usually associated with the stress-end. It can be experienced that extreme stress, for example because a loved one is missing, leads to acute psychiatric symptoms like anxiety, irrational behaviour, aggression, etcetera. Perception of colours and sounds may change, becoming too bright and hard. Other people can be perceived as hostile. During extreme stress, it is usually difficult to sleep without medication. If a person does fall asleep, the sleep is often restless, with nightmares. The majority of etiological theories consider heightened levels of autonomic, cortical, cognitive and emotional arousal to be a stable feature of patients with insomnia (Rieman et al., 2010; Harvey, 2002; Espie, 2002; Perlis et al., 1997). This state is usually experienced as unpleasant and the body becomes exhausted if the stress is prolonged.

On the other end, extreme relaxation often induces a blissful feeling of rest and calmness. Sounds and colours are usually experienced as soft and pleasurable. The relationship between bodily reactions associated with stress and subjective experience may be a crucial link between body and mind and possibly holds a key to treatment of psychiatric disorders. This observation is not new, as reflected in the ancient wisdom of (Zen) Buddhism and Hinduism. Modern life is becoming more and more stressful, among other things because mobile phones and iPads make it possible to be online most of the time.

Physiology of the stress–relaxation continuum

In the physiology of the stress–relaxation continuum, the autonomic nervous system plays an important role (Schmidt and Thews, 1989). This system is a division of the peripheral nervous system that influences the function of the internal organs. The autonomic nervous system is a control system that acts largely unconsciously, and regulates bodily functions such as muscle tension, heart rate and respiratory rate. The autonomic nervous system can be divided into the parasympathetic and sympathetic nervous system. While the sympathetic nervous system is responsible for the fight-or-flight response, the parasympathetic nervous system is responsible for the complimentary rest-and-digest state. The fight-or-flight response, also called hyperarousal, occurs in response to a perceived harmful event or threat to survival, and primes the animal/person for fighting or fleeing.

For example, you are driving through the centre of a big city and suddenly another car toots very loudly, and it looks like as if a collision will occur. The sympathetic nervous system increases muscle tension to provide the body with extra speed and strength, and with increased blood pressure, heart rate, blood sugars and fats to supply the body with extra energy to be able to fight-or-flight. At the same time, a down-regulation takes place of neurobiological systems that hinder the adaptive reaction such as digestion, reproduction and growth (Grippo and Scotti, 2013). These alterations are associated with changes in brain activity (e.g. in EEG, hormones, neurotransmitters, etcetera). When an accident has been averted and you drive out of the city, the parasympathetic nervous system helps switch of the fight-or-flight response and return all hormones, organs and systems back to pre-stress levels. Your heart rate decreases, muscles become less tense, blood pressure returns to normal, and food is digested. Often a sigh of relief is the harbinger of a slower, more relaxed breathing pattern. The fight-or-flight and opposing rest-and-digest response have evolved over millions of years, and work well in the face of imminent threats such as predators. However, these responses also occur in modern times, for instance when your boss is negative about your work. The fight-or-flight response is associated with psychological effects, making us more alert, angry, fearful, etcetera. If the perceived threat is prolonged, assisted by worrying, the rest-and-digest response does not set in, and the continuous hyperarousal can be associated with prolonged anxiety, depression, irritability, etcetera.

The problem with hyperarousal can be that awareness of this state occurs only at the moment one is able to relax. Then you feel how tense your muscles were, and relaxation is sometimes accompanied by muscle pain. Unfortunately, if you have no possibility to relax, for example because of a continuous perceived threat, muscles become more and more tense. Sleeping problems start to occur, and attempts to reduce stress, for example by increased alcohol or drug intake, fail. It is like a frog in a pan that is slowly heated. The frog does not notice the increase in temperature until it is too late. Finally, the body stops an individual from continuing with too much stress and too little relaxation. Exhaustion sets in, accompanied by anxiety and depression, referred to as burn out. Depression may be a sign of exhaustion, and induces extreme lack of activity. Depressed people have no energy whatsoever to undertake activities, forcing one to rest.

It is difficult to find methods to relax. Many psychotropic drugs like benzodiazepines (anti-anxiety drugs) and antipsychotics induce an artificial relaxation, leading to suppression of psychiatric symptoms. The problem with these medications is that once they are stopped, a rebound effect occurs leading to worse symptoms than before the start of the medication. It is more difficult to use natural techniques to relax, but these techniques can lead to long-term benefit without rebound or withdrawal effects. Sometimes people think that relaxation comes with activities like going to a theme park. But this may cause too much stimulation and may lead to more stress. An important method is to stop the continuous stream of thoughts as described in meditation. This can be achieved by counting to 5 during breathing in and to 5 during breathing out. If attention is focused in this task, the continuous stream of thoughts is stopped. However, it requires some exercise to keep the focus on counting. Thoughts evoke emotions and physiological reactions. Stopping the continuous stream of thoughts is an effective way to relax naturally.

Another natural method to relax is physical exercise. During the exercise muscles are strained, expiration is deep and, after the exercise, muscles naturally relax. Physical exercise may be more effective than SSRI's especially at longer term follow up (Hoffmann et al., 2011). Perhaps if the public was better informed about the down side of psychotropic drugs and the risk of chronicity, and clinicians were more reticent in prescribing these drugs, people would be more inclined to take the effort to do physical exercise, or try meditation instead of taking a pill.

The case example of Mira illustrates the initial heavenly feeling of muscle relaxants such as benzodiazepines. Unfortunately, these drugs are addictive, and after weeks to months of use, more and more of the substance is needed to reach the same effect, and the body loses its ability to relax naturally.

CASE EXAMPLE: MIRA

Mira's problems started when her father died suddenly in a car accident. She was 42 then, a mother of two, married to Ben and working 4 days a week as a personal assistant. She had always been close to her father. Her mother died when she was 6 years old. She missed her father very much and started to sleep poorly. She felt irritable and depressed for months. Because of her responsibilities to her family and boss she kept on going, but she became more and more stressed and tired. She also lost weight, and some days when she woke up she felt very afraid. A few times she even had a panic attack. She went to her general practitioner, and he said that she could try oxazepam, a benzodiazepine which she could take when needed. She was amazed how oxazepam could make her feel. When she lay in bed worrying about her life, unable to sleep and she took a pill, she felt her muscles relax and it took her to a peaceful place where she could rest. She loved that feeling. In the morning when the coming day loomed upon her, she took a pill and the feeling went away. It had a numbing effect and that comforted her. Each time she got the medication from the pharmacy, she felt safe. Her family and boss were happy that she could function again, although she was not as sharp and lively as she used to be. However, after a few weeks, she could not fall asleep without the oxazepam anymore. She also needed more and more of the pills to sleep through the night, and to dampen her anxiety. She tried to stop taking the pills but her body craved for it. After a few months, she threw all her oxazepam pills away because she felt much worse than before she started with the medication, she was not herself anymore. She used to be enthusiastic and vibrant, but now she was just a shadow of the person she used to be, hollow and numb. She had lost her interest in her friends and family, sex and her job. She was determined to find herself, and swore not to touch any psychotropic medication ever again. She could not sleep all night and was extremely anxious the next day. All her muscles were cramped up and she felt dizzy and nauseous. Sounds and colours seemed to explode in her skull. She called in sick from work. She was alone at home, and the walls closed in on her. Even in bed with a pillow on her ear, her nerves were so highly strung that it was unbearable. Sometimes she heard a foul voice that whispered that her husband cheated on her. A week later, she was admitted to hospital and treated with antipsychotic medication.

References

Espie, C. (2002). Insomnia: conceptual issues in the development, persistence and treatment of sleep disorders in adults. *Annual Review of Psychology* 53, 215–43.

Fritz, C., Sonnentagg, S., Spector, P.E. and McInroe, J.A. (2010). The weekend matters: Relationships between stress recovery and affective experiences. *Journal of Organizational Behavior* 31, 1137–1162.

Grippo, A.J. and Scotti, A.L. (2013). Stress and neuroinflammation. In: Halaris, A. and Leonard, B.E. (eds.). *Inflammation in Psychiatry.* Modern Trends Pharmacopsychiatry 28. Basel: Karger.

Harvey, A. (2002). A cognitive model of insomnia. *Behaviour Research and Therapy* 40(8), 869–93.

Hoffman, B.M., Babyak, M.A., Craighead, W.E., Sherwood, A., Doraiswamy, P.M., Coons. M.J. and Blumenthal, J.A. (2011). Exercise and pharmacotherapy in patients with major depression: one-year follow-up of the SMILE study. *Psychosomatic Medicine* 73(2), 127–33.

Perlis, M.L., Giles, D., Mendelson, W.B., Bootzin, R.R. and Wyatt, J.K. (1997). Psychophysiological insomnia: the behavioural model of a neurocognitive perspective. *Journal of Sleep Research* 6(3), 179–88.

Riemann, D., Spiegelhalder, K., Feige, B., Voderholzer, U., Berger, M., Perlis, M., and Nissen, C. (2010). The hyperarousal of insomnia: a review of the concept and its evidence. *Sleep Medicine Reviews* 14(1), 19–31.

Schmidt, A. and Thews, G. (1989). Autonomic nervous system. In: Janig, W. (ed.). *Human Physiology* (2nd edn.). New York, NY: Springer-Verlag.

Walker, A.J., Kim, Y., Price, J.B., Kale, R.P., McGillivray, J.A., Berk, M. and Tye, S.J. (2014). Stress, inflammation, and cellular vulnerability during early stages of affective disorders: biomarker strategies and opportunities for prevention and intervention. *Frontiers in Psychiatry* 5, 34.

11

REDEFINITION OF HEALTH AND ILLNESS IN PSYCHIATRY

In modern western societies, reflected in psychiatric practice, mental health is regarded as a relative absence of depression, anxiety, psychosis. If you look on the website Facebook (www.facebook.com), life as it should be may be defined by many these days as having fun with other people. If mental health is regarded as a relative absence of depression, anxiety, psychosis, it is not surprising that 1 in 4 suffers from a mental illness. To come to a redefinition of health and illness in psychiatry, it may be important to investigate the true nature of social interaction, mystic experiences and the mind-brain problem, and not follow preconceptions of the majority. It may not be possible to live a life, face death, and come to terms with limitations and difficulties in social relationships without, what is labelled as, psychiatric symptoms.

Living through negative, overwhelming emotions can lead to personal development. As Rilke (1929) wrote in *Briefe an einem jungen Dichter*:

> Why do you want to shut out of your life any discomfort, any misery, any depression, since after all you don't know what work these conditions are doing inside you?

Realizing that human beings do terrible things to each other, and crying about it, can result in acceptance, quiescence and a melancholic undertone. Suppressing this feeling with medication leads to an artificial state of mind. Similarly, facing mortality and incorporating it in your existence may be an important task in life (Heidegger, 1962; Rilke, 1929) which cannot be accomplished by artificially manipulating anxiety and depression with psychotropic medication.

According to various philosophers, scientists and persons who have experienced psychiatric symptoms, those who deviate from what is considered normal may in fact be more aware of certain truths of life. Mental health, as defined in current psychiatry, may consist of being able to suppress (to a great extent) these truths. This possibility is not often taken into consideration. An important function of art may be uncovering truths that most people notice glimpses of from time to time. Art shows the transience of our existence, the harshness people often display, intense despair, grief, fear. It is a short interruption in the bubble of safety that healthy people are able to create for themselves. The difference between art and mental illness may be that during severe mental illness patients are immersed in these truths, and have no control over what is happening.

Rilke (1933) wrote:

> God and death were now outside, were the Other, while inside was our life, that at the cost of this exclusion, seemed to become more human, intimate, bearable, something that could be completed; it became entirely our own.

Rilke (1933) wrote about the Russian author Leo Tolstoy:

> Tolstoy observed many forms of death fear in others and in himself because his self-restraint enabled him to reflect on his own fear. His relationship with death must have been characterized by an omnipresent fear, a magnificent construct, a tower of fear with hallways and stairs, with ledges without railings and abysses on all sides…were it not that the intensity with which he experienced it and the realization of how much it cost him, transformed into distant reality; and suddenly this intensity became the tower's safe flooring to him, the landscape and air that surrounded it as well as the wind and a flock of birds.

Facing death and staring its accompanying fear in the eye leads to a floor from which to build an authentic existence. Death is inherent to living, and that does not change by trying to push it out of daily life.

Currently, psychiatric symptoms are seen as a result of a dysfunctional brain. However, this interpretation has yielded little or no progress in the understanding and treatment of psychiatric symptoms. Works of art or philosophy are better at giving a realistic interpretation of the 'human condition'. Acknowledging the human condition in scientific research may be one part of the puzzle. As an illustration, research has shown that depressed people may sometimes be more accurate in their perceptions and judgements than non-depressed people, which is designated as the depressive realism hypothesis (Seidel et al., 2012; Yeh and Liu, 2007; Alloy and Abrahamson, 1979). Bortolotti and Antrobus (2015) also conclude in their review that the recent studies confirm people with depression are able to make more accurate judgments and more realistic predictions in some contexts, and nonclinical samples have overly optimistic beliefs.

Furthermore, paranoia may also contain an element of realism. Many patients with schizophrenia and other psychotic disorders are socially isolated. Bhatia et al. (2004) found in a sample of 144 patients that only 4 per cent of the 38 year old men and 7 per cent of the 40 year old women were married. The origin of social isolation in psychotic disorders is a much debated issue. One main hypothesis suggests that patients with a psychotic disorder isolate themselves because they are more paranoid than other people.

In a famous experiment in social psychology, Milgram (1974) investigated subjects taking orders from a scientist-experimenter in a laboratory setting. To what extent would the subjects deliver a shock with increasing intensity, up to 450 volts (a life threatening shock) to an innocent, likeable victim who has to perform a learning task? The victim was an actor who does not actually receive the shocks, but the subjects do not know that. This experiment is often cited as the Obedience to Authority Study. How many psychologically normal people would administer the 450 volts shock? When Milgram posed this question to a sample blind to the results of the experiment, the average estimate was no more than one in a hundred. A group of psychiatrists guessed one in a thousand (Milgram, 1974). The results of the experiment were otherwise: 63 per cent of the subjects obeyed the scientist-experimenter to the limit and delivered 450 volts. The Milgram experiment has been reproduced many times and in many countries, and always with similar results (Blass, 1999).

Considering the results of the Milgram experiment, being paranoid to a certain extent would lead to a more realistic estimation of the percentage of subjects that would deliver the life threatening shock. As a clinician who treats patients with a psychotic disorder describes:

> It is in the relationship, and the one who is psychotic makes the bad condition visible. He or she 'wears the symptoms' and has the burden to carry them (Whitaker, 2010)

Treatments in contemporary psychiatry are usually focused on restoring 'normality'. Normality can be conceptualized as the majority, that which is most common (see Figure 11.1).

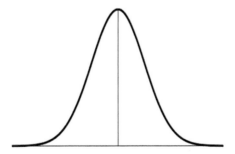

FIGURE 11.1 The normal distribution plot; this plot shows that normality is that what occurs most (top of the graph line)

However, a society needs people who are different from the majority, from Das Man. Many creative individuals who were struggling with despair about the human existential situation would have been diagnosed with a major depressive disorder or other psychiatric illness and treated with medication if they were living today, e.g. van Gogh, Camus, Rilke, Kafka, Woolf, Nietzsche, Beethoven. Would they have been able to create their masterpieces then? Irving Taylor (cited in Maddi, 1975) suggests that they may have had faculties of self-reflection so highly developed that they had a keener vision than most of us of the human existential situation and, with a ferocity born of desperation, plunged into creative efforts (Yalom, 1980). Beethoven expressed that art kept him from suicide (Yalom, 1980). At the age of thirty-two he wrote (cited in von Andics, 1947):

> Little kept me back from putting an end to my life. Art alone held me back. Alas, it seems to be impossible for me to leave the world before I have done all that I feel inclined to do, and thus I drag on this miserable life.

For children it is even more important that a wider variety in existential modes than normality is tolerated. In western societies, children who have a lot of energy and are very active have a considerable chance of being diagnosed with ADHD and medicated. Then they are told that there is something wrong in their brain, and that this can be restored with medication. Is it really necessary that everyone in a classroom is brought to the same norm? As Whitaker (2010) writes:

> Not too long ago, goof-offs, cut-ups, bullies, nerds, shy kids, teachers' pets and any number of other recognizable types filled the schoolyard and all were considered more or less normal. Nobody knew what to expect from such children as adults. That was part of the glorious uncertainty of life – the goof-off in the fifth grade might show up at his high school's twenty year reunion as a wealthy entrepreneur, the shy girl as an accomplished actress. But today children diagnosed with mental disorders – most notably ADHD, depression, and bipolar illness – help populate the schoolyard. These children have been told that they have something wrong with their brains and that they may have to take psychiatric medications the rest of their lives, just like a 'diabetic taking insulin'. That medical dictum teaches all of the children on the playground a lesson about the nature of humankind, and that lesson differs in a radical way from what children used to be taught.

Why not allow the wide diversity in behaviour, mood and personality that is inherent and even beneficial to society, and appreciate what suffering, despair, solitude (deviances from the norm) can lead to? If society in general and psychiatry in particular is of the opinion that everybody needs to be able perform their roles (as spouse, employee, pupil, productive member of society) all the time, and that deviances from 'normality' need to be treated, it is not surprising that the number of disabled mentally ill has increased between 1955 and 2007 6-fold in adults, and between 1987 and 2007 35-fold in children (Whitaker, 2010). These numbers are even more disturbing because normality may mean being able to suppress the harsh facts of life, creating a safety bubble, which may not be the ultimate state in life to wish for.

Environmental factors

The environment can play an important role in the causation and remission of psychiatric symptoms. Research shows that green environments and access to nature lead to better mental as well as physical health and less access to nature is linked to exacerbated ADHD symptoms, higher rates of anxiety disorders and clinical depression (Faber Taylor and Kuo, 2009; van den Berg and van den Berg, 2011; Kuo, 2010). Growing up and living in an urban environment is associated with a 2–3 fold increase in the chance of developing a non-affective psychosis (Heinz et al., 2013). Urbanicity is an environmental risk factor for schizophrenia (Vassos et al., 2012; Saha et al., 2005). Findings suggest it is unlikely that social drift alone can fully account for geographical variation in incidence (Heinz et al., 2013). Chan et al. (2015) investigated urbanization and the prevalence of schizophrenia in China between 1990 and 2010. In recent decades, urbanization has been occurring at a massive scale in low- and middle-income countries (United Nations Population Division, 2013; Cohen, 2006). In China, there were 3.09 million persons affected during their lifetime in the year 1990. Twenty-seven per cent of the cases were from urban areas, which corresponds to the overall proportion of urban residents in China in the same year (26.4 per cent). By 2010, the number of persons affected with schizophrenia rose to 7.16 million, a 132 per cent increase, while the total population of China only increased by 18 per cent during this period (United Nations Population Division, 2013). Moreover, the contribution of expected cases from urban areas to the overall burden increased from 27 per cent in 1990 to 62 per cent in 2010, well above the proportion of urban residents in China in 2010 (49.2–49.7 per cent). The rapid urbanization in many parts of the world may result in an increased global prevalence of schizophrenia.

The mechanisms underlying the relationship between urbanicity and schizophrenia are still unclear. Psychosis is often associated on a phenomenological level with the experience of overstimulation, alienation and perceived environmental hostility. These are characteristics of urban areas. In the city, there is an abundance of stimuli caused by traffic, busy people, shops trying to sell their products, etcetera. The atmosphere in densely populated urban areas can be hostile because most people are in a hurry and try to get ahead. There is often a lack of trees, fields and nature in general. In addition, modern architecture can be abominable and alienating with massive, grey, concrete walls, small rooms with a view on trash, public transport, highways, etcetera. Our species lived and evolved in green, natural environments for millennia. Every animal on our planet thrives in the environment in which it evolved and can become ill in alien environments such as cages without natural elements

(Kuo, 2010). This is one aspect of urbanicity that needs to be further explored for its contribution to increased risk for psychosis.

The case example of David shows how the environment can play an important role in the pathogenesis of mental ill health.

CASE EXAMPLE: DAVID

David was offered a job by a famous professor in a big city in the USA. David lived with his wife and two young sons in the country in France. He loved it there, he cycled to work and his sons could play in the green fields around the house. David was flattered by the offer. He thought hard about it and discussed it with his wife, sons and others. It would be a very good career move and they decided that David should take the offer. It took half a year of preparation, they sold their house quite quickly and then they left with a lot of hope for a bright future. David had dreams of writing articles in excellent journals with the professor, and of buying a big house in the USA where they would all be happy.

When they arrived at the airport in the USA, David already felt the hairs on his back rise. The barren, grey concrete walls in the airport gave him an alienated feeling. When they took a taxi to their hotel he started to feel very scared and desolate. He disliked the abundance of traffic, the concrete everywhere, the scarceness of trees and green fields. He already regretted his decision to leave his hometown. A few weeks later, they settled into an apartment in the city because it would take at least an hour and a half of driving if they wanted to live outside the city. The only apartment they could afford was in a northern suburb. When he walked to the bus stop to go to work, there was a 6 lane highway road that was always full with cars, noise, exhaust fumes. After the bus, he caught a train to go to work. The trains were so packed with people that often they stood crammed together going to and coming from work. With all the people and their urgent goals, it felt like an ant heap burying him. Often he longed terribly for the green fields around his former house. He felt very guilty that he took his wife and children to this repulsive environment. There were hardly any possibilities for the children to play outside, so they sat in front of the television or computer. Everybody was eating hamburgers and fries, and so their children did as well; they were slowly becoming pale and overweight.

David tried to be strong and make the best of it but he could not prevent sinking in a swamp of regret, longing, tension and repulsion. The environment was opposite to his nature, his needs. There was noise, ugliness, concrete, people, graffiti and cars everywhere. He tried to find a job again in France, but he became desperate after writing 50 letters and being turned down all the time.

His wife noticed a stare lately in his eyes. He hardly smiled anymore, and lay awake a large part of the night. He also started drinking more and more. The

> doctor prescribed him tranquilizers and antidepressants. One day he just could not go on. He woke up and all his muscles were so tense that they felt like ice. He just could not move one leg before the other. He called in sick from work, and he was admitted to hospital 4 weeks later because he tried to kill himself.

Currently, if an individual goes to his/her general practitioner and describes difficulty sleeping, weight loss, low mood, energy loss for more than two weeks, there is a big chance that he/she is diagnosed with a major depressive disorder and gets a prescription for antidepressant medication (SSRI's). It is questionable whether this is a good approach in all instances. In some subjects (like the case example of David above and of Thomas in Part III) the depression may be a sign one has taken a wrong direction in life. Depression can occur as a result of not following your own nature, and this problem is not solved by taking antidepressants.

Perhaps it is not possible to define in general terms when mental health becomes mental illness, or to formulate diagnostic categories. People may just be too different from each other with respect to existential concerns, previous experiences, genetic make-up, etcetera. However, it may be possible to find biomarkers that can have an individual prognostic value and that can help define treatment targets such as the P300 event-related potential described in Chapter 8. The blend of biological, environmental, psychological causal and maintaining factors in the psychiatric symptoms has probably as many variations as there are people. Therefore, each person deserves an idiographic, personalized approach in which his/her blend of causal and maintaining factors is investigated. Some factors could be influenced (preferably not with psychotropic medication), but others not. This approach may lead to a more enduring recovery than trying to fit individuals in broad diagnostic DSM categories that have not much value for understanding the problems of the individual patients or for possible solutions for these problems.

Patients with psychiatric symptoms are often searching for meaning in their life, and struggle with estrangement from themselves. They often say that they do not feel themselves anymore in the consulting room. Sometimes depression is the result from being estranged from who you really are and what you really want. Of course, not all psychopathology can be traced back to fundamental questions, but we need to consider that it may not be possible to have a sensible definition of mental health and mental illness without taking fundamental questions into account. We need to understand a healthy human mind before it is possible to determine its illnesses. In orthopaedics, these definitions are less complicated: a straight bone is healthy, a broken bone is not. But in psychiatry, is a happy person healthy and an unhappy person not? Or is a person who dysfunctions ill? Is prolonged sadness an illness, or is one just being realistic? Making arbitrary cut-offs as in the DSM is strangely artificial. A person having obsessive compulsive symptoms for 59 minutes a day is not ill but someone with these symptoms for an hour and a minute is. Such definitions may seem scientific because they can be quantified, but the consequences are unscientific and show the flaws of the reductionist paradigm in psychiatry: increased disability caused by psychiatric symptoms, despite a steep increase in psychotropic medication prescription. Psychiatry should have a separate status in between medicine, philosophy and art. In some subjects with psychiatric symptoms, physiological disturbances predominate, but others struggle with an existential crisis. In each individual there is a unique combination of contributing factors, and therefore it is almost impossible to divide them into diagnostic categories. Across individuals, there may be organizing dimensions, like the stress–relaxation continuum. It is possible to investigate scientifically the relationship between a physiological stress reaction and parameters such as sleep or mood. Thus, what would psychiatry based on the aforementioned principles look like?

Each subject with psychiatric symptoms is regarded as an individual with a unique combination of causal and maintaining factors. Symptoms are treated as early as possible, with the least invasive treatment method. Symptoms do not always need to be labelled as an illness, certainly not at the early stages. Regarding moods as fundamental states that can disclose suppressed truths (Heidegger, 1962) can instigate subjects to examine their life, their choices and their authentic self (see next Chapter). Natural ways of influencing the stress–relaxation continuum (by relaxation exercises, normalizing psycho-education, doing more of what you want and less of what you ought to do) can be very effective in the early illness stages. In the later stages, medication may be indicated but new, curative medications need to be developed on the basis of transdiagnostic research.

References

Alloy, L.B. and Abrahamson, L.Y. (1979). Judgement of contingency in depressed and non-depressed students: Sadder but wiser? *Journal of Experimental Psychology* 108, 441–85.

Bhatia, T., Franzos, M.A., Wood, J.A., Nimgaonkar, V.L. and Deshpande, S.N. (2004). Gender and procreation among patients with schizophrenia. *Schizophrenia Research* 68, 387–94.

Blass, T. (1999). The Milgram paradigm after 35 years: some things we now know about obedience to authority. *Journal of Applied Social Psychology* 29, 955–78.

Bortolotti, L. and Antrobus, M. (2015). Costs and benefits of realism and optimism. *Current Opinion in Psychiatry* 28(2), 194–198.

Chan, K.Y., Zhao, F.F., Meng, S., Demaio, A.R., Reed, C., Theodoratou, E., Campbell, H., Wang, W. and Rudan, I. (2015). Urbanization and the prevalence of schizophrenia in China between 1990 and 2010. *World Psychiatry* 14(2), 251–2.

Cohen, B. (2006). Urbanisation in developing countries: current trends, future projections, and key challenges for sustainability. *Technology in Society* 28, 63–80.

Faber Taylor, A. and Kuo, F.E. (2009). Children with attention deficits concentrate better after walk in the park. *Journal of Attention Disorders* 12, 402–409.

Heidegger, H. (1962). *Being and Time*, Macquarrie, J. and Robinson, E. trans. New York: Harper & Row.

Heinz A., Deserno, L. and Reininghaus, U. (2013). Urbanicity, social adversity and psychosis. *World Psychiatry* 12(3), 187–197.

Kuo, F.E. (2010). Parks and other green environments: essential components of a healthy human habitat. *Australasian Parks and Leisure* 14, 10–12. http://www.nrpa.org/uploadedFiles/nrpa.org/Publications_and_Research/Research/Papers/MingKuo-Research-Paper.pdf

Maddi, S. (1975) The strenousness of the creative life. In: Taylor, I.A. and Getzels, J.W. (eds.). *Perspectives in Creativity*. Chicago, IL: Aldine.

Milgram, S. (1974). *Obedience to Authority: An Experimental View*. New York: Harper and Row.

Rilke, R.M. (1929). *Briefe an einem jungen Dichter*. Leipzig: Insel Verlag.

Rilke, R.M. (1933). *Über Gott*. Leipzig: Insel-Verlag.

Saha, S., Chant, D., Welham, J. and McGrath, J. (2005). A systematic review of the prevalence of schizophrenia. *PLoS Medicine* 2, e141.

Seidel, E.M., Satterthwaite, T.D., Eickhoff, S.B., Schneider, F., Gur, R.C., Wolf, D.H. and Derntl, B. (2012). Neural correlates of depressive realism-An fMRI study on causal attribution in depression. *Journal of Affective Disorders* 138, 268–376.

United Nations Population Division. (2013). *Total Population: Urban and Rural Population*. New York: United Nations Population Division.

Vassos, E., Pedersen, C.B., Murray, R.M. Collier, D.A. and Lewis, C.M. (2012). Meta-analysis of the association of urbanicity with schizophrenia. *Schizossphrenia Bulletin* 38, 1118–23.

von Andics, M. (1947). *Suicide and Meaning of Life*. London: William Hodge.

Whitaker, R. (2010). *Anatomy of an Epidemic: Magic Bullets, Psychiatric Drugs, and the Astonishing Rise of Mental Illness in America*. New York: Crown.

van den Berg, A.E. and van den Berg, C.G. (2011). A comparison of children with ADHD in a natural and built setting. *Child: Care, Health and Development* 37(3), 430–439.

Yalom, I.D. (1980). *Existential Psychotherapy*. New York: Basic Books.

Yeh, Z.T. and Liu, S.I. (2007). Depressive realism: evidence from false interpersonal perception. *Psychiatry and Clinical Neurosciences* 61, 135–41.

12
THE AUTHENTIC SELF

Although the self has always played a more or less important role in psychiatry (Gallagher, 2000), in the DSM the self is not taken into account (van de Kraats et al., 2012). However, many psychiatric patients report that they feel that they are no longer themselves. Do we know what the self is and how we can lose or find it? In the work of many philosophers, scientists and writers, the topic of finding one's true self (also called self-actualization, individuation, authenticity, true identity) is of great importance. Finding yourself can be a road to connect to a deeper, ancient, ego-transcendent part of the human mind (see also Chapter 4). To take the subjective experience of patients more seriously than in the current paradigm, we should define the authentic self and try to formulate an answer to the question: How do people lose themselves and how can they find themselves again? To gain more insight into the concept of authentic self, the following paragraphs will summarize the work of some of our greatest thinkers, writers and scientists who wrote about this topic. Subsequently their ideas are synthesized and the relevance to psychiatry discussed.

Martin Heidegger

Martin Heidegger (26 September 1889–26 May 1976) was a German philosopher. He developed a ground breaking and widely influential philosophy. In his book *Sein und Zeit* (1927) he describes 'being' (Dasein) on a fundamental level. He invented new words to express his accurate, precise, true observations of human nature. His accounts on human conditions such as uncanniness (Unheimlichkeit), existential anguish (Angst), being-toward-death are very relevant for understanding people with psychiatric symptoms. Irvin Yalom incorporates the insights of Heidegger in his textbook *Existential Psychotherapy* (1980).

Authenticity plays an important role in Heidegger's philosophy. People are prone to follow the majority (Das Man) in their choices and opinions, which leads to a sense of homeliness (Heimlichkeit), a superficial day to day reality in which harsh existential facts are suppressed.

Being-with (Mitsein) refers to the ontological concept of a human being in relationship to other human beings. We all have relationships and we cannot live without them. However, as described in Chapter 3, Mitsein has the inherent difficulty of the opinions of others about ourselves. We are inauthentic when we fail to recognize how our social surroundings influence us. We are authentic when we pay attention to that influence and decide for ourselves whether to go along with it. This is very difficult. Firstly, to recognize the influence and secondly to decide for ourselves what we want to do. This difficulty is hardly acknowledged in contemporary psychiatry. We all want to feel safe, loved and respected and therefore we are inclined to make choices that lead to approval of Das Man. However, these choices are not always the choices that we want to make ourselves (see also the story of Thomas in Part III of this book).

Mitsein (being with others) also has the unfortunate consequence that people want to have the same social status as, or preferably a higher social status than the others. Although Heidegger investigates the nature of Dasein without offering ethical or normative judgements, it is clear that he holds authenticity in very high esteem. He describes 'publicness' (mass society) as something that destroys Dasein's authenticity because of the induction of vain pride and the subsequent obsession with comparing oneself to and competing with others. Furthermore, mass society leads to levelling down to a sort of averageness (for example, mainstream television and movies). Publicness controls how the world, Dasein, is interpreted and this way seems to involve a dumbing down of everything according to Heidegger. The importance of mass society to Dasein is expressed in Heidegger's statement that 'everyone is the other, and no one is himself.'

Heidegger calls the state of Dasein's inauthentic Being-in-the-world 'fallenness' and the possible cure for fallenness is anxiety. Anxiety is a disclosive state of mind that can be used to reveal aspects of Dasein and the ultimate conditions of existence, it is the harbinger of authenticity (Magrini, 2006). Heidegger is concerned with bringing Dasein back to face its own being with honesty and integrity, similarly to Rilke. Moods are fundamental states of attunement that colour Dasein's disposition and awareness, out of which it uncovers, or discloses, things that matter (Magrini, 2006). Following Heidegger, moods such as anxiety are essential for 'unconcealment'. In current psychiatric practice, (prolonged) anxiety or depression are often not explored for their disclosing potential but rather suppressed with medication. Perhaps contemporary psychiatry holds the implicit assumption that authentic existence should be brought back to the averageness of Das Man. Although the current classification system in psychiatry pretends to be objective and scientific, it is based on subjective expert-consensus. This means that it could be replaced by another approach that takes into account a deeper understanding of human beings and their moods. Of course, this change would take a long time to realize but considering the extent of the unsolved problems in contemporary psychiatry, change is overdue.

Friedrich Nietzsche

Friedrich Nietzsche (15 October 1844–25 August 1900) was a German philosopher, poet, cultural critic, composer and Latin and Greek scholar.

Nietzsche's (2001) term for Das Man (Heidegger) is The Herd:

> Today… when only the herd animal is honoured… the concept of 'greatness' entails being noble, wanting to be oneself, being capable of being different, standing alone and having to live independently; and the philosopher will betray something of his own ideal when he posits: He shall be the greatest who can be the loneliest, the most hidden, the most deviating, the human being beyond good and evil.

Nietzsche's quote (1882) 'Was sagt dein Gewissen? – Du sollst der werden, der du bist' (What does your conscience say? – You shall become the person you are) is at the heart of his philosophy. The exemplary human being must craft his/her own identity through self-realization. In contrast to Jung and Rilke, Nietzsche acclaimed that man must do so without relying on anything transcending that life, such as God or a soul.

Nietzsche's project of bringing the human being from religion and eternity back to earth turned him towards the biological dimension of human existence, its irrational instincts and drives: what he called will-to-power. Psychologically, it is the drive to dominate and control. 'Man is an evaluating animal,' Nietzsche wrote, and moral and aesthetic values coalesce in the project of consciously making one's life a work of art. This union of morality and the aesthetic can save us from ourselves and from the despair that the universe does not care. To Nietzsche, art is to supplant religion (Flynn, 2006).

Søren Kierkegaard

Søren Kierkegaard (5 May 1813–11 November 1855) was a Danish philosopher, theologian, poet, social critic and religious author who is widely considered to be the first existentialist philosopher. Much of his philosophical work deals with the issues of how one lives as a 'single individual', giving priority to concrete human reality over abstract thinking and highlighting the importance of personal choice and commitment (Gardiner, 1969). His psychological work explored the emotions and feelings of individuals when faced with life choices (Ostenfeld and McKinnon, 1972).

Like Heidegger, Kierkegaard (1847) wrote about the threat of social comparison to individuality:

Alas, those great, uplifting, simple thoughts, those first thoughts, are more and more forgotten, perhaps entirely forgotten in the weekday and worldly life of comparisons. The one human being compares himself with others, the one generation compares itself with the other, and thus the heaped up pile of comparisons overwhelms a person. As the ingenuity and busyness increase, there come to be more and more in each generation who slavishly work a whole lifetime far down in the low underground regions of comparisons. Indeed, just as miners never see the light of day, so these unhappy people never come to see the light: those uplifting, simple thoughts, those first thoughts about how glorious it is to be a human being. And up there in the higher regions of comparison, smiling vanity plays its false game and deceives the happy ones so that they receive no impression from those lofty, simple thoughts, those first thoughts.

Kierkegaard wrote extensively on the project of becoming an individual in his overarching concern with 'what it means to exist; … what it means to be a human being.' According to Kierkegaard, anxiety is the 'dizziness of freedom', the awareness of the possibility of 'being able'. Therefore anxiety is, as well as despair, not a defect but a mark of a human beings possibility of becoming an authentic self.

Upanishads

The Upanishads are a collection of texts which contain the earliest emergence (centuries BCE) of the central religious concepts of Hinduism, some of which are shared with Buddhism. The Upanishads are considered by Hindus to contain revealed truths concerning the nature of ultimate reality and describing the character and form of human salvation. The concepts of Brahman and Ātman are central ideas in all the Upanishads (Radhakrishnan, 1956; Raju, 1985), and 'Know your Ātman' their thematic focus (Doninger, 1990). The Brahman is the ultimate reality and the Ātman is individual self. At the deepest level and in the state of self-realization, Ātman and Brahman are identical (Varghese, 2008).

Baruch Spinoza

Baruch Spinoza (24 November 1632–21 February 1677) was a Dutch philosopher whose work was very influential in Western philosophy. Spinoza's life testifies to his authentic choices and courage. He developed controversial ideas regarding the nature of the divine and the Jewish bible, which lead to his excommunication from the Jewish community at age 23. Spinoza lived a humble life as a lens-grinder, and turned down several rewards and honours during his life, including teaching (professor) positions. In his magnum opus *The Ethics* Spinoza argues that there is only one substance, which is absolutely infinite, self-caused and eternal, opposing the Descartes' mind–body dualism. He calls this substance

'God', or 'Nature'. He takes these two terms to be synonymous (in Latin the phrase he uses is *Deus sive Natura*). This pantheist position is comparable to the one described in the Upanishads. The term pantheism is constructed from the Greek *pan* 'all' and *theos* 'god' and is described as 'the belief that every existing entity is only one Being; and that all other forms of reality are either modes (or appearances) of it or identical with it' (Stanford Encyclopaedia of Philosophy).

Albert Einstein wrote in a letter in 1929:

> We followers of Spinoza see our God in the wonderful order and lawfulness of all that exists and in its soul as it reveals itself in man and animal.

Joseph Campbell

Joseph Campbell (26 March 1904–30 October 1987) was an American mythologist, lecturer and writer, and his work covers many aspects of human experience. He is best known for his work in comparative religion and mythology. His philosophy is often summarized by his phrase: follow your bliss. He derived this idea from the Upanishads:

> Now, I came to this idea of bliss because in Sanskrit, which is the great spiritual language of the world, there are three terms that represent the brink, the jumping-off place to the ocean of transcendence: Sat-Chit-Ananda. The word 'Sat' means being. 'Chit' means consciousness. 'Ananda' means bliss or rapture. I thought, 'I don't know whether my consciousness is proper consciousness or not; I don't know whether what I know of my being is my proper being or not; but I do know where my rapture is. So let me hang on to rapture, and that will bring me both my consciousness and my being.' I think it worked.

Doing what you want to do, and perhaps were meant to do (considering your constitution, interests, past experience, etcetera), often leads to a state of bliss. Joseph Campbell said (1988):

> If you follow your bliss, you put yourself on a kind of track that has been there all the while, waiting for you, and the life that you ought to be living is the one you are living. Wherever you are – if you are following your bliss, you are enjoying that refreshment, that life within you, all the time.

However, it is important to note that 'following one's bliss', as Campbell saw it, is not merely a matter of doing whatever you like, and certainly not doing simply as you are told. It is a matter of identifying that pursuit which you are truly passionate about and attempting to totally give yourself to it. In so doing, you may reach your fullest potential and serve your community to the greatest possible extent. Thus, an emotional state (bliss) can help someone in his search for who he really is and what he really wants in life. Campbell believed in the psychic unity of mankind and its poetic expression through mythology and that the religions of the world are the various culturally influenced 'masks' of the same fundamental, transcendent truths.

Paolo Coelho

Paolo Coelho (born 24 August 1947) is a Brazilian lyricist and novelist. His books are read by millions of people worldwide. Paolo Coelho expresses a kind of wisdom in his books that encompasses elements of those whose work is described in this chapter. He combines insight into the path of personal growth with literary capabilities, which could explain the worldwide popularity of his books.

In his novel *The Alchemist* (1993) he tells a story about finding your destiny. To find your destiny you should follow your heart and there you will find your treasure. With 'find your treasure' he refers to a spiritual meaning. Thus, finding yourself can be a road to connect to a deeper, ancient, ego-transcendent part of the human mind (see also Chapter 4).

William James

William James (11 January 1842 – 26 August 1910) was an American philosopher and psychologist. James wrote widely on many topics, including psychology, epistemology, religion, metaphysics and mysticism.

William James provided a description of the mystical experience in his famous collection of lectures published in 1902 as *The Varieties of Religious Experience*. He proposed that the following four marks may justify us to call an experience mystical:

1 *Ineffability* – The handiest of the marks by which I classify a state of mind as mystical is negative. The subject of it immediately says that it defies expression, that no adequate report of its contents can be given in words.
2 *Noetic quality* – Although so similar to states of feeling, mystical states seem to those who experience them to be also states of knowledge. They are states of insight into depths of truth unplumbed by the discursive intellect. They are illuminations, revelations, full of significance and importance, all inarticulate though they remain; and as a rule they carry with them a curious sense of authority for aftertime.
3 *Transiency* – Mystical states cannot be sustained for long.
4 *Passivity* – Although the oncoming of mystical states may be facilitated by preliminary voluntary operations, as by fixing the attention, or going through certain bodily performances, or in other ways which manuals of mysticism prescribe, when the characteristic sort of consciousness once has set in, the mystic feels as if his own will were in abeyance, and indeed sometimes as if he were grasped and held by a superior power.

As described in Chapter 4, James regarded mystic experiences as 'stemming from that great subliminal or transmarginal region of which science is beginning to admit the existence, but of which so little is really known.' James took a more pantheist approach, comparable to Baruch Spinoza.

Karl Jaspers

Karl Jaspers (23 February 1883–26 February 1969) was a German psychiatrist and philosopher who had a strong influence on modern theology, psychiatry and philosophy. After being trained in and practicing psychiatry, Jaspers turned to philosophical inquiry and attempted to discover an innovative philosophical system. He was often viewed as a major exponent of existentialism in Germany, though he did not accept this label.

Erklären und Verstehen

In 1913 Jaspers published his classical work *Allgemeine Psychopathologie (General Psychopathology)*. Many of his ideas described in this comprehensive book are of great importance to current psychiatry.

Jaspers makes the distinction between the method of 'understanding' (*Verstehen*) and the method of 'causal explanation' (*Erklären*). Verstehen is the phenomenological method of trying to understand the individual world of the patient. Erklären stands for the method of scientific investigation. According to Jaspers, both methods are required in psychiatry and cannot be reduced to one another. In psychiatry, biologically and psychologically oriented paradigms have alternated historically. When Jaspers published his handbook in 1913, the paradigm was biologically oriented with an emphasis on a natural-scientific approach (based on empirical or measurable evidence). In an epistemological debate about whether psychiatry should adopt a natural-scientific approach or follow the methods of the human sciences (the study and interpretation of the experiences, activities and constructs associated with human beings), Jaspers adopted an intermediate position. This position can be described as a hybrid approach, partly following the methods in natural sciences and partly following those in the humanities. In his book *General Psychopathology*, he describes psychiatric symptoms objectively to facilitate recognition in other cases, but combines it with a focus on the subjective part of psychopathology; the individual patient with his own existential concerns (Fusar-Poli, 2013).

On page 459 of *General Psychopathology* (1947) Jaspers writes:

> It could be formulated as *mental illness is a cerebral illness (Griesinger, Meynert, Wernicke)*... we know that in general no psychic events exists without the precondition of some physical basis. There are no 'ghosts'. But we do not know a single physical event in the brain which could be considered the identical counterpart of any morbid psychic event. We only know conditioning factors for the psychic life; we never know the cause of a psychic event, only a cause.

On page 766 he writes:

> What the individual is *manifests itself at three levels*. (a) He is shown to be an empirical reality in various ways in which he becomes *objectively explorable* as a creature of this world. (b) He *illuminates himself* from his own sources in making use of the different encompassing modes of his Being. (c) As he searches in the world and founders there he *unifies* and becomes conscious of his true origins and destination. It is only at the first level that he is accessible for scientific investigation.

With respect to (b), Jaspers describes earlier on that page that man struggles with inner resistance:

> a continual *process of covering up and distorting everything that is,* everything that he feels, thinks and wishes. ... Against the process of covering up and distorting he sets up a process of illumination.

This is comparable to Heidegger's concept of 'unconcealment'. Dreams can play an important role in illumination or unconcealment (see also the paragraph about Jung). What Jaspers wrote in 1913 is not much different from current psychiatry. Level (a) can be studied scientifically, but level (b) and (c) that are at least as important for understanding psychiatric symptoms, cannot. It makes no sense to form groups of patients with their individual backgrounds, existential concerns, specific resistances, etcetera and define statistical outcome parameters. As Jaspers put it (p. 462):

> ... the occasion is always a rather new, historical source for concrete understanding in the personal form of this doctor and this patient. It is the most intense presentation of what is entirely individual.

Thus, a mature psychiatry should combine Erklären with Verstehen. It is not necessary to solve the mind–brain problem, it just needs to be taken seriously: the mind cannot be reduced to the brain, not now and perhaps never.

Psychosis and neurosis

Jaspers also played an important role in distinguishing psychosis from neurosis (such as anxiety and depression). He wrote in *General Psychopathology* that neurosis elicits empathy because it is understandable, psychosis on the other hand is un-understandable in many instances. This distinction was adopted in the first version of the DSM (Grob, 1991) and psychosis is still considered by many to be qualitatively different from neurosis.

Although the term neurosis is not often used anymore these days in clinical practice, recent empirical evidence is not congruent with the thought that psychosis is qualitatively different from neurosis (anxiety and depression). Psychotic experiences occur in the general population in a continuum with normality (Allardyce et al., 2007). During sensory deprivation, sleep deprivation, solitary confinement and grieving, delusions and hallucinations frequently occur (Leff, 1968; Babkoff et al., 1989; Grimby, 1993). There are also results that show that psychosis as well as neurosis can be luxated by life events (Bebbington et al., 1993). Patients with schizophrenia often show partial insight in their symptoms, whereas anxious and depressed patients can have irrefutable convictions. Psychotic symptoms are often understandable in the way dreams can be understood, in an affective, associative manner. Psychosis also becomes understandable if one takes into consideration the element of realism in paranoia, and the essential religious nature of human beings (see Chapter 4). The Dutch philosopher and writer Wouter Kusters, who experienced psychosis himself, demonstrates the intelligibility of psychosis in his book *Philosophy of Madness* (2014).

Furthermore, Jaspers believed that psychiatrists should diagnose symptoms, particularly of psychosis, by their form rather than their content. This is still general practice in clinical psychiatry. The content of the delusion is deemed irrelevant, perhaps because mystic experiences and paranoia are regarded as expressions of neurotransmitter dysfunctions. However, this can be derogatory to the patient, and many patients experience it this way. Psychotic experiences are often meaningful to them, but their treating health care professionals often dismiss these experiences as psychotic expressions of a dysfunctional brain. Of course there is a biological component in psychosis, just as there is in anxiety and depression, but the problem is more complex than just this biological component. Allowing the reality of mystic experiences, paranoia and existential issues to play a role in a new paradigm in psychiatry, could lead to a more truthful understanding of psychiatric symptoms.

Perennial philosophy

In his book, *The Perennial Scope of Philosophy* Jaspers (2007) wrote:

> The subjective and the objective side of faith are a whole. If I only take the subjective side, there remains a faith that is merely a believing state of mind, a faith without object, which in a manner of speaking believes only itself, a faith without inner content. If I only take the objective side, there remains a content of faith, as object, as proposition, as dogma, as dead something. ... Accordingly, when we speak of faith, we shall have in mind this faith that comprehends subject and object. Therein lies the whole difficulty of defining faith.

Faith and mystic experiences are difficult to define objectively, because their experience is essential. As William James wrote, one of the descriptions of a mystic experience is its ineffability. The experience itself is an essential component. It is hardly possible to evoke the experience in someone else just by describing it. This magnifies the mind–brain problem in psychiatry: the main topic of study in psychiatry is the subjective side, the experience itself, but we try to investigate it, define it through the objective side (the brain). If a great mystic dies and you examine his brain post-mortem, would one find mystic experiences (or any other experience) in there? No, one would not. The solution of the past decennia has been to ignore difficult topics such as mystic experiences, or to just state that they are signs of aberrant neurotransmitter systems, but that means depreciating an essential part of human experience. Throughout history, in philosophy and in the subjective reports of psychiatric patients, God and faith have played a major role. Looking at it only from the objective side is insufficient, the subjective side needs to acknowledged, taken seriously on its own merits.

As Jaspers wrote (2007):

> If faith is neither solely content nor solely an act of the subject, but is rooted in the vehicle of phenomenality, then it should be conceived only in conjunction with that which is neither subject nor object in one, with that which manifests itself in the duality of subject and object.

Since we cannot 'catch' the subjective experience in the brain, it can only be incorporated in psychiatry through a phenomenological approach. A patient is treated differently when a psychiatrist is trained to regard mystic experiences as superstitious beliefs, or a sign of aberrant neurotransmitters, than when he is trained to understand these experiences as pivotal and sometimes containing elements that can lead to a natural recovery. Mohr et al. (2012) report that spirituality is helpful in a majority of schizophrenia patients (87 per cent) and harmful (a source of despair and suffering) in a minority (13 per cent) of 276 outpatients with schizophrenia or schizoaffective disorder in Switzerland, Canada and the US. Cohen et al. (2010) conclude that religiousness may have a favourable impact on the quality of life of older adults with schizophrenia, and it must be considered along with other therapeutically important agents. Furthermore, Kirov et al. (1998), conclude in a study of 52 patients with psychosis that the experience of a psychotic illness is likely to lead to an increase in religious beliefs. Such beliefs are commonly used for coping with the illness, and some patients attach a great importance to them.

In conclusion, Jaspers has made a significant, still very relevant contribution to psychiatry. His insights into the mind–brain problem (Verstehen-Erklären) and perennial philosophy should be taught in (clinical) training of psychiatrists, psychologists and researchers. However, his views on the distinction between psychosis and neurosis (e.g. anxiety and depression) may have been overtaken by recent developments in research and treatment.

Mihály Csíkszentmihályi

Mihály Csíkszentmihályi (born 29 September 1934) is a Distinguished Professor of Psychology and Management at Claremont Graduate University, USA. He is most known for his work on 'flow' a state of concentration or complete absorption with the activity at hand and the situation. It is a state in which people are so involved in an activity that nothing else seems to matter (Csíkszentmihályi, 1990). The idea of flow is identical to the feeling of being 'in the groove'. The flow state is an optimal state of intrinsic motivation, where the person is fully immersed in what he is doing. This is a feeling everyone has at times, characterized by great absorption, engagement, fulfilment and skill during which temporal concerns (time, food, ego-self, etcetera) are typically ignored.

A flow state can be entered while performing any activity, although it is most likely to occur when one is wholeheartedly performing a task or activity for intrinsic purposes (Csíkszentmihályi, 1975). Passive activities like watching TV usually don't elicit flow experiences (Moneta, 2012).

Rainer Maria Rilke

Rilke (4 December 1875–29 December 1926) was an Austrian poet and novelist. Rilke showed a deep understanding of human nature in his letters, prose and poems. As discussed in previous chapters, his work is mystic in the sense that he describes communion with the ineffable as a highly relevant subjective experience in life.

Rilke expresses that those who live on the surface, ruled by conventions, forfeit experience of the mystery. Rilke (1929) describes God, mysticism, as a sealed letter that can be opened and if not, it is handed on. This is similar to the ancient domain, the collective unconsciousness, perennial philosophy:

> Let the surface not distract you; it is in the depths where everything becomes law. And those who live the mystery falsely and badly (and there are many) forfeit it only for themselves and still hand it on like a sealed letter, unknowingly.

Rilke was driven by what could be called a quest for God. The relationship with the transcendent is most explicit in *Das Stundenbuch* (1905). God hides in the ordinary, in the easily overlooked, in the core of the person's interior and not necessarily in the church. Rilke's view of God is experiential: it cannot be separated from life in the here and now, the human body, the things in the world or nature. By unreservedly receiving and accepting life's suffering, humans can feel close to God. God is hidden and mysterious. People are likely to discount and ignore God, thereby constructing a sanitized, arid version of life. For God is the essence of life, and God's apparent distance from us diminishes to the degree that we become open to life's questions, to the presence and reality of love and death, in short, to life itself (Kidder, 2012).

Thus, the experience of God is not an experience of superhuman eternal divinity but one of humility, permeated by life's realities of finitude, sorrow and dread. For Rilke, recovering God's presence in life does not necessarily fall to the church's office bearers but to artists (poets, painters and sculptors). He saw the artist's role as mediator between God and the people through art. Artists can be mediator between God and people because a poem, sculpture or painting can convey a truth that many try to ban out of their life. In *Briefe an einem jungen Dichter* (1929), Rilke describes the importance of solitude for an artist to discover God.

To acknowledge, experience, feel all that is within, composes the path of personal growth that Rilke describes. The important thing is to go through the emotion, and the best situation for that is solitude. In company, despair, grief, anxiety are often repressed with idle conversations, diversions and distractions. If grief is shown in company, others may become embarrassed by the crying or try to stop it as soon as possible. It is better to face it and undergo it in all its intensity alone, or with others who do not become embarrassed by negative emotions. The best moments in psychotherapy are those in which the patient becomes aware of a truth he has covered for himself, and cries about it intensely. That can be a break-through situation, the start of recovery.

It is widely recognized that Rilke showed a profound understanding of man's deepest and most valuable experiences, and his works are read by many all over the world. To contrast his conceptions with those of mainstream contemporary psychiatry shows the huge gap between Erklären and Verstehen (Jaspers, 1947). The method of Erklären (scientific research) usually does not take into account God, personal growth, etcetera whereas the method of Verstehen (understanding) does. Had Rilke lived today, and had he fallen into the hands of psychiatry because of his depression and anxiety, he would probably have been treated with antidepressants that may have prevented his personal growth.

Psychiatry can learn from Rilke because he gives valid answers to questions about how to live a meaningful life, how to cope with life's difficulties and tasks. The first important step would be to acknowledge that life is a struggle, especially if you try to live it authentically. Defining the resulting anxiety and depression as a brain disorder that needs treatment with medication does not do justice to the complexity of the problem. Of course, a biological brain element plays a role, in one patient more than in the other, but existential difficulties may play an important role as well. Although most patients with mood and anxiety disorders prefer psychotherapy to medication, in the USA they are increasingly likely to receive the latter (Markowitz and Milrod, 2015). To implement more natural, less harmful treatments or coping skills in psychiatry, insights from our greatest writers and thinkers concerning human nature should be employed to understand psychiatric symptoms and redefine illness and health.

A view of human existence as formulated by Rilke has at least as much truth in it as the mechanistic, reductionist brain view of human existence. Both views can and should be combined to find an optimal approach in psychiatry.

Jean-Paul Sartre

Jean-Paul Sartre (21 June 1905–15 April 1980) was a French philosopher, novelist, playwright and political activist. He was one of the key figures in phenomenology and existentialism.

In his play *Huis clos* (*No exit*, 1944) the famous sentence '*L'enfer, c'est les autres*' occurs, which is usually translated as 'Hell is other people' or 'Hell is The Other.' In this play the three main characters have been judged; they are in hell, sentenced to spend eternity in a room they will never be able to leave.

Sartre says that the Other is, or can be, a source of our distress. Sartre spelled out this meaning in a talk that preceded a recording of the play issued in 1965:

> ...'hell is other people' has always been misunderstood. It has been thought that what I meant by that was that our relations with other people are always poisoned, that they are invariably hellish relations. But what I really mean is something totally different. I mean that if relations with someone else are twisted, vitiated, then that other person can only be hell. Why? Because ... when we think about ourselves, when we try to know ourselves, ... we use the knowledge of us which other people already have. We judge ourselves with the means other people have and have given us for judging ourselves. Into whatever I say about myself someone else's judgment always enters. Into whatever I feel within myself someone else's judgment enters. ... But that does not at all mean that one cannot have relations with other people. It simply brings out the capital importance of all other people for each one of us.

Thus, the hell in the play consists of the situation that the three characters can only define themselves by mirroring themselves in the eyes of others, who reflect them badly. With his play Sartre says: 'We construct a hell for ourselves, when we refuse to take responsibility for our own actions, leaving us at the mercy of the opinions of others.'

An escape from this hell is not defining yourself through the distorting mirror of others, but through your choices that come from within. Man is free to choose whatever he wants and needs to take responsibility for these choices.

This is also very important in psychiatry. When a patient blames others for his problems or expects others to relieve him from his symptoms, remission of the symptoms is unlikely (Yalom, 1980). We are the authors of our lives, and breaking away from Das Man, the opinions of others, may be scary in the beginning but very rewarding in the end. The conflict between oppressive, spiritually destructive conformity (*mauvaise foi*, literally, bad faith) and an authentic way of being is the dominant theme of Sartre's early work, a theme embodied in his principal philosophical work *L'Être et le Néant* (Being and Nothingness, 1943).

Irvin Yalom

Irvin Yalom (born 13 June 1931) is emeritus professor of Psychiatry at Stanford University, USA, existential psychiatrist and author of both fiction and nonfiction. Yalom's work also bears witness of a true understanding of human nature. In his highly acclaimed textbook *Existential Psychotherapy* (1980), he combines the work of philosophers, writers, psychiatrists into a guideline how to accompany or guide, as a psychotherapist, those who struggle with life's difficulties. The book is divided in four parts that cover the major challenges that we all grapple with during life: death, freedom, isolation and meaninglessness. Much psychopathology can be brought back to denial, avoidance, evasion of these themes. For example, people fear death because it is an annihilation of one's own personal world. A self-evident solution may seem to avoid confrontation with death by not thinking about it, keeping yourself occupied with superficial pursuits, and escaping situations in which death is intruding. However, the fundamental death anxiety that is present in everyone cannot be suppressed that easily. It surfaces in psychopathology, and uncovering this anxiety in all its intensity can be healing (unconcealment, Heidegger). Living through the anxiety and sadness associated with the finitude of all life is the starting point of personal growth into living authentically.

Similarly with responsibility. Fleeing our freedom to choose is to live 'inauthentically' (Heidegger) or in 'bad faith' (Sartre). According to Sartre, one is entirely responsible for one's life, not only for one's actions but also for one's failures to act. To be aware of this great responsibility is a deeply frightening insight. It may seem easier to deny our responsibility. This may explain the success of the notion that 'we are our brains'; our brain will decide for us how our life turns out. In many instances these days, psychotherapy focused on assuming responsibility in life is replaced by the prescription of psychotropic medication to alleviate 'a brain dysfunction'. However, as discussed in previous chapters, medication has a mostly suppressing, not curative effect. In advanced stages of psychiatric disorders though, medication may be necessary.

In the case example of Thomas in the next Part of this book, the main character has been led by what his social environment expects from him. He becomes a banker like his father, and not the writer that he always wanted to be. It is difficult to choose against what others expect from you, or against rational reasons such as making money. However, the choices we make can greatly influence our mood, our relationships, our feeling of really being alive. It may be safe to choose on the basis of expectations, making money or gaining social status, but these choices are not always the same choices that lead to fulfilment. Realizing that one has a choice to take steps to do more of what one wants, and less of what one ought to do, is frightening but healing.

In the part about isolation, Yalom distinguishes interpersonal isolation (isolation from other individuals), intrapersonal isolation (partitioning off parts of oneself) and existential isolation (an unbridgeable gulf between oneself and any other being or the world itself). Intra- and interpersonal isolation are closely related to existential isolation. As Yalom writes, in everyday, ordinary life

> ...we are lulled into a sense of cozy, familiar belongingness; the primordial world of vast emptiness and isolation is buried and silenced, only to speak in brief bursts during nightmares and mythic visions.

Like Rilke, Yalom writes that facing aloneness ultimately allows us to engage with others deeply and meaningfully. Relationships cannot eliminate isolation, but love can compensate for the pain caused by it. If we evade the experience of isolation, we may cling at others to keep us safe. If one engages with others to ward off loneliness, then one uses the other as a tool. The relationship between therapist and patient can be healing, independent of the therapists theoretical orientation, if the therapist responds in a genuine manner, is truly with the patient, and displays a high degree of accurate empathy. A true encounter between two individuals is one of the most powerful consolations that life can offer (Yalom, 1980).

Several philosophers and writers such as Tolstoy, Camus and Sartre elaborate on the inherent meaninglessness of life, because all experiences are annihilated by a certain death. People need meaning in their life. Severe experiences of meaninglessness can lead to the decision to end one's life. Although there is no cosmic meaning, we can give our life personal meaning. According to existentialists as Sartre and Camus, one must invent one's own meaning and commit oneself fully to fulfilling that meaning. Meaning can be found in altruism, dedication to a cause, creativity, hedonism, self-actualisation or self-transcendence.

The textbook of Yalom about existential psychotherapy describes in a very clear and understandable way a dynamic approach that focuses on concerns rooted in human existence. On page 485 Yalom writes:

> Each of us craves perdurance, groundedness, community, and pattern; and yet we must all face inevitable death, groundlessness, isolation, and meaninglessness. Existential theory is based on a model which posits that anxiety and its maladaptive consequences are responses to these four ultimate concerns.

Yalom said in a recent interview (*Volkskrant*, April 26, 2015) that he never prescribes medication these days. If medication is necessary he refers the patient to another psychiatrist.

Unfortunately, existential psychotherapy as described by Yalom does not have the place in the psychotherapy refer-landscape that it deserves in most countries. There are not many existential psychotherapists, and it is not taught in many universities. Patients mainly receive medication and/or cognitive behavioural therapy. Perhaps the limited number of scientific papers about existential psychotherapy has led to the preference for other forms of psychotherapy in practitioners. However, as Yalom justly writes, it is very difficult to catch the relevant outcome of existential psychotherapy in the statistics required for scientific papers. This relates to Chapter 2 (entitled Scientific research and its omissions). Adoption of a sole scientific method may not be sufficient in psychiatry because humans are too diverse, too complex, too individual to calculate a mean of. How does one express personal growth in statistical significance? For the biology of mental illness the method of Erklären (Jaspers, 1947) is necessary, but for psychotherapy the method of Verstehen may be required. As Yalom (1980) writes:

> ... to study all beings with some standard instrument as though they inhabited the same objective world is to introduce monumental error into one's observations.

People constitute the world, interpret the world in their own idiosyncratic way. The great popularity of Yalom's books worldwide shows that many people, including psychotherapists, recognize the truth in his work. It is a pity that the knowledge and insights of Yalom are not more widely taught and practiced. In many cases it may offer an enduring alternative to psychotropic medication.

Carl Jung

Carl Jung (26 July 1875– 6 June 1961) was a Swiss psychiatrist and psychotherapist. He is the founder of analytical psychology, but his work has also been influential in anthropology, philosophy, literature, archaeology and religious studies.

Individuation plays a central role in the work of Jung. The realization of the uniqueness in the individual man is the goal of individuation. In the process of individuation a supra-personal force is actively interfering in a creative way, which can amongst others be grasped through the investigation of one's dreams. Jung calls the organizing centre from which this regulatory effect stems, the 'Self', that is distinguished from the 'ego' which constitutes only a small part of the total psyche. How far a human being develops depends on whether or not the ego is willing to listen to the messages of the Self. The ego must be able to listen attentively and to give itself to that inner urge toward personal growth. Jung believed that our main task is to discover and fulfil our deep innate potential. This journey of individuation is at the mystical heart of all religions. It is a journey to meet the Self and therewith to meet the divine.

Many other cultures than our own understand that it is necessary to give up the utilitarian attitude of planning in order to make way for inner growth. Unfortunately, in many western societies the utilitarian mode is the prevalent, daily mode (Von Franz, 1964).

Archetypes are an important concept in Jung's work. Archetypes are universal, archaic images that derive from the collective unconsciousness and are the psychic counterpart of instinct. For Jung, 'the archetype is the introspectively recognizable form of *a priori* psychic orderedness' (Jung, 1991). Jung saw the human psyche as 'by nature religious' and made this religiousness the focus of his explorations (Jung, 1992).

Jung stressed that for self-knowledge, it is important to acknowledge all within, including those qualities and impulses that one would rather deny such as egotism, mental laziness and cowardice. Jung calls this part of the personality 'The shadow'.

There are many similarities between the ideas described in this book and Jung's work. The ancient domain is consistent with the collective unconscious and its archetypes. The essential religious nature of man is caused by the existence of the ancient domain. Unfortunately, the influence of Jung on modern psychiatric practice is very limited. Dream analysis plays a marginal role these days. In many countries, psychoanalysis is not reimbursed by insurance companies anymore, because it is deemed unscientific. The number of randomized clinical trials that investigate therapies based on Jung's ideas is small. The critics of Jung's ideas forget that they entail a living experience charged with emotion, by nature ever changing and irrational, which does not lend itself to a scientific research design except in the most superficial fashion. The psychoanalytic society has fewer and fewer members, and Jung's ideas are not prominent in the training of modern psychotherapists. I do not want to argue that psychoanalysis should be reinstated as a main form of psychotherapy. I would like to argue that the insights of the philosophers, scientists, psychiatrists described in this chapter should be included in the understanding of the human mind and its illnesses, and taken seriously in a redefinition of concepts in psychiatry.

Synthesis

The problems in contemporary psychiatry show that it is not possible to reduce psychiatric symptoms to brain dysfunctions. For answering the fundamental questions that inevitably play a role in psychiatry, one should consider the deep insights of our greatest thinkers. One such question is: how should one live a life worth living? A common theme in the work of authors discussed in this chapter is authenticity as an answer to this question; finding a path to personal growth and therewith connecting to a deeper level of the human psyche. Combining the ideas of Jung, Spinoza, Einstein, Rilke, Jaspers, Coelho and James leads to a view of God, spirituality, mysticism as emanating from the human psyche, subject to the laws of nature and encompassing the accumulated wisdom of the human species. It is a concrete part of human experience, not a vague, new-age notion of something outside us. Furthermore, the work of Sartre, Rilke, Jung, Kierkegaard, Nietzsche, Yalom, Jaspers, Heidegger attest to a major difficulty in human life: the natural urge for authenticity and personal growth on the one hand, and living in a society with its conventions and coercion on the other. People want to feel safe, liked and respected, and because of that they are inclined to make choices that lead to approval of Das Man, the herd, mass society. However, these choices are not always the choices that they want to make themselves (see also the story of Thomas in Part III of this book). Relying on others for safety and approval leads to inauthenticity, because we view ourselves through the eyes of others (Sartre). Realizing that others cannot keep us safe (each of us dies alone and death is inevitable), and that we need to make our own choices from within, can be therapeutic (Yalom). The frightening realization that life is finite can instigate new choices to make life worth living before one dies. On the contrary, psychotropic medication has a suppressing, dampening effect and it has usually no disclosing potential.

The authentic self can be defined as the traits, the likes and dislikes, the goals, the aspirations that come naturally to a person and that are not imposed by the social environment. A basic principle of all life on earth is apparent: a seed contains a plan, and this plan is carried out if conditions are sufficient for its growth. As Aristotle wrote in *Physics II*, an acorn has an inherent tendency to grow into an oak tree. A human embryo contains the plan for a person, and part of the plan is present in the genes. Babies are born with certain inclinations. Parents of more than one child usually notice a difference in the temperament and likes/dislikes between siblings from a very young age. Also, differences exist between individuals in what is necessary for personal growth. Some individuals need lots of stimulation from the environment, whereas others are easily overstimulated. A basic organizing principle in mental health and mental illness may be knowing yourself, and being able to provide yourself with what you need. If you have a sensitive nervous system that responds to even the mildest level of stimulation, failing to provide yourself with sufficient tranquillity may lead to overstimulation, stress and mental illness.

Thus, a common theme in the work of the thinkers and writers described in this Chapter is authenticity; being or becoming yourself. Psychiatric patients also often bring up this theme in the consulting room. When children grow up, they are taught to take up roles as responsible adults. They learn to compete with others for social status, and fool themselves in believing that that is important in life.

Concealment is a defence mechanism that may have been formed during evolution to cope with intense negative emotions and keep on going. To be able to continue with daily life in the face of a terrible event, such as the loss of a loved one, has of course an evolutionary advantage. But most people who have experienced such a situation know that the negative emotions do not disappear by suppressing them, but these emotions linger and surface at a later moment. Heidegger (1962) wrote 'Hiding itself is a main characteristic of Being.' Unconcealment seems to be a prerequisite for advancing on the path of personal development. Unconcealment means knowing your true, authentic self, and this can be achieved through the experience and exploration of moods, feelings and the interpretation of dreams (Jung). The symbolic images in dreams can be understood through the emotions they convey. Interpreting dreams rationally and literally is usually not the road to unconcealment. Furthermore, it is important to find out what activities lead to a state of bliss (Campbell, Upanishads) or flow (Csíkszentmihályi).

It cannot be ascertained with modern brain imaging technology whether someone is him/herself, because a person can only experience it. Perhaps this is the reason why this important concept has been relatively neglected in the past decennia in psychiatric research and treatment. It does not fit in the biomedical model of psychiatric disorders. However, that it is not possible to assess it with brain imaging technology does not mean that it is not relevant. I would like to argue that this concept should be granted the central role in psychiatry that it deserves. Opponents may say that it is unscientific. But listening to what patients have to say about their subjective experience it is not more unscientific than using the polythetic checklists of the DSM in clinical practice. The road to finding your authentic self is being open to experiences without the conventions of Das Man, the Herd, the majority. It also involves experiencing all emotions, including anxiety and despair. A certain degree of solitude may be important in this respect.

References:

Allardyce, J., Suppes, T. and van Os, J. (2007). Dimensions and the psychosis endophenotype. *International Journal of Methods in Psychiatric Research* 16, Suppl 1, S34–40.

Babkoff, H., Sing, H.C., Thorne, D.R., Genser, S.G. and Hegge, F.W. (1989). Perceptual distortions and hallucinations reported during the course of sleep deprivation. *Perceptual and Motor Skills* 68(3), 787–98.

Bebbington, P.E., Wilkins, S., Jones, P., Forester, A., Murray, R.M., Toone, B. and Lewis, S. (1993). Life events and psychosis: results from the Collaborative Psychosis Study. *British Journal of Psychiatry,* 162, 72–9.

Campbell, J. with Moyers, B.(1988). *Joseph Campbell and the Power of Myth* Flowers, B.S. (ed.). New York: Doubleday and Co.

Coelho P. (1993). *The Alchemist.* San Francisco, CA: Harper.

Cohen, C.I., Jimenez, C. and Mittal, S. (2010). The role of religion in the well-being of older adults with schizophrenia. *Psychiatric Services* 61(9), 917–22.

Csíkszentmihályi M (1975). *Beyond Boredom and Anxiety.* San Francisco, CA: Jossey-Bass Publishers.

Csíkszentmihályi, M. (1990). *Flow: The Psychology of Optimal Experience.* New York: Harper and Row.

Doniger W. (1990). *Textual Sources for the Study of Hinduism.* Chicago, IL: University of Chigago Press.

Einstein, A. (1929). 'Letter to Eduard Büsching', Oct 29; after Büsching sent Einstein a copy of his book 'Es gibt keinen Gott'

Flynn, T.R. (2006). *Existentialism.* Oxford: Oxford University Press.

Fusar-Poli, P. (2013). One Century of *Allgemeine Psychopathologie* (1913 to 2013) by Karl Jaspers. *Schizophrenia Bulletin* 39 (2), 268–269.

Gallagher, S. (2000). Philosophical conceptions of the self: implications for cognitive science. *Trends in Cognitive Sciences* 4, 14–21.

Gardiner, P. (1969). *Nineteenth Century Philosophy.* New York: The Free Press.

Grimby, A. (1993). Bereavement among elderly people: grief reactions, post-bereavement hallucinations and quality of life. *Acta Psychiatrica Scandinavia* 87(1), 72–80.

Grob, G.N. (1991). Origins of DSM-I: A study in appearance and reality. *American Journal of Psychiatry* 148(4), 421–31.

Heidegger, H. (1927). *Sein und Zeit.* Tübingen: Max Niemeyer.

Heidegger, H. (1962). *Being and Time,* Macquarrie, J. and Robinson, E. trans. New York: Harper & Row.

James, W. (1902). *The Varieties of Religious Experience: A Study in Human Nature.* Gifford lectures. New York: Random House.
Jaspers, K. (1947). *General Psychopathology.* Vols 1 & 2. Hoenig, J. and Hamilton, M,W., trans. Baltimore, MD: Johns Hopkins University Press. First published as: Jaspers, K. (1913). *Allgemeine Psychopathologie.* Berlin: Springer.
Jaspers K. (2007). *The Perennial Scope of Philosophy.* Manheim, R., trans. New York: Philosophical Library.
Jung, C.G. (1991). *The Archetypes and the Collective Unconscious*, 2nd edition, Collected Works of C. G. Jung, London: Routledge.
Jung, C.G. (1992). *Two Essays on Analytical Psychology*, 2nd Edition, Collected Works of C.G. Jung, London: Routledge.
Kidder, A. (2012). Introduction to R.M. Rilke, *Letters on God and Letters to a Young Woman.* Kidder, A. trans. Evanston, IL: Northwestern University Press.
Kierkegaard, S. (1847). *Upbuilding Discourses in Various Spirits.* In: The Essential Kierkegaard (2000), Hong, H.V. and Hong, E.H., trans. Princeton, NJ: Princeton University Press.
Kirov, G., Kemp, R., Kirov, K. and David, A.S. (1998). Religious faith after psychotic illness. *Psychopathology* 31(5), 234–45.
Kusters, W. (2014). *Filosofie van de waanzin (Philosophy of Madness).* Rotterdam: Lemniscaat (in Dutch).
Leff, J. P. (1968). Perceptual phenomena and personality in sensory deprivation. *British Journal of Psychiatry* 114, 1499–1508.
Magrini, J. (2006). 'Anxiety' in Heidegger's Being and Time: The Harbinger of Authenticity *Philosophy Scholarship.* Paper 15. http://dc.cod.edu/philosophypub/15
Markowitz, J.C. and Milrod, B.L. (2015). What to do when psychotherapy fails. *The Lancet Psychiatry* 2, 186–7.
Mohr, S., Borras, L., Nolan, J., Gillieron, C., Brandt, P.Y., Eytan, A., Leclerc, C., Perroud, N., Whetten, K., Pieper, C., Koenig, H.G. and Huguelet, P. (2012). Spirituality and religion in outpatients with schizophrenia: a multi-site comparative study of Switzerland, Canada, and the United States. *International Journal of Psychiatry Medicine.* 44(1), 29–52.
Moneta, G. (2012). On the measurement and conceptualization of flow. In: Engeser, S. (ed.). *Advances in Flow Research.* New York: Springer.
Nietzsche, F. (1882). *Die Fröhlichen Wissenschaft.* Leipzig: Insel-Verlag
Nietzsche, F. (2001). *Beyond Good and Evil.* Cambridge: Cambridge University Press.
Ostenfeld, I. and McKinnon, A. (1972). *Søren Kierkegaard's Psychology.* Waterloo, ON: Wilfrid Laurer University Press.
Radhakrishnan, S. (1956). *History of Philosophy: Eastern and Western.* Crows Nest, NSW: Allen & Unwin.
Rilke, R.M. (1905). *Das Stundenbuch.* Leipzig: Insel-Verlag
Rilke, R.M. (1929). *Briefe an einen jungen Dichter.* Leipzig: Insel-Verlag.
Raju, P.T. (1985). *Structural Depths of Indian Thought.* New York: State University of New York Press.
Sartre J.P. (1943). *L'Être et le Néant.* Paris: Gallimard.
Varghese, A.P. (2008). *India: History, Religion, Vision and Contribution to the World*, Volume 1. New Delhi: Atlantic Publishers & Distributors.
van de Kraats, G.B., de Haan, S.E. and Meynen, G. (2012). Self-experience in the early phase of psychosis: a phenomenological approach. *Tijdschrift voor Psychiatrie* 54(12), 1021–9.

Von Franz M.L. (1964). The process of individuation. In C.G. Jung. *Man and his Symbols*. (pp. 159–229). London: Aldus Books Limited.

Yalom, I.D. (1980). *Existential Psychotherapy.* New York: Basic Books.

PART III
Case examples

The following case examples illustrate various aspects of the preceding chapters. Because subjective experience is the primary object of study in psychiatry, the case examples are presented from a phenomenological viewpoint. To elucidate the relationship with the previous chapters of this book, each case example is followed by a short discussion.

Part III

Case studies

13
THOMAS

Although Thomas had not done any exercise the day before, all his muscles ached when he woke up. He felt nauseous. He had no energy whatsoever to get out of bed. The morning was grey and cold. The curtains were opened a bit, and the outside world penetrated his room with too loud sounds of cars and people on the street. He tried to cheer himself up ('It WILL be spring again, I WILL get out of this mess, I WILL get myself together') but nothing helped. Immediately the worries started to cloud his mind. He worried about his work, he worried about his relationship, he worried about his children. He had been away from work for 12 weeks now. He worked at a bank and had a good salary.

'They will probably think of me as a wimp, in a way I am. Why can't I snap out of it? I have a nice wife, great children, a house and work. What on earth is the matter with me?'

He could not answer this question. He stayed in bed for two hours, stiff as a plank. Then he slowly sat up, yawned for a long time and started to dress himself. He went to the kitchen and got himself a glass of water. He sat at the kitchen table staring into the garden.

'I should have chosen another career', he thought.

He could not remember ever being happy at his job, or in any other situation in his life. He shuffled to the doormat and picked up the paper. He stared at the front page but he could not comprehend what he was reading. He had had problems with his attention for months, and his memory was a sieve. He slowly got up and went upstairs. He got into bed again. He was so tired he could not imagine doing anything else for the coming years than lie in bed. At that moment, he heard the door open. His two boys of 10 and 12 years came home. He wanted something to calm his nerves. He went to the bathroom and took 4 tranquilizing pills when only 2 were permitted. He loved his boys but hearing them in the hallway was already too much stimulation for his highly strung nerves. When they argued or yelled to each other, he just could not bear the sound of their loud and harsh voices.

When he was young, he wanted to become a writer. When he wrote he forgot everything around him. He felt intensely alive and close to the core of his being. He was immersed in a world he wanted and needed to be in. His dream was to travel around the world, think about human nature and write great novels. His father was a banker, and always ridiculed this plan.

'You will end in the gutter,' he used to say. 'You had better choose a profession.'

Thomas loved poetry and literature. He wrote poems and prose himself, but as he never was satisfied with the result he doubted if he was any good at it. Thomas started to study economics, and thought that he could still write if he wanted. However, his studies took too much time to be able to write as well. Then he got married and they had two children. His life became even busier. He either worked or took care of the kids. In the evening, he was so tired that he could only land on the couch and not get up for the rest of the evening. He disliked his work, but he made good money and he needed that to take care of his wife and children. His parents were proud of him, and he was well respected by his peers. Everything he wanted when he was young became buried in his busy life. He had sometimes a flare in which he longed so terribly for something. He did not even know exactly what it was he longed for. He did not have the time to find out.

Lately he felt frozen. He could not even cry. It was as if all the grief for lost dreams was frozen inside of him. He tried several medications but nothing worked.

That evening his father came to visit. They went outside in the garden.

His father said: 'I do not understand son, you have everything a man could wish for, a beautiful wife, two healthy sons, a great job, house and car. Why are you not happy?'

'I do not know. I say the same thing to myself every day but it does not help to lift the depression. I feel as if I am dead alive, do you know what I mean?'

'I am trying', his father said. 'Is there any way I can help you?'

Later that evening he told his wife that he wanted to take a walk alone. He saw the fear in her eyes.

'It is all right' he said, 'I'll be back in an hour or so.'

He walked along the deserted streets. A drizzle moistened his face. He looked in the lit living rooms of the houses he walked by. Some people were watching television, staring into the flickering light of the screen, their faces focused and blank. Others were reading the paper at the living room table.

'Why is everybody so alone and pretending that they are not? Nobody can feel exactly what I feel. In essence, it is impossible to really share experiences. Most people aren't even interested in sharing. They just want to take what they need to get by. I have been betrayed by friends, co-workers, family. Before I became depressed, I was able to not pay too much attention to this, but now I cannot ignore it. It keeps coming back to the centre of my mind. I do not know how to live with this,' he thought.

He walked to the small train station. The train passed by. He saw the iron wheels and they appealed to him. He went on the platform and sat there for ten minutes. He saw a train coming from far because of the headlights.

'Shall I jump,' he thought?

He could picture the wheels crushing his body and he was almost comforted by it.

'Finally, rest,' he thought.

He walked to the rails. The train came closer. He was in a desperate struggle. He wanted to kill himself, but the thought of his wife and sons made him doubt. The train came closer. He stood there frozen. The driver blew his horn. He could not get himself to jump. The thought of other mornings like this morning loomed upon him. He could not imagine that he would ever be happy again. He walked back home. When he came into the back door, he saw the relief on his wife's face. That night he lay awake, like most nights lately. He saw the clock at 12.10 am, then at 1.45 am at 3.02 am and 3.47 am.

The next morning he woke up and he immediately felt a paralysing fear. He felt like an insect about to be crushed by the world. He felt powerless to do anything. He could not decide whether to get out of bed or to stay under the covers. Finally, he got up and went downstairs. He tried to smile at his wife but he felt no joy whatsoever. He felt disconnected from his wife, his children, his past and his future. It was as if he was totally lost without direction and bearing. He tried to make conversation with his wife but the sentences were stiff and dead.

That night he was so tired that he managed to fall asleep an hour after he went to bed. He woke up from a nightmare. He dreamt that is father was standing on his chest wearing big black boots. Thomas could hardly breathe and could not move. He felt totally powerless. Later that night, he dreamt that his father and he were arguing.

'I want you to hit me,' Thomas shouted, 'because I know I deserve it.'

He even felt that he wanted to be hit by his father. When he woke up the next morning, he immediately felt the fear and lack of looking forward to anything. He felt so tired and wanted to sleep some more, but he could not. He felt worthless, ashamed of who he was.

Memories of his childhood came to his mind. His mother and father cared for him, but he always had to adjust to them. They were never really interested in what he felt or what he wanted. When he was about 6 years old, he found his mother crying in the kitchen. His brothers and he had been playing with paint, and their new shoes and clothes were spoiled. His mother tried to clean the shoes and clothes, but she could not get it off. He felt very guilty to be the cause of his mother's sorrow. Unconsciously he decided that he would avoid making his mother cry again. He did everything to appear as a happy, well-adjusted boy. When he was bullied by his peers, he did not speak to anybody about it and tried to cope with it alone. He remembered being very scared on Sunday evening, because he had to go to school the next morning. His classmates sometimes took his coat and hid it, or took his books out of his bag when he was not looking and never gave them back. He was unable to do anything about it, because he acted as if nothing was the matter. He did not speak to anyone about it. It was as if there was no emotional bond between him and his parents. They never noticed it when he was scared or sad, and he could not remember ever being comforted by them. They were certainly not interested in giving him what he needed to become who he was. The whole family played tennis, so he also had to play tennis. It just did not come to their minds to ask him what sport he wanted to do, or even if he wanted to join a sports club. By the time he hit puberty, he was totally estranged from himself. He did not know who he was and what he wanted. He remembered puberty as a horrific period. He could not pretend anymore that everything was fine, because he felt very depressed. His mother thought he was weak for not being able to get his emotions under control. Whenever he had to do something with his family, he felt trapped, as if he could not breathe. One time he tried to talk with his mother about how unhappy and alone he was in his childhood, and that he was bullied, but his mother just said that it was not true. She never noticed that he was bullied. She just did not believe him, and that was the end of the conversation.

When he went to college, his depression disappeared. He lived in an apartment with two other students and it was a very relaxed, fun period. It was only years after he started his first job that he could not function anymore.

Slowly over a period of months, he became very afraid of other people. He noticed that the more depressed he was, the more others had to make an effort to be friendly to him, as if there was a very hostile undercurrent in interactions. People did their best to be friendly, but their posture, tone of voice and expression emanated irritation. He felt utterly alone and scared, and could not find any comfort anywhere.

Before his depression, he sometimes preferred the icy wind above the clammy cosiness of the company of other people. People were always talking, so he could not think. Of all the daily babbling, maybe only 10 per cent consisted of true interactions that touched the core. In such interactions, it was as if he was connected to another, and he loved that.

Maybe he had difficulty with the babbling because he was so angry about what human beings were capable of. It started when he learned about the holocaust in school. He could not imagine how a human being could draw up the plan to gas so many other human beings. And that was only one of the massacres in the history of human kind. It was always in the back of his head, and it made the tone of his mood dark. Why could many other people born after World War II live with it so easily, or why could he not forget it? Why could he not read the books of Primo Levi about the holocaust without crying? Was that the reason that he was not afraid of his death? He did not want to commit suicide because of his family, but it would be a relief for him if he could die when he was old and his children were independent. He noticed often enough in other people, including himself, a small onset of excluding someone else, because it was easy to let that happen. Or ridiculing someone who was unable to defend himself because it was an easy point to score. He knew that he himself was not better than other people, and that he had to live with it, and accept how he and other people are. But it made him melancholic. He was so afraid that real, unconditional love did not exist, not deep down. Of course there were gradations of love. He loved some people more than others, but if it came down to it, would someone be able to save him? Would someone stand by him whatever he did or however he felt? He still did not know for sure. He thought not. He started to avoid visiting family. It became more and more difficult to keep up the mask. The family did not tolerate his suffering, his silence, his pain.

His mother said: 'you should just try harder to get out of it.' His brothers agreed. They were annoyed that he was not stronger.

In his work, he was unable to let it go. When he came home from work, he opened his laptop and checked his email. It became a compulsion, he had to do it. Perhaps the positive reinforcement had become stronger than the negative reinforcement. What was he waiting for in his email? An affirmation of his existence? Self-esteem? Why not leave the computer turned off, like he really wanted. He longed so much for a powering down, plugs out of the sockets, dark, quiet, rest, no movement. Perhaps he was running for so long, that he did not know how to stand still anymore. He did not dare to pull the plugs out of the sockets. What would happen? Was he running to escape something? What was he escaping from? There was a foul voice that did not let him rest. If he wanted to do nothing, he started feeling scared. The voice made him feel worthless for not working. Keep on running was the gateway to his exhaustion. He hardly ever took a day off because at home there was more noise, more duties to fulfil, less time to think than at work. So he worked and worked and worked. He started having very quick heartbeats with some irregular beats but he had no means to make a change. Was he running from the despair of looking too deeply into human nature? He needed to change the world, while knowing he would not succeed. Trying that was the only possible way to bear his existence. At times, he thought there was someone who could save him, who really understood him. He always fell in love with this person only to discover later that it was just his imagination.

Now he was so scared, he craved a bit of warmth of another human being. He wanted shallowness, not the quicksand that was threatening to suffocate him.

One year later, Thomas was on his way up from the desert of deadness he had been through. He realized that nobody was going to save him, and that the only person who could save him was he himself. He quit his job and started reading a lot. The novels of the Russian authors Dostoyevsky and Tolstoy gave him consolation, because he recognized his own suffering in their characters. He even wrote short stories himself from time to time, and when he read what he had written, he started to understand himself better. When he wrote about experiences, feelings that stirred inside him and that were elusive before, they became tangible. He could look at it from different angles and it helped him to accept the horrors that were unbearable before, and live with them. Sometimes when he was alone he cried for 15 minutes, and felt pain to the bone, but afterwards he was relieved and calm. The tears melted his frozen muscles. It was as if a vale, suffocating blanket had lifted. He could breathe and feel again.

When he looked back, he thought that it was good that his body and mind took over and made it impossible to continue with the life that he never wanted in the first place. In the eyes of others, he was a loser now because he did not have a huge salary anymore and he lacked social status. He was a social drop out, and he avoided occasions such as birthday parties. But to his surprise, he did not miss it at all. When he compared the shallow satisfaction of high social status with the deep satisfaction of creating something that was true and valuable to him, it was very clear what had more meaning.

Discussion

The story of Thomas shows the entanglement of psychological, existential and biological factors in his symptoms. In Thomas' case, a large part of the problem may be that he did not follow his own nature. He never wanted to become a banker. The job failed to give him any joy and fulfilment in life. The absence of bliss (the bliss that he did feel when he was younger during writing) may have played a part in his exhaustion. Exhaustion is often the result of prolonged stress that can be caused by going against your authentic self. The fact that he felt frozen, and as if he cannot breathe, as well as the sleeping difficulties are signs of stress. He tried medication but it did not work, which is not surprising because it would not solve the underlying problem. In addition, during his depression he realized certain harsh truths, and he is struggling to cope with it. The way out of his existential struggle is making a choice to start doing more what he wants and less what he is expected to do.

14
LIZZIE

Lizzie was sitting in front of the television. It was 4 pm and she had been sitting there since 11 am when she got out of bed. She heard sounds of the busy world outside, from behind the closed curtains, that both scared her and made her long for sunlight, laughter and lightness. Lizzie was prone to anxiety, and always had been as long as she could remember. Her biggest fear was to become psychotic again. Six years ago, she was diagnosed with major depressive disorder. She was admitted to hospital when she tried to commit suicide. In the years after, she had three more admissions and received several diagnoses: borderline personality disorder, psychosis not otherwise specified, and schizophrenia. In these years, she had periods of weeks in which she wandered the streets in the city she lived in. She had memories of having sex with men she did not know for money, and sometimes she was convinced that she had been married and had kids who all died in a car accident. Her parents said that money had been taken out of the cash machines at strange places during this period. The past two years she had been treated with a high dose of the antipsychotics leponex and additional haloperidol. She took about 3 oxazepam a day to manage her anxiety. She did not dare to go outside, because voices told her to jump in front of the metro, and she was afraid that she would listen. She also experienced dizziness now and then when she walked on the pavement, and she panicked that she was hit by a car. She called her parents or the centre where she was treated but she called 10 times in a row because the reassurance lasted just a few minutes. She was also often afraid that she had taken too much or too little medication, that her hair would catch fire when she cooked, that she was in danger when she heard a crying voice, and that a berry would fall into her mouth when she walked below a tree and she would suffocate. She had no confidence in herself that she could cope with situations, and this led her to spend most of her time alone in front of the TV. She really wanted to go outside, and make something of her life. Before she became ill she was very good in school and at playing the piano, but now it felt as if she wasted her life. She was referred to the academic medical centre because there was no progress in her treatment.

She takes an oxazepam but she does not dare ride the metro to her first psychotherapy appointment. On the metro, it is just a 20 minute journey. By bus it is about 2 hours, but she makes it in time. It feels good to talk to someone about her situation. The therapist (Dr. Marcia Modine) is in her mid-thirties. She listens carefully to what Lizzie says, speaking in a soft voice, with little emotion. Her face is pale and expressionless. She is about 15 kilo overweight. Marcia is moved by the excruciating fears, desolation and confusion Lizzie had been through. She wants to help her out of the hell she is in. Lizzie is very motivated to change her situation, she wants to live again, and do something with her life. In the first sessions, the tragic history of Lizzie unfolds piece by piece. Marcia invites Lizzie's parents, with her permission, and they describe the period of years in which Lizzie was in and out of hospital. She lived for some time alone in a room, but she could not keep it clean and look after herself. Her parents frequently came and helped her. Her mother is very supportive, a bit over-concerned maybe. Her father is more distant, and critical from time to time.

Lizzie suffers most because of her constant worrying. She is anxious and tense all day. She is worried about all sorts of situations: being psychotic while not being aware of it, being in an accident and committing suicide even though she does not want to. She tries to find reassurance all the time in her environment, because she does not dare to trust herself. However, other people cannot reassure her for longer than a few minutes. In addition, she experiences problems with attention and memory. All these factors together lead to very low self-esteem. She feels unable to cope, spends a lot of time alone on the couch, calling others to get reassurance, leading to even lower self-esteem. Part of her complaints and fears can be traced back to the period in which she wandered the streets while she was floridly psychotic.

In therapy Lizzie discovers that the thought which makes her most afraid is that she is not in control and very vulnerable. An example is that she hears a voice that says she should commit suicide by jumping in front of the metro. Her immediate thought is that she may do it, and thus that she is not in control. This leads to high levels of anxiety and anger towards herself. As a consequence, she avoids all situations that may evoke these intense adverse emotions. When they discuss what she would like to work on in therapy, Lizzie says that she wants to be less anxious, so she would be able to do more. She would like to study, meet people, etcetera.

The following interrelated goals for the therapy are formulated by Lizzie and Marcia together:

1 Increasing self esteem
2 Decreasing the frequent phone calls to get reassurance

3   Decreasing anxiety
4   Decreasing the use of oxazepam
5   Initiating activities, e.g. volunteer work
6   Reduction in burden caused by hearing the voices
7   Being able to travel on the metro.

Lizzie's thoughts about her voices are explored, and she discovers that she holds the thought that the voices represent part of herself, and therefore she might listen to them. She also recollects that she listened to the voices when she was floridly psychotic. When Marcia and Lizzie discuss possible arguments why it is not likely that she will listen to the voice Lizzie comes up with:

- The voices say things that I do not want to do.
- I have not listened to the voices since I am not floridly psychotic anymore.
- The voices are a symptom of an illness.

Together they come up with the additional arguments:

- Voices cannot force me to do anything, they have no hands and feet.
- The voices never say anything that helps me.

Lizzie is able to formulate a reasonable alternative thought to replace the dysfunctional thought 'I may listen to the voices': 'The voices say nothing that helps me, they cannot force me to do anything and thus I can ignore them.' Lizzie writes this sentence on a flashcard. The only way to conquer the fear is facing it, and experiencing that the expected negative outcome does not occur. They make a fear hierarchy ranging from standing on a metro platform with a companion to riding the metro alone.

Lizzie dares to take the first small step and goes to a metro station one day the next week with her mother. At the metro station she is very relieved and thinks: 'Is this what I have been so afraid of all these years'?

Her mother buys something at a shop and Lizzie is alone for 10 minutes on the platform. A voice says that she should jump in front of the metro. She takes out the flashcard with the sentence 'The voices say nothing that helps me, they cannot force me to do anything and thus I can ignore them' and she becomes less afraid.

Lizzie describes her experience in the next session and Marcia praises her extensively. Lizzie is very proud and happy that she had taken the first step in conquering her fear. For the next session, she will travel by the metro with her mother. This went well. She took the initiative to travel one stop by herself in the same week. In the session, she describes humourously how she said goodbye to her mother in a dramatic way, because she may not survive it. In the metro she could laugh about herself. She hears voices but they do not affect her. She decides to travel alone by the metro to the therapy appointment next week. She has taken a few oxazepams in the previous weeks but not as many as 3 a day, like she used to.

Marcia and Lizzie also discuss her invalidating fear of being hit by a car when she is outside. When she is dizzy, Lizzie thinks that she may have been hit and injured badly which could lead to her death. She totally panics then, takes oxazepam and calls others to be reassured.

The next session Marcia and Lizzie design a behavioural experiment to test the thought: 'When I am dizzy, I may have been hit by a car'. The alternative thought is: 'When I am dizzy, I am not necessarily hit by a car'. Evidence for the first thought would be that:

- I am bleeding
- I have fracture(s)
- someone has seen it
- someone has done it
- an ambulance is present
- people try to help.

Evidence that would support the alternative thought includes:

- I feel no pain
- I am not bleeding
- I have no fractures
- nobody in the surroundings tries to help
- there is no ambulance present.

She writes all evidence on the behavioural experiment form, and next week she will go outside with the form, check all the evidence and come to a conclusion then. They agree that for an accident, at least two of the first list should be present. If it cannot be avoided, she may take an oxazepam but it would be better if she would not.

Next session Lizzie is very proud that she came alone by the metro without taking an oxazepam. She noticed that the voices are still there but in the background. Voices live on anxiety and stress and when she is no longer afraid of them they disappear to the background.

She performs the behavioural experiment. When she is dizzy on the sidewalk she checks the evidence: There is no ambulance, nobody has seen it, nobody has done it, I have no fractures or blood, I can move and I have no pain. After checking everything on the form she comes to the conclusion that nothing is the matter. She is a lot less anxious than before, but still she calls her mother to confirm.

Marcia and Lizzie discuss her dizziness, how it causes her to panic, leading to more dizziness because of shallow breathing. Marcia gives her exercises to relax, and to change breathing patterns. They also discuss that it would be good to do physical exercise like jogging, which can also induce relaxation and better breathing patterns. Lizzie agrees to that.

Next session Lizzie says that she is better able now to reassure herself, and that she has an improved ability to distinguish reality from irrational thoughts. Marcia brings up that it would be a step forward if Lizzie would reduce the frequent phone calls for reassurance. Lizzie agrees that the phone calls help her for a moment, but in the longer term it is not good for her self-confidence. Her goal is to become more independent and she will not succeed when she keeps calling so frequently. Lizzie will record for the next session in which situations she calls, to whom and what her thoughts were at that moment. Lizzie can travel alone by the metro, and her fear of being hit by a vehicle when she is outside is much reduced. Marcia brings up whether Lizzie would like to do a course at a rehabilitation facility. This facility offers educational and social activities for young people with psychiatric complaints like herself. Lizzie agrees.

The record about the phone calls shows that Lizzie calls her mother or the hospital about 10 times a day, and they reassure her. Lizzie knows that the fear subsides even when she does not call, and then she can relativize the situation. However, when she is so afraid she does not reflect, but calls immediately. In addition to the reassurance, Lizzie appreciates the social contact. Marcia discusses that it would be beneficial if Lizzie would get more social contacts that not only entail reassurance, e.g. at the rehabilitation facility. Lizzie and Marcia make a plan that Lizzie may only phone for reassurance once a day the next week. Lizzie is largely able to keep to the agreement. She notices that if she goes through the anxiety, it just subsides. She says to herself: 'You can freak out all you like, it will go away no matter what.'

In the meantime, Lizzie starts the course at the rehabilitation facility and she likes it very much. She meets a man there who is her age to whom she feels connected. She is able to reduce the calling further and takes only 4 oxazepams in a week. She says that she is starting to 'Find her way in her head'. She also feels more grounded. Together with the rest of the staff of the medical centre it is decided that it would be a good idea if the clozapine was reduced and the haloperidol stopped. Lizzie hardly experiences psychotic symptoms anymore. Lizzie is afraid to reduce the medication, but she wants the reduction because the medication sedates her. At the next session, Lizzie is panicking that she is psychotic again. Although Marcia notices that Lizzie has intact reality testing, Marcia mentions that perhaps Lizzie should be admitted to the medical centre, but Lizzie replies hastily that that would not be necessary. Lizzie is able to realize at that moment that she is doing all right. She is going to the rehabilitation facility two days a week, and she even went for coffee with the man she met there. She can also start at a care farm, and she is excited about that because working at a farm with animals was something she always wanted to do. She also notices the positive effects of the reduced medication. She is less sedated, she feels more and she is able to lose weight.

At session 29 Lizzie mentions that it can sometimes be delightfully quiet in her head. The man from the rehabilitation centre and she admitted to each other that they are in love, and they spend quite some time together. In addition, Lizzie can start a part-time education in biological farming, which she can combine with her work at the care farm. In many instances she is able to exchange her initial automatic frightening thoughts for the thought: 'I can judge for myself what is happening; I do not have to rely on others for that; I can trust myself.' Marcia and Lizzie discuss the approaching end of the therapy. In the last session, the therapy is evaluated. Lizzie says that she has received tools to help her cope with difficult situations for the rest of her life. She has more self-confidence than when she started therapy, but it still needs to grow. She has much more activities than a year ago, and she loves that. She is even able to laugh now and then, while this had not happened in the years before that. She has accepted her illness and says: 'I know I have that chance of becoming psychotic again, but that does not prevent me from doing the things I want in my life'. She also says that the therapy has taught her how anxiety works, and that she is able to do something about it herself. She feels less helpless. She is also able to take care of herself and her apartment. Her goals for the coming period are really enjoying how she is doing now and becoming more independent.

Lizzie is referred to low frequency, regular care in her neighbourhood. They agree on several booster sessions to see how Lizzie is doing.

During the period of half a year of booster sessions, Lizzie sometimes experiences some difficulties. Her education and work sometimes cause stress, but she is able to balance this by taking more rest. After the booster sessions, Lizzie keeps in contact with Marcia. Although she sometimes still struggles with her symptoms, she is able to study and have meaningful relationships. A year later she writes Marcia a card to invite her for her graduation. It also says: 'Thank you for giving me myself back'. Marcia of course is happy to read this, but she realizes that she only held Lizzie's hand in the process, because Lizzie had done all the hard work herself.

Discussion

The case example of Lizzie shows that medication is necessary in some instances, but medication alone often is not sufficient to reach the desired effect. Medication can suppress symptoms to some extent, but it usually does not cure patients. With additional, more benign treatments such as cognitive behavioural therapy, people can learn coping skills that can help reduce the medication dosage, and it can offer enduring relief of symptoms. Furthermore, low self-esteem can be a very important mediating factor in symptoms and their remission. Research needs to focus on the role of self-esteem, and methods for improving it.

In addition, just as in the other case examples, the stress–relaxation continuum plays an important role in the onset, maintenance and remission of Lizzies symptoms. Last, the story of Lizzie shows the interweaving of anxiety, personality traits, depressive, obsessive-compulsive and psychotic symptoms. The course of the therapy also shows that going through the emotions, for example enduring anxiety until it subsides, is the best way to incorporate the emotions into one's life and move on. Avoiding emotions leads to a false sense of safety and a lingering of the emotion on the background. Going through the emotions and learning to cope with it is associated with an outcome that seems most important to many patients: becoming themselves (again).

15
MARTIN

Martin heard the laughter and voices out on the street when he walked to the apartment of his cousin Guy, who was celebrating his 21st birthday. Martin felt stressed and wanted to turn around and go home. He did not know why. He walked to the door and rang the doorbell. There was no response. He rang again. Now the buzzer sounded, Martin pushed the door open and walked to the second floor. When he opened the door, a group of his peers laughed and turned to where Martin stood hesitant. Martin felt a rush of anxiety.

'They're laughing about me', he thought. 'They probably think I'm a weirdo – and they're right'.

He saw Caitlin also laughing. 'Oh no,' he thought, 'she also thinks I'm weird.'

Martin had a big crush on Caitlin, he could not get her out of his mind. Especially when he was doing nothing, his mind wandered to her: Caitlin laughing at him, Caitlin kissing him, walking with Caitlin through fields of high grass and flowers, picnicking and making love with Caitlin. When he thought about her, his body felt all warm inside and he was happy for a moment. But then he ached, because she was not with him and he missed her terribly. Caitlin had long blonde hair and she emanated a kind of sweetness. He could not figure out whether she liked him as much as he liked her. He tried to interpret all her looks and actions. Sometimes he thought it was clear that she liked him, but other moments he was sure that she could never like a weirdo like him. Caitlin thought that Martin was very good looking. He had lots of thick dark hair that seemed resistant to combing. His face was very finely lined and had a sort of melancholic expression. She would like to know him better, but she was unsure if this feeling was mutual. His actions and words were not at all clear.

Martin tried to convince himself that the group in the room was probably not laughing about him, but could not convince himself entirely. He thought he heard a boy whispering his name to another boy in the group while he looked at Martin tauntingly.

Martin tried to find his cousin Guy. He saw him across the room, talking to a girl. Martin stood next to Guy but he could sense that he was interrupting something. A few moments later, Guy pretended that he had only just noticed Martin.

'Congratulations,' Martin said to Guy and he gave him a present. He had bought one of his favourite books *Zen and the art of motorcycle maintenance* by Robert Pirsig and he wanted to tell Guy what he liked about the book, but his cousin beat him to it.

'Thanks,' he said, while he hardly noticed the author and title of the book.

He focused his attention again on the girl, with far more interest. Martin walked to the table with the drinks and got himself a beer. He did not know where to go next and he felt very shy. Luckily his aunt came up to him and hugged him.

'How is my favourite nephew?' she asked.

Without waiting for his answer, she took him to her husband, his uncle. 'Say hi to Martin,' she yelled.

His uncle gave him a hand and patted his shoulder a few times.

Across the room he saw Caitlin looking at him, he caught her eye and he looked back, but he did not know what to do next. Should he smile, or look away because otherwise he would be staring, or should he go to her? He became very stressed and opted for looking at his shoes. When he looked up again, Caitlin was talking to a boy standing next to her. He assembled all his courage and he went over to them.

'Hi,' he said.

Caitlin smiled at him broadly and said 'Hi' back.

She introduced him to the boy she was talking to.

'Please meet Ben,' she said.

Ben was studying philosophy and Caitlin was a sophomore philosophy student. Martin had dropped out a few months ago, because he got bad grades all the time. He was unable to focus because his thoughts wandered off. When he read a text, he could not get the meaning of what he was reading anymore. This problem had started in high school, but became progressively worse. Martin felt a wave of anxiety and jealousy. He wanted to study but was unable to.

His anxiety at that moment seemed to freeze him, make him rigid and unable to respond naturally. Ben and Caitlin seemed to sense the anxiety that Martin radiated. He felt as if he was a sitting duck for mean jokes, and he was unable to defend himself. Ben looked him up and down as if he was dressed inappropriately. Martin felt himself blush.

'Ben was just telling me about his paper on religion,' Caitlin said. 'Ben was trying to convince me that mankind invented God to reduce anxiety. He thinks that people who believe in God are fooling themselves.'

'I don't agree,' Martin said, a bit too hard and rigid. 'I think that believing in some sort of God is a natural inclination of human beings. If God was just an invention, the majority of the world population throughout the centuries would not have believed in some God and fought wars to protect their belief.'

Martin was never able to explain in words his philosophy and experiences concerning God, he could only feel it when he had a certain state of mind. This state of mind could be described as being carried by life, a weightless existence just for a moment, never longer. He remembered one such moment when he was hiking alone in Nepal. He walked about 8 hours a day from hostel to hostel, surrounded by massive mountains with snow on the top. It was late September, and the nights were becoming cold but the days were still warm. Nature was prominent, and other people were scarce. After a day of walking, he came into a little town. The smell of a wood fire was hanging in the air. The bells of yaks were tinkling in the fields nearby. The sun was low, casting long shadows. Martin walked through a field of high yellow grass that was swaying in the wind.

'Fields of gold,' he thought and felt.

He existed intensely during that moment in time. He felt a connection to the past, the past of humankind. It felt like a mystic experience. For Martin, God had nothing to do with an Almighty Father who created the world and who determined what happened. He considered God as an inner force that sometimes comforted him with the benevolence of a kind sun, or a desired surrounding. Considering God as the legacy of evolution did not make Him less sacred and important. However, Martin was aware that it was very difficult to convey what he meant to someone who had never had such an experience, whereas others who experienced it before needed only a couple of words to understand.

Ben sighed and did not try to conceal his contempt.

'Believing in God is something like believing in Santa Claus,' he said. Caitlin did not seem to have any opinion on the matter.

Later that evening he watched Caitlin and Ben talking intimately. He bent his ear towards her mouth because the music was rather loud. Ben even touched her arm. A moment later they smiled to each other. It felt as if someone had punched him very hard in the stomach, it took his breath away. He wanted to storm up to them and stand between them but knew that that would not work. A few moments later they left together. Ben helped her with her coat and put his hand on her back when he escorted her out of the room. Martin left ten minutes later. He walked alone and frozen in the deserted streets. He did not want to go home but there was no other place to go to. He was really tired and went to bed but, as usual, he could not fall asleep. His body felt cold and hard. The duvets could not warm him. He kept thinking about Caitlin and that she probably liked Ben more than him. He imagined them together in bed making love, and he almost threw up. It was as if his thoughts were like leaves that were twirling in the wind, and they would not settle down and let him sleep. Suddenly he heard a whispering sound in the room, a voice calling him in an eerie tone. He jumped up and switched on the light. No-one was there, but Martin was sure that he had heard someone calling him. He looked out of the window and in the corridor but he saw nobody.

'I'm losing my mind,' he thought, and that thought kept him up the rest of the night.

The next morning he made an appointment with his general practitioner. He told the doctor that he could not sleep, could not focus, that he was disorganized and was afraid that he was going crazy. The doctor gave him a prescription for sleep medication. At first the pills helped him to fall asleep, but after a few weeks he was unable to sleep without the medication. He needed more and more sleeping pills to sleep through the night. Some days he was sitting for hours at his kitchen table, and felt empty, without energy to do anything.

His mother visited him unexpectedly. His place was a mess, he had not done the dishes for days and clothes were strewn all around his apartment. Martin saw the worry in his mom's eyes.

'How are you Martin?' she asked.

Martin had no energy to lie and pretend that everything was fine. 'It feels as if I'm losing myself,' he said.

'How do you mean?' his mother asked.

'I don't know, I feel alien to myself.'

'What can I do to help?'

'I'm sorry Mom, I don't think you can.'

His mother looked very sad and tired, and he wished he had not said anything. He noticed that she had become more and more grey in the past months.

'I'm sure it'll be alright. It's probably just a phase.'

His mother looked a bit less worried.

His mother thought that Martin had always been different from his brother. He was always a bit on edge, he could not stand loud sounds and very crowded places. He was somewhat uncomfortable around other people. But he had seemed to be doing alright until about a year ago. Now he was even more on edge and distant. He also seemed unable to organize his life. His apartment was a mess every time she visited, and he dropped out of college because he was unable to get the required grades. Often, when she was alone, she cried and felt hopeless because she was unable to help him.

The next morning when Martin woke up, he felt that something was wrong. He did not know exactly what it was. The muscles all over his body were as hard as ice. His room seemed unfamiliar; it did not feel like his own room anymore. At certain moments, the walls were moving a bit.

'Perhaps I'm still dreaming' he thought.

He did not know how to check if he was dreaming or awake. He pinched himself but nothing changed.

'I have to get out of the house,' he thought but he did not know where to go to.

He was not hungry, so he skipped breakfast. He also avoided the shower because lately he heard murmurs as soon as he ran the water. He walked on the pavement and all the noises around him seemed too loud and the colours too bright. He always had been sensitive to sounds and colours, but lately he could hardly bear it. People walking by seemed to look angrily at him. Martin could not figure out why.

'Perhaps people are conspiring against me, to lock me up,' he thought.

A moment later he was able to reflect on this thought. 'These people don't even know me – that's impossible.'

He walked to a pub and ordered a Belgian beer. He hoped that he would be able to relax with alcohol. After the first beer, he felt less tense, but started to feel nauseous. He ordered another beer. But instead of feeling better as he had hoped for, he felt worse.

'I'm in a hopeless situation,' he thought. 'How am I going to get out of this? I don't know what's real or imaginary anymore. I'm unable to study or have relationships, and I'm afraid all the time. If my situation stays like this for another year, I might as well kill myself.'

After the third beer he paid and went on the street again. The world looked strange. As if the foreground and background had changed places. Certain details were very pronounced – like the pigeons in a tree. Buildings seemed to glow.

'Are these omens of a dark future event?' he thought for a moment and he became very afraid. 'Nonsense,' he said to himself. 'You're just drunk'.

In the park, he sat down on a bench. He felt horrible, hopeless and alone. People walking by were in a hurry to go to their work or family. A group of five boys looked at him from a distance, estimating their chances. They were loud and tough. They approached Martin.

'Do you have a light?' one of them asked.

The other boys looked around. There were no other people near at that moment.

'Now give me your wallet and phone,' one of the boys said.

'No,' Martin answered.

The boy punched him hard in the face. The pain was sort of a consolation for Martin, he did not know why. Martin fell on the ground and the boy forced his hand into Martin's pockets until he found Martin's wallet and phone.

'Help!' Martin yelled, but no one responded.

A woman in the distance looked in his direction, but hastily continued on her way. The group of boys ran off, leaving Martin on the ground with blood dripping from his mouth. Martin closed his eyes and lay there for some time until a police officer helped him up.

'Perhaps someone in the park called the police after all,' Martin thought.

The police officer took Martin to the police station and gave him a strong coffee. Then he took his statement. Martin could not remember well what had happened. He was afraid that the police officer was also against him and would throw him into jail without a reason. The officer saw that Martin had difficulty concentrating, and he gave a disorganized impression. He called in the psychiatrist who was on duty. Martin told the psychiatrist that he could not focus and had difficulty with planning and had dropped out of college. He often felt on edge, for as long as he could remember. Martin fidgeted with his keys because he was nervous. He got of his chair a few times to stretch his legs and walked across the room. He told the psychiatrist nothing about his voices because he was afraid that he would think he was crazy.

'You have symptoms of ADHD,' the psychiatrist told him. 'I'll give you a prescription for Ritalin, and you need to go to your general practitioner to get a referral for psychiatric treatment.'

Martin went to the pharmacy the same day, in the hope that the medication would help him. He would love it if he could focus and study again.

The Ritalin helped him a bit with focusing, but he became even more alienated from himself. He sometimes felt as if someone else was controlling him. He made movements with his hands, that were not his own movements. He tried to calm his nerves with music but at the same time he thought that the lyrics had a message for him personally.

He heard, 'It's no use going to the doctor, you're going to die anyway.'

The sentence haunted him for days.

One evening a few months later at 2 am, he heard banging on the wall and footsteps on the stairs.

'They're coming to get me,' Martin thought. He jumped out of bed.

'Get out of the house,' he heard a voice yelling.

In panic, he grabbed his trousers and a t-shirt. He did not even have time to put on his jacket. He ran onto the street, fearing for his life. He ran for an hour, then he was exhausted and sat on a bench in a park.

'I need something to calm my nerves,' Martin thought.

He went to a bar and ordered the strongest beer. Suddenly he saw that a guy sitting at another table had red eyes.

'He must have the devil inside of him,' Martin thought.

Martin was terrified. He looked around, and all the people in the bar had red eyes, and grinned at him. The surroundings had a red glow. He stormed out onto the street.

At 6 am he went to the metro station to go back home. It was built of grey concrete blocks. The architect had tried to lighten the station up with brightly coloured benches, but time had made these rusty and dark. A drizzle wet his face. A few other lonely souls were shivering in the cold. When the train arrived, Martin walked to the opening doors. He saw people staring at him.

'What do they want?' he thought.

He could not hide from their gaze.

'I bet they think I'm crazy', he thought.

He always became very tense when he had to take the metro. He was relieved when he could get out. He was afraid to go back to his house, but there was no other place to go.

'Watch out,' he suddenly heard somebody yell, and he ran away as fast as he could.

When he looked back, he saw nothing that explained why someone had yelled that.

He dare not go back to his apartment and he walked all day and evening through the streets. He tried to stay away from the busy, crowded parts of the city. He was continuously scanning his environment for threats.

'They must have been watching me for months.'

This thought entered his mind and he could not get rid of it. The fear it caused told him that the thought was true.

'Maybe they've been interfering with my mind, and that's why I can't concentrate. They're transmitting messages to my brain through the voices. The Turkish mob must have done it. I read in the paper that these people are totally ruthless.'

Suddenly all the pieces of the puzzle fell together. He was the victim of a conspiracy that had been going on for months, maybe even years.

It was 2 am and he was very tired. He lay down on a bench in the park. All his muscles were tense, and he was very cold. Finally, he fell asleep. He woke at 6 am. He decided to confide in his mother, and walked to her place. He rang her doorbell, and it took some time for her to open the door. She was still in her pyjamas, and looked very pale. When she opened the door and saw her son, she was startled. He looked bewildered and anxious.

'I have to speak to you,' he said. She opened the door and they sat at the kitchen table.

'Mom, I'm in great danger. The Turkish mob is after me, I don't know why. They've been watching me for months and they've planted a chip in my brain.'

'Martin, I don't understand. That's not possible. How could they plant a chip in your brain and why on earth would they be watching you?' his mother said, panicky.

Martin looked suspiciously at his mother. 'Would she be in on it?' he thought. He scanned the room for cameras.

'You cannot trust her,' he heard a voice say. He stormed out of the room.

'Martin,' his mother yelled in agony.

She tried to grab him to keep him from leaving the room, but she failed and he sprinted for the door. She ran after him, but he slammed the door in her face.

'Martin, please listen to me,' she yelled, but she saw only the back of her son as he turned the corner.

She closed the front door and sank down to her knees. She started to sob. She felt a terrible pain to see her son like this. She was unable to get through to him, to comfort and protect him as she had always done. She did not know what to do. She had to take him to the general practitioner to get help and treatment. She quickly got dressed and went to his apartment but he was not there. She phoned her ex-husband, and he suggested that they start searching for him. She went to a pub that she knew he sometimes visited, but they had not seen him for days. She walked through the streets near his house, and sometimes she thought she saw him and her hopes flared, but when she approached she saw that it was not her son.

Finally, she found her son in the park. He smelled of alcohol and he was sedated. He hardly recognized her and gazed at her with a blank stare. She hugged him for a long time. Together they stumbled to the nearby hospital.

Martin slept with his head on her lap. When it was finally their turn, she had trouble wakening him up. The psychiatrist asked some questions, but Martin hardly gave an answer. His mother told him what Martin said earlier about not trusting her and other people, how he acted, and his problems with other people, his study and alcohol and cannabis use, and that a previous psychiatrist had diagnosed ADHD and had prescribed medication.

'I think it's a personality disorder, combined with alcohol and drug misuse, and ADHD,' the psychiatrist said at the end of the conversation. 'I'm going to refer Martin to the psychiatry department of the hospital so that he can be treated there.'

A few weeks later Martin received his hospital appointment, and his parents were also invited. He did not want to go to the hospital, but the alternative, going on like this, was also not an option. At the day of the appointment, his mother, father and Martin drove to the hospital.

At the hospital Martin spoke with a psychiatrist and a psychologist, and his parents were seen by a psychiatric nurse. He said as little as possible, because he did not trust the hospital staff. His voices warned him not to speak about them, or they would punish him. When he was asked whether he heard people speak to him when there was nobody near, he denied it. He was sure that they could not protect him against his persecutors. He checked the room carefully for cameras but he could not see them. He expected that they were so small that he could not detect them. In the meantime his mother told the nurse that Martin said that he thought the Turkish mob had planted a chip in his brain. She was happy that finally someone asked her to talk about her experiences. In the past years she had seen her son deteriorate from someone who was basically alright into a scared, disorganized wreck, and she was unable to stop it. A week later, the outcome was discussed with Martin and his parents. The team had concluded that Martin may be suffering from a psychosis. Martin denied it. The psychologist said that they could offer Martin a diagnostic admission. If Martin was not ill, it would show during the admission but if he was, they could help him with treatment. Martin said that he did not think it was necessary, but his parents urged him to accept the offer.

A few days later Martin was admitted. About six people of his age were also at the clinic. They hardly spoke to each other. After a few days he was prescribed antipsychotic medication. The doctors asked him to stay a bit longer, so they could monitor his reaction to the medication. It took some time before the pills had an effect, but then Martin noticed that he became less afraid. He slowly started to realize that he was not being persecuted by the Turkish mob. But his fear and paranoia were replaced by fatigue and numbness. He started sleeping much longer, for 11 hours or more. When he woke up, he was still very tired. He had no motivation to do anything, he felt like a zombie. He also experienced other side-effects like weight gain. In the past months he had gained 8 kilos. He could not stand the sight of himself in the mirror. Slowly he started to realize that he had a severe mental illness. He had read on the internet about psychosis and schizophrenia, and it was described as a debilitating brain disorder, often with a chronic course.

'My future is gone,' he thought.

He did not want to be a psychiatric patient for the rest of his life. He thought about Caitlin. He could not imagine her wanting a schizophrenic patient as a boyfriend. One day he woke up and realized that he had nothing left to live for. He could not live with or without the antipsychotic medication. He did not want to hurt his parents, but perhaps he would even help them to get on with their lives if he ended his own, he thought. Then they would not have to see him struggle and fail all the time. It was very early in the morning. He walked to the nearby station and sat on a bench for a while. Then he saw a train approaching. He walked to the edge of the platform and jumped. He was killed instantly.

Commuters grumbled all morning because the trains were not on time.

'Another jumper,' the rumour went.

His doctors had a meeting in which they discussed whether his suicide could have been prevented. The treating psychiatric resident, in whom he had partly confided, felt guilty that she had been unable to save him. She went to his funeral, and afterwards wept for hours because of the tragedy of it all.

Discussion

The story of Martin shows the problematic side of the use of the DSM in clinical practice. Before Martin has a florid psychosis, he seeks professional help several times but on each occasion the symptoms are misdiagnosed, and some of the medication prescribed may have had iatrogenic effects. If community centres like headspace, described in the conclusion of this book, were available widely, the at risk mental state symptoms could have been recognized and stepped care would have been employed. A benign treatment like cognitive behavioural therapy could have been offered. Cognitive behavioural therapy can reduce the chance of transition to a first psychosis, with 50 per cent without side effects. If Martin was treated with cognitive behavioural therapy, he would still have the biological vulnerability (as expressed by the cognitive impairment) but the vicious circle of anxiety, stress, university drop out, sleeping problems, social isolation may have been broken.

Martin's story also shows that antipsychotic medication can suppress the psychotic symptoms that are most disruptive for society, but that it does not cure the disorder and creates other problems such as apathy and weight gain. New treatment options are needed that are more acceptable to patients, and that have fewer side-effects.

CONCLUSIONS AND FUTURE DIRECTIONS

The reductionist biomedical model in psychiatry in the past decennia is associated with a steep increase in psychotropic medication prescription but not with better prognosis of psychiatric symptoms. An invalid classification system has supported this worrying development. To understand and better treat psychiatric symptoms, alternatives to the DSM should be investigated. One such an alternative is clinical staging and profiling. Furthermore, it has become apparent that only investigating psychiatric symptoms by including patients with a certain DSM diagnosis in a scientific research design, may not lead to a true understanding of psychiatric symptoms. For a true understanding of psychiatric symptoms we first need to understand a human being and for this we need to take a broader perspective, including insights from philosophers and artists.

How can this broader perspective help in advancing knowledge and treatment in psychiatry? First by redefining mental health and mental illness. This is necessary to stop the ever increasing number of people and especially children, who are treated for mental illness as defined by the current classification system with psychotropic medication. Second, listening to what subjects with psychiatric symptoms go through (e.g. mystic experiences, alienation, isolation, fear of death) and taking it seriously instead of regarding it as just the consequences of a deregulated neurotransmitter system can fill the gap between patients and mental health care professionals that is often experienced by those with psychiatric symptoms. In addition, the content of fears, depression and psychosis can convey meaning and a direction for a more natural path to recovery than suppression with psychotropic medication. Third, trying to treat psychiatric symptoms in an early stage with benign treatments, without diagnosing these symptoms as a psychiatric disorder can reduce the chance that these symptoms progress to more chronic stages.

In a new biological-philosophical-art paradigm, psychiatric symptoms can be regarded from several perspectives and treated in a stepped care model. Stepped care means that the least invasive and harmless evidence-based treatments are employed first. Psychotropic medication should be avoided until the safer, less invasive methods have shown to be ineffective (McGorry et al., 2007; Nieman and McGorry, 2015).

Seeking help in low stigma settings

While neurodevelopmental, behavioural disorders and certain anxiety disorders emerge during childhood, most of the high prevalence disorders (anxiety, mood, personality and substance use disorders) have their onset during adolescence and early adulthood, as do the bulk of the psychotic disorders (McGorry et al., 2011). Yet, although having the highest incidence and prevalence across the life span, young people show a relatively low level of professional help-seeking and access to care for mental health problems (Slade et al., 2009). It is difficult for young subjects with emerging psychiatric symptoms to 1) recognize what is happening to them and 2) take the step to seek help (McGorry et al., 2014).

Help-seeking may be easier in low stigma settings such as 'headspace' in Australia (www.headspace.org.au) where not only young people (12–25 years) with severe psychiatric problems seek help but also young people with early and mild to moderate problems are encouraged to seek assessment and care. Young people and/or their parents and friends can seek help for problems ranging from general health, education, to drug use, anxiety and other (emerging) psychiatric symptoms. Evidence-based interventions are provided in a stepped care manner. Many young people can be helped with just information or a listening ear. Others may be helped with eHealth chat groups or a group-therapy focusing on, e.g. building self-esteem. Furthermore, it is also possible to seek help anonymously by telephone or online (via eheadspace). There are already 74 headspace centres (soon to be 100) in Australia and over 100,000 subjects have been helped. It is not necessary to be referred or receive a DSM or ICD diagnosis before or even after help is provided. Indeed most patients are demonstrably in the early stages of disorder (Rickwood et al., 2013). Considering its successful implementation in Australia, a promising direction in clinical staging is adoption of this model in other parts of the world. This would enable evidence-based interventions given in a stepped care manner to help-seeking youth, and reduce the level of undertreatment as well as the risk of premature and overtreatment with medication provided by health care professionals who are not yet familiar with the ARMS and staging concepts. A preliminary independent evaluation of headspace was done in 2009 (Muir et al., 2009) and another independent evaluation has been completed recently but results have not yet been published. Furthermore, a comprehensive study has commenced to assess the outcomes and fidelity of the headspace programme, of which results are expected in 2017 or 2018.

While many other countries (e.g. Denmark, Ireland, Israel, USA, Canada) are exploring similar approaches, there are some obvious barriers. Only in countries with a strong and universally funded primary care system augmented by government support of psychosocial interventions will find it easy to restructure the frontline to enable stigma-free multidisciplinary care for young people to be provided without barriers and with a soft entry mechanism. When it comes to specialist outpatient mental health care in many countries, patients are only reimbursed by insurance companies for their mental health treatment costs if they have particular levels of formal DSM or ICD diagnosis, such as schizophrenia. The bar is set very high through these arrangements which are discriminatory in that they do not apply to physical illness such as cancer, where early diagnosis is of great importance. Such funding models therefore fail to support the principles of clinical staging and should be reformed. New investments in youth mental health are required to catalyse such reforms and are feasible even in countries like Ireland where primary care is not yet generally subsidized by the government and health funding has been otherwise constrained (McGorry et al., 2013b). Economists and policy makers are beginning to understand that investing in effective mental health care for young people is truly an investment rather than a cost (Nieman and McGorry, 2015).

On the basis of meta-analyses and reviews it can be concluded that treating ARMS leads to a significant reduction in transition rate to a first psychosis (about 50 per cent within 12 months). The number needed to treat is better than in several other medical specialties where preventive treatment has been implemented in clinical practice. Furthermore, individualized risk estimation is feasible but promising research results need to replicated. Overall, there is a critical need for longitudinal studies of biology and clinical manifestations in psychiatry, agnostic to the traditional diagnoses, to chart the evolution of distinct trajectories (McGorry et al., 2014). The literature on stigma in ARMS suggest that stigma is due in large part to negative societal views on psychiatric disorders rather than the act of providing care, especially in low stigma settings. Perhaps if psychiatric symptoms could be regarded more by the general public in the way physical ailments are regarded (e.g. all areas of a person's health may need some access to care from time to time) and also treated that way then societal stigma would be greatly reduced. A clinical staging approach would also be helpful in this respect and should be supported by substantial health system reform and investment (Nieman and McGorry, 2015).

Individual approach

In psychiatry, an individual approach may be important instead of trying to fit individuals in diagnostic categories. Hopefully in the future, subjects can be helped in the early phase of psychiatric illness. The individual situation of the subject should be evaluated, taking into account that anxiety, depression and other negative emotions can convey a message about someone's life. It is not necessary and can even have an adverse effect to consider it as something that has to be suppressed as soon as possible with medication.

Research into biomarkers can hopefully validate the promising results concerning profiling. Biomarkers such as the P300, stress-indicators, cognitive deficits could aid individual prognosis and treatment in the future. Treatment should be guided by what is the matter with a specific individual not by a broad diagnostic category that has no prognostic or treatment-selection value for that individual.

In Maastricht, the Netherlands an interesting personalized diagnostic method has been developed: the PsyMate. The patient receives an app on his phone that makes a sound 10 times a day at random moments by which the patient is invited to fill out some questions about experiences (mood, psychosis, anxiety), behaviour (drug- or food intake), environment (stressors, company) and activities (work, study, household chores). After 6 days of self-quantification, the data are processed and the patient and professional receive a comprehensive graphical diagnostic overview in which complaints are shown dimensionally, in relationship to each other and in relationship to events, activities, etcetera. In addition, the PsyMate assesses cognitive functions such as memory, problem solving and processing speed (van Os, 2014).

The data are ecologically valid because subjects fill out the questions at the moment they have the experiences, which makes the answers more reliable than from memory. The PsyMate can reveal what someone's strengths and vulnerabilities are, e.g. which activities lead to improvement in mood and which activities to an increase in psychotic symptoms?

It may not be possible to categorize psychiatric symptoms. Human beings are just too diverse with respect to subjective experience, memories, aspirations, etcetera to generalize in categories. In psychotherapy, the primary task of the therapist is to try to understand the world and experiences of a particular patient. This is important to be able to reach someone in despair, psychosis, profound anxiety. Feeling understood, taken seriously and supported may be the most healing ingredient of psychotherapy. Labelling the existential struggle of a patient with a DSM diagnosis often does not help recovery (Yalom, 1980). There may be a part of psychiatry that does not lend itself to a scientific research design because subjective experiences of patients cannot be studied in the same way as broken legs or heart attacks. Other parts of psychiatry (the biological component, e.g. physiological stress reactions) can be studied the same as in most medical illnesses. As Jaspers (1947) already described in his handbook *General Psychopathology*, Verstehen and Erklären are both necessary and complementary.

Although it is not formalized in psychotherapy protocols, most experienced psychotherapists know that a road to recovery from psychiatric symptoms can be to help patients find their authentic self and a way to realize what they really want in life even though this is not always easy. Considering the work of the philosophers, scientists and psychiatrists discussed in Chapter 12, finding your authentic self and living life accordingly may be a road to cure. Going against what you really want usually leads to stress whereas following your own nature facilitates relaxation. Questions that can help are: When did you feel most alive? Was there a period in your life in which you were happy, in which life seemed less effortful than at the moment? Do you have hobbies or are there activities that lead to a sense of fulfilment? These questions often instigate a sudden joyous expression. The motto of Joseph Campbell 'Follow your bliss' also applies to psychiatry.

Wellness Recovery Action Plan

This idea is partly formalized in Wellness Recovery Action Plan (WRAP) that has been developed by a group of people who experience mental health and other health and lifestyle challenges. These people learned that they can identify what makes them well, and then use their own Wellness Tools to relieve difficult feelings and maintain wellness and a higher quality of life. These are activities that you enjoy or that help you feel better and that you may have used in the past or would like to use in the future. The result has been recovery and long-term stability (Copeland, 2011).

With WRAP it may be possible to find out what gives an individual consolation. There are no rules here that apply for everybody. By 'following your bliss' one can find out what is meaningful and healing for oneself, which may be not meaningful and healing for the next person. Patient-empowerment is important in this respect. Most patients know what can make them well and WRAP is a self-management tool. The usual stance in mental health care that entails 'What is wrong' as assessed by the health care professional is replaced by 'What is strong' as assessed by the individual that experiences the symptoms.

In traditional psychiatry, recovery is defined as remission of symptoms and restoration of functioning. These are elements of recovery but as the case examples in Part III of this book show, people can recover without restoration of functioning and sometimes psychotic symptoms are in remission but the patient does not experience this as recovery because he perceives his life as meaningless. The definition of recovery should include finding meaning in life, independently of functioning and symptoms. People with symptoms can experience their life as meaningful whereas those numbed by medication may be symptom-free but may have lost themselves, and with that, the sense of living a meaningful life. Therefore, just as the diagnosis and treatment should be personalized in psychiatry, so should the definition of recovery. The definition of a meaningful life is personal and depends on what people really aspire to and what is important to them (Shrank and Slade, 2007). Zimmerman et al. (2006) found that the three factors that were the most frequently judged to be very important by patients themselves in determining remission of depression were the presence of features of positive mental health such as optimism and self-confidence; a return to one's usual, normal self. Thus, according to the patients themselves, these features are a better indicator of remission than the absence of the symptoms. Law and Morrison (2014) report that 93 per cent of the service users agree that recovery is present 'When the person is able to find time to do the things they enjoy'. Thus, there is a clear discrepancy between recovery as defined by the psychiatric profession and as defined by those who experience psychiatric symptoms themselves and use mental health services. The important question arises: Whose interests are primary in psychiatry, those of the patient or those of the professionals/society? Considering the limited use of the definition of recovery of service users in research and clinical practice it appears the latter. However, this should change to a more balanced approach, taking both perspectives into account.

Of course, (re)finding your authentic self and especially realizing it is a struggle. There is a certain unfulfilment inherent to life. For example, you want to be a writer but you cannot provide for your family with selling your books. Therefore you take another job with which you can make money but that you do not like. The resultant unfulfilment and sadness is not a brain dysfunction but the result of life's difficulties.

Another example, if one is lucky, one falls in love, marries, has children; life is like a fairy-tale. However, most people do not stay in love for decades although being in love can pass into love. The possibility exists that one falls in love with someone else. One is then faced with a difficult choice: following one's feeling and leaving one's partner and children often to much grief of those involved, adultery or trying to stop being in love (which is very difficult especially when you cannot avoid the person you are in love with). There is no easy solution for such a common problem.

Acceptance and Commitment Therapy

The goal of Acceptance and Commitment Therapy (ACT) is getting to know unpleasant feelings, then learning not to act upon them, and to not avoid situations where they are invoked (Hayes et al., 2012). The objective is not happiness, rather it is to be present with what life brings us either positive or negative. Suppressing inevitable negative emotions does not make them go away. For example, someone can drink a lot to suppress negative feelings. In the short term this may work but the next day when the negative feelings surface, the person drinks again. In the long-term, this will lead to the additional problem of addiction. If emotions are experienced as they come, its therapeutic effect is a positive spiral which leads to a better understanding of the truth (Shpancer, 2010). ACT aims to help the individual clarify their personal values and to pursue them, bringing more vitality and meaning to their life in the process and increasing psychological flexibility (Zettle, 2005). In meta-analysis of 39 randomized controlled trials on the efficacy of ACT, including 1,821 patients with mental disorders or somatic health problems it was reported that ACT is more effective than treatment as usual or placebo and that ACT may be as effective in treating anxiety disorders, depression, addiction and somatic health problems as established psychological interventions (A-Tjak et al., 2015).

Antipsychiatry

What is the difference between the ideas in this book and the antipsychiatry movement in 1960–70? An important difference is the acknowledgement that there is a transdiagnostic biological component in psychiatric disorders and that future research efforts need to elucidate the relationship between transdiagnostic phenomenological symptom dimensions and biological dysfunctions to find new treatment options. Psychotherapy is not sufficient in all cases. Another difference is that prevention, clinical staging, profiling and stepped care is given an important place in the new model. Furthermore, it is not necessary anymore to oppose to large asylums where psychiatric patients are treated because these asylums have already been broken down to a large extent.

New treatments for psychotic disorders

(This section is an adaptation of: D.H. Nieman (2015) New treatments for psychotic disorders *The Lancet Psychiatry* 2(4), 282–3.)

Treatments for psychotic conditions, such as schizophrenia, need substantial improvement. As discussed in previous chapters, the first-line treatment of schizophrenia – i.e. antipsychotics – can suppress delusions and hallucinations, but patients still suffer from other symptoms such as negative symptoms, and often report adverse side-effects from the medication (e.g. apathy, neurological side-effects, serious weight gain and sexual dysfunction). The percentage of non-compliance with medication in patients with schizophrenia is as high as 40–50 per cent, (Lacro et al., 2002) and 74 per cent of patients discontinue their medication within 18 months (Lieberman et al., 2005). Furthermore, Wunderink and colleagues (2013) report that dose reduction or discontinuation of antipsychotics during the early stages of remitted first-episode psychosis is associated with superior long-term (7 years) recovery rates (40.4 per cent) compared with the rates achieved with antipsychotic maintenance treatment (17.6 per cent). Additionally, Morrison and colleagues (2014) reported that cognitive therapy significantly reduced psychiatric symptoms and seems to be a safe and acceptable alternative for people with schizophrenia and related disorders who have chosen not to take antipsychotic medication. In consideration of low patient compliance with antipsychotics (Lacro et al., 2002; Lieberman et al., 2005), evidence for improved long-term functional recovery with dose reduction or discontinuation of antipsychotic medication (Wunderink et al., 2013) and the promising results from trials of psychological treatments (Morrison et al., 2014), intervention options for patients with a psychotic disorder are clearly needed that are effective, have fewer side-effects, and are more acceptable to some patients than antipsychotics.

Freeman and colleagues (2015) show in their randomized controlled trial of 150 patients with persecutory delusions that a six session, worry-reduction cognitive behaviour therapy (CBT) intervention added to standard care led to significant reductions in both worry and persecutory delusions compared with standard care alone. The intervention aimed to reduce time worrying and did not directly target the delusions themselves. In addition to significant reductions in worry and persecutory delusions, the intervention also led to significant improvements in overall psychiatric symptoms, paranoid thinking, psychological wellbeing and rumination. Furthermore, the results of a mediation analysis were consistent with a causal role for worry in paranoia (i.e. the change in worry accounted for 66 per cent of the change in delusion).

A few important questions about this study need to be addressed in future research. First, can the worry CBT intervention in combination with modular interventions targeting other key causal factors, such as sleep disturbance and low self-esteem, reduce the dose of antipsychotics needed for patients with psychotic disorders? Second, do these modular interventions improve outcome for patients with an At Risk Mental State (ARMS) for developing a first psychosis (McGorry et al., 2003) when they are added to a more comprehensive CBT? As discussed in Chapter 9, a CBT developed especially for ARMS patients that targets the effects of cognitive biases, such as jumping to conclusions, and encompassing psycho-education about prepsychotic symptoms, has been shown to reduce the chance of transition to a first psychosis by about 50 per cent (van der Gaag et al., 2012, 2013). The first treatment option for ARMS patients should be CBT because there is cumulative evidence that this type of intervention is effective and without adverse effects in this patient group (Hutton et al., 2014), and international treatment guidelines advise against treating ARMS patients with antipsychotics (International early psychosis writing group, 2005). In ARMS patients, worrying, stress, sleep disturbances, negative effects of reasoning biases and low self-esteem often have an important role in the onset, maintenance and exacerbation of psychotic symptoms. Targeting these factors with optional modules that are incorporated in a more comprehensive CBT could further improve prognosis in ARMS patients.

The study by Freeman and colleagues (2015) is an important contribution that fits with the current movement towards evidence-based, benign treatment options for patients with a psychosis spectrum disorder. Furthermore, the study fits with the trend towards transdiagnostic interventions in psychiatry. Cumulative evidence suggests that the DSM categories for mental disorders might not be valid, both from a biological and a clinical perspective (see Chapter 2). Worrying occurs in many psychiatric disorders, in the ARMS phase as well as in later illness stages, and targeting worry could lead to improved outcomes, irrespective of DSM diagnosis.

The Open dialogue approach

In some areas in Finland, a method is employed to treat psychosis that involves listening to the patient, including the social environment in the treatment and use of as little antipsychotic medication as possible. According to one of the developers of this method, Jaakko Seikkula, psychotic experiences are a metaphorical way of communicating and are therefore understandable. The patient and family are involved in all decisions and each voice is important. Outcome studies show that open dialogue treatment is very successful. Areas in Finland that use this approach have now the best documented outcomes of psychotic disorders in the Western World. For example, around 75 per cent of those experiencing psychosis have returned to work or study within 2 years and only around 20 per cent are still taking antipsychotic medication at 2 year follow-up. Furthermore, in these areas spending on psychiatric services dropped 33 per cent from 1980–1990 and today is the lowest among all health districts in Finland (Seikkula, 2006; Whitaker, 2010). Because of these positive results, other countries started to show interest in this method as well.

What could be underlying the success of this approach? The recognition that psychosis is partly associated with inherent difficulties in social relationships (in the family, at school, work or in society in general). Excellent art-house films of Lars von Trier (Breaking the waves, Melancholia) and of Jane Campion (The Piano, An Angel at my Table) show how people sometimes interact without caring about what the other person needs. Psychiatry can learn from films like this to comprehend the subtle, often concealed mechanisms in social interactions that play a role in psychiatric symptoms.

The vision of the staff in Finland who employ the open dialogue method is that psychosis arises from severely frayed social relationships that have led to extreme stress. Everybody can become psychotic if stress levels arise too high. The main intervention is focused on the social relationships. Truly listening to what the patient and the family say and just being with them without the necessity to intervene with medication creates room for openness and truth in relationships. In addition, the very limited use of antipsychotics facilitates regaining grip on reality in a more natural way and reduces the numbness of sedation to a minimum.

Biomarkers

As discussed in Chapter 7, biomarkers could provide insight into progression or remission of biological disease processes in psychiatric disorders. Biomarkers can be studied scientifically because they signify biological changes. For example, EEG biomarkers can signify information processing deficits. New treatments targeting biomarker abnormalities may improve psychiatric symptoms in some patients. For example, N-acetylcysteine has been shown to improve EEG abnormalities (see Chapter 8). A comprehensive study is currently performed, funded by the National Institute of Mental Health in which biomarker research in ARMS subjects is harmonized, leading to samples of hundreds of ARMS subjects and healthy controls. The Academic Medical Center in Amsterdam is one of the including sites. Such a study could increase insight into biomarkers as predictors of a severe course and possible new treatment options. However, biomarkers are only a component of the clinical picture and will at best be a part of the solution in many patients. The phenomenological component is at least as important. Furthermore, the relationship between biomarkers and narrowly defined symptom dimensions should be the focus of future research.

The role of cognition

Future research needs to clarify the role of cognition in psychiatric symptoms. Cognitive training before psychiatric symptoms emerge could play a role in the prevention of these symptoms. Furthermore, cognitive behavioural therapy can be effective (especially in the early stages of psychiatric disorders) but for many patients it should be combined with elements from Acceptance and Commitment Therapy, Wellness Recovery Action Plan and existential psychotherapy to give way to intense emotions and experiences that cannot be steered by cognition.

Primary prevention

Secondary prevention, when subjects already have symptoms and start to drop out psychosocially, is more effective than tertiary prevention, when patients have severe symptoms and psychosocial dysfunction. However, it would be even better when it would be possible to prevent the symptoms and psychosocial drop out from occurring, i.e. primary prevention. Of course, this will never be possible entirely but in other areas of medicine, this approach has been highly effective. For example, in dentistry education in brushing teeth has improved the teeth of many and dentures are less common than decades ago. In psychiatry, a reduction in childhood adversity, trauma and bullying would lead to primary prevention.

Furthermore, less phoney behaviour may be beneficial for everybody. We constantly pretend that we are successful, happy, fulfilled, not afraid. Why do especially the pictures and stories about happy moments appear on facebook? Because we want to be at least as happy and successful as our peers. If we all would just be more honest and share our pain, desperation, longing, fear, sadness as well as our happiness and success, those who are suffering would not feel so alone.

The ultimate step in despair is suicide. According to the World Health Organization, almost 1 million people kill themselves every year. That is more than the number that die in homicides and war combined. A further 10 million to 20 million people attempt it. Suicide is one of the three leading causes of death in the economically most productive age group – those aged 15–44 years (Aleman and Denys, 2014). In the Netherlands suicide numbers increased by 30 per cent from 1353 in 2007 to 1854 in 2013. In comparison, the number of traffic casualties declined from 791 in 2007 to 570 in 2013 (Centraal Bureau voor de Statistiek, 2015). The rise in suicide may express the loneliness, and unconnectedness of those who are in despair. If western societies would find some of their old wisdom back, give room to personal growth, spirituality, retreat, solitude, literature, philosophy instead of the emphasis on gathering material things, performing roles and gaining social status, primary prevention would benefit.

For most, life is a struggle. It is difficult to reach your goals, people can be ruthless to each other, we need relationships in our life but true contact is more the exception than the rule. People in despair may become more desperate by the appearance of success and ease people try to display. They often keep their despair to themselves (Jack, 2015).

People with suicidal ideation can be helped by just talking about their despair and make a 'map' of it (Kerkhof and Luyn, 2011). Which areas of their life, which events and situations luxate the feelings of hopelessness? Just acknowledging and talking about it with friends or in psychotherapy can help subjects who struggle with suicidal thoughts or plans. There is an unfounded fear that talking about suicide can instigate it but research does not support this fear (Kerkhof and van Heeringen, 2000). Furthermore, art can be healing because it often shows the true universal suffering that most recognize in their own life (de Botton, 2012).

Essential and existential redefinition

The World Health Organisation (WHO, 2012) reports that at least 350 million people are suffering from depression worldwide and they list as symptoms persistent sadness, low energy and difficulty in functioning normally. 350 million people is more than 20x the complete population of the Netherlands, an incredible lot of people. Depression is the leading cause of disability worldwide. Considering the insights of the existentialist discussed in Chapter 12, it is questionable if persistent sadness, low energy and reduced functioning is actually an illness. Of course for a proportion of the 350 million people it is, but another proportion may just be confronted with the harsh reality of failure, deceit, societal pressure, alienating environments, lack of meaning, the ultimate hollowness of gathering material things. The Dutch 'happiness professor' Ruut Veenhoven (2015) reported that the mean happiness score of Dutch people is 8 on a scale of 0 (very unhappy) to 10 (very happy). This score is in sharp contrast with the rise in suicide, psychotropic medication prescription and disability associated with psychiatric symptoms. Perhaps mechanisms of social comparison as described in Chapter 12 also play a role in upgrading the score. One does not want to be less happy than the next person. If society and resultant psychiatric practice expects from life that it can be given a mean happiness score of 8 it is not surprising that so many people present to the primary health care with depression complaints. Mojtabai and Olofson (2011) report that between 1996 and 2007, the proportion of visits at which antidepressants were prescribed but no psychiatric diagnoses were made, increased from 59.5 per cent to 72.7 per cent. Antidepressants are now the third most commonly prescribed medication class in the United States (Hsiao et al., 2010). With annual sales of approximately $10 billion, antidepressants are also one of the most costly medication classes (Deacon, 2013; IMS Health, 2010). Prescription by non-psychiatrist physicians have been growing; 60 per cent of antidepressant prescriptions in the USA are written by such providers (Takayanagi et al., 2015). Research into the long-term consequences of this practice is urgently needed.

According to Heidegger, Rilke, Kierkegaard and many others, negative emotions such as despair, sadness, anxiety are essential for personal growth. If they are regarded as abnormal because the average person in a society has a happiness score of 8, it is understandable that people seek 'treatment' for these emotions. General practitioners describe en masse antidepressants to 'help' these people but antidepressants are not indicated when people present with these symptoms and may even make matters worse in the long-term (Whitaker, 2010). A better approach would be to ascertain in a low stigma community setting such as headspace what this particular person is so desperate, sad, anxious about. Just talking about it to an empathic listener, acknowledging and undergoing the negative emotions can be helpful. Furthermore, regarding these emotions not as abnormal but helpful may also reduce the necessity to get rid of these emotions as soon as possible. These emotions may tell you something about your life. Stepped care may reduce the chance of becoming a revolving-door patient (in and out of the hospital); psychotropic medication may suppress the symptoms in the short-term but lead to a neurotransmitter disequilibrium and resultant chronic psychopathology in the long-term. It would be wise to try more benign interventions with fewer side-effects first. In addition, stepped care is cost saving because expensive chronicity becomes less likely (Ising et al., 2015).

Paradigm change

We have to be realistic, it will be an enormous struggle to change the current biomedical reductionist paradigm because so many have adhered to it for so long. Luckily more and more people notice the limitations and the problematic side of the current diagnostic system and the biomedical model (Dehue, 2010, 2014). The results of biomedical research may seem objective but many subjective decisions with respect to research design, data-analysis, etcetera of the researchers play a role. In addition, it is implied that the mean in a group included patients in research says something about an individual in this group, but that does not have to be true. Two individual patients in a group can have very diverse outcomes. The mean of these outcomes is a totally different value than the two outcomes separately.

The individual stories of patients are as important as research results (Brinkgreve, 2014; Dehue, 2014; The, 2014). For patients with Alzheimer's disease, a story-bank has been instated where people with Alzheimer's disease and their family can deposit stories about their experiences, grief, consolations and daily life solutions. Reading these stories can be helpful for those with Alzheimer's disease and their social network but also for professionals to understand what people are going through. A similar story-bank would be very useful for psychiatry in general.

The public and those diagnosed with a psychiatric disorder are also becoming more critical of current psychiatric practice. The voice of the public, of patients and critical professionals combined with evidence-based alternatives as implemented in Australia, should give this change movement enough impetus in the real world. The change should start in the psychiatric profession. Debates should be organized at psychiatric conferences about the DSM and the biomedical model. Unfortunately, insurance companies base reimbursement of health care costs on a DSM diagnosis in many countries. Policy makers and insurance companies may only change this if the psychiatric profession comes up with an alternative. In the meantime, stepped care of the successful headspace model can already be implemented in other countries than Australia (Nieman and McGorry, 2015).

Conclusion

Mental illness results from the interplay of biological, psychological and environmental factors. Furthermore, part of the experiences labelled these days as psychiatric symptoms are not symptoms but just normal human experiences that everybody needs to go through during their life. Creating a safety bubble by placing death, horrors, deceit, loneliness, failings, imperfections outside daily life may lead to a happiness score of 8 but is just not very truthful and realistic. A more general adoption of the view about human nature of some of our greatest thinkers would be truly destigmatizing: those succumbing to sadness, despair, psychosis, anxiety are not suffering from a debilitating brain disorder but have the courage to step out of the safety bubble and face the harsh facts of life. Once these facts are integrated into one's life, they are not that hard to bear. Although we are essentially alone, we can still have comforting, true encounters with others; although we are going to die, this does not mean the end of the world because others will keep on living and life is not just individualistic. By authenticity and self-actualization, it is possible to have moments of concurrence with that amazing part of our mind that connects us with others and the world. In addition, the finitude of our existence results in a necessity for spending the time you have as good and as truthful as possible. Being intensely sad and anxious from time to time should not be suppressed or avoided but paves the way for unclouded happiness at other moments.

References

Aleman, A. and Denys, D. (2014). Mental health: A road map for suicide research and prevention. *Nature* 509(7501), 421–3.
A-Tjak, J.G., Davis, M.L., Morina, N., Powers, M.B., Smits, J.A and Emmelkamp, P.M. (2015). A meta-analysis of the efficacy of acceptance and commitment therapy for clinically relevant mental and physical health problems. *Psychotherapy and Psychosomatics* 84(1), 30–6.
Brinkgreve, C. (2014). *Vertel: Over de kracht van verhalen*. Amsterdam: Atlas Contact.
Centraal Bureau voor de Statistiek (CBS). (2015). The Netherlands. http://statline.cbs.nl/Statweb/ (accessed July 6, 2015).
Copeland, M.E. (2011). *Wellness Recovery Action Plan*. Dummerston, VT: Peach Press
de Botton, A. (2012). *Religion for Atheists*. London: Hamish Hamilton.

Deacon, B.J. (2013). The biomedical model of mental disorder: A critical analysis of its validity, utility, and effects on psychotherapy research. *Clinical Psychology Review* 33(7), 846–61.

Dehue, T. (2010). *De depressie-epidemie*. Amsterdam: Uitgeverij Augustus.

Dehue, T. (2014). *Betere mensen*. Amsterdam: Uitgeverij Augustus.

Freeman, D., Dunn, G., Startup, H, , Pugh, K., Cordwell, J., Mander, H., Černis, E., Wingham, G., Shirvell, K. and Kingdon, D. (2015). Effects of cognitive behaviour therapy for worry on persecutory delusions in patients with psychosis (WIT): a parallel, single-blind, randomised controlled trial with a mediation analysis. *The Lancet Psychiatry* 2, 305–13.

Hayes, S.C., Strosahl, K.D. and Wilson, K.G. (2012). *Acceptance and Commitment Therapy: The Process and Practice of Mindful Change*, (2nd edn.). New York: Guilford Press.

Hsiao, C.J., Cherry, D.K., Beatty, P.C.and Rechtsteiner, E.A. (2010). National Ambulatory Medical Care Survey: 2007 summary. *National Health Statistics Report* 27, 1–32.

Hutton, P. and Taylor, P.J. (2014). Cognitive behavioural therapy for psychosis prevention: a systematic review and meta-analysis. *Psychological Medicine* 44(3), 449–68.

IMS Health (2010). *Top Therapeutic Classes by U.S. Sales*. Norwalk, CT: IMS Health.

International Early Psychosis Association Writing Group. (2005). International clinical practice guidelines for early psychosis. *British Journal of Psychiatry* 187, S120–4.

Ising, H.K., Veling, W., Rietdijk, J., Dragt, S., Klaassen, R., Savelsberg, N., Boonstra, N., Nieman, D., Wunderink, L., Linszen, D., Smit, F. and van der Gaag, M. (2015). Cost-utility and cost-effectiveness of the prevention of a first episode psychosis in ultra high risk subjects. *Psychological Medicine* 45, 1435–46.

Jack, A. (2015). *A Suicide in the Family*. BBC documentary, viewed on 24 October 2015 at http://www.bbc.co.uk/programmes/b05rcrx0

Jaspers, K. (1947 [1997]). *General Psychopathology*. Vols 1 & 2. Hoenig, J. and Hamilton, M.W., trans. Baltimore, MD: Johns Hopkins University Press. First published as: Jaspers K. (1913). *Allgemeine Psychopathologie*. Berlin: Springer.

Kerkhof, A.J.F.N. and Luyn, B. (2011). *Suicidepreventie in de praktijk (Suicide Prevention in Clinical Practice)*. Houten: Bohn Stafleu van Loghem.

Kerkhof, A.J.F.N. and van Heeringen, C. (2000). *Behandelingsstrategieeen bij suicidaliteit*. Houten: Bohn Stafleu van Loghum.

Lacro, J.P., Dunn, L.B., Dolder, C.R, Leckband, S.G. and Jeste, D.V. (2002). Prevalence of and risk factors for medication nonadherence in patients with schizophrenia: a comprehensive review of recent literature. *Journal of Clinical Psychiatry* 63, 892–909.

Law, H. and Morrison, A.P. (2014). Recovery in psychosis: a Delphi study with experts by experience. *Schizophrenia Bulletin* 40(6), 1347–55.

Lieberman, J.A., Stroup, T.S., McEvoy, J.P., Swartz, M.S., Rosenheck, R.A., Perkins, D.O., Keefe, R.S., Davis, S.M., Davis, C.E., Lebowitz, B.D., Severe, J., Hsiao, J.K., and the CATIE investigators. (2005). Effectiveness of antipsychotic drugs in patients with chronic schizophrenia. *New England Journal of Medicine* 353, 1209–23.

McGorry, P.D. (2007). Issues for DSM-V: clinical staging: a heuristic pathway to valid nosology and safer, more effective treatment in psychiatry. *American Journal of Psychiatry* 164(6), 859–60.

McGorry, P.D., Yung, A.R. and Phillips, L.J. (2003). The 'close-in' or ultra high-risk model: a safe and effective strategy for research and clinical intervention in prepsychotic mental disorder. *Schizophrenia Bulletin* 29, 771–90.

McGorry, P.D., Purcell, R., Goldstone, S. and Amminger, G.P. (2011). Age of onset and timing of treatment for mental and substance use disorders: implications for preventive intervention strategies and models of care. *Current Opinion in Psychiatry* 24(4), 301–6.

McGorry, P., Bates, T. and Birchwood, M. (2013). Designing youth mental health services for the 21st century: examples from Australia, Ireland and the UK. *British Journal of Psychiatry* 202: s30-s35.

McGorry, P., Keshavan, M., Goldstone, S., Amminger, P., Allott, K., Berk, M., Lavoie, S., Pantelis, C., Yung, A., Wood, S. and Hickie, I. (2014a). Biomarkers and clinical staging in psychiatry. *World Psychiatry* 13(3), 211–23.

McGorry, P.D., Goldstone, S.D., Parker, A.G., Rickwood, D.J. and Hickie, I.B. (2014b). Cultures for mental health care of young people: an Australian blueprint for reform. *The Lancet Psychiatry* 1, 559–68.

Mojtabai, R. and Olfson, M (2011). Proportion of antidepressants prescribed without a psychiatric diagnosis is growing. *Health Affairs* 30(8), 1434–42.

Morrison, A.P., Turkington, D., Pyle, M., Spencer, H., Brabban, A., Dunn, G., Christodoulides, T., Dudley, R., Chapman, N., Callcott, P., Grace, T., Lumley, V., Drage, L., Tully, S., Irving, K., Cummings, A., Byrne, R., Davies, L.M. and Hutton, P. (2014). Cognitive therapy for people with schizophrenia spectrum disorders not taking antipsychotic drugs: a single-blind randomised controlled trial. *Lancet* 383, 1395–403.

Muir, K., Powell, A., Patulny, R., Flaxman, S., Mcdermott, S., Gendera, R., Vespignani, J., Sitek, T., Abello, D. and Katz, I. (2009). *Independent Evaluation of Headspace: The National Youth Mental Health Foundation*. Sydney. Social Policy Research Centre, University of New South Wales.

Nieman, D.H. (2015). New treatments for psychotic disorders. *The Lancet Psychiatry* 2(4), 282–3.

Nieman, D.H. and McGorry, P.D. (2015). Detection and treatment of at risk mental state for developing a first psychosis: Making up the balance. *The Lancet Psychiatry* 2, 825–34.

Rickwood, D.J., Telford, N.R., Parker, A.G., Tanti, C.J. and McGorry, P.D. (2013). Headspace – Australia's innovation in youth mental health: who are the clients and why are they presenting? *Medical Journal of Australia* 200, 108–11.

Schrank, B. and Slade, M. (2007). Recovery in psychiatry. *Psychiatric Bulletin* 31, 321–25.

Seikkula, J (2006). Five-year experience of first-episode nonaffective psychosis in open-dialogue approach. *Psychotherapy Research* 16, 214–28.

Shpancer, N. (2010). Emotional acceptance: why feeling bad is good. *Psychology Today*. https://www.psychologytoday.com/blog/insight-therapy/201009/emotional-acceptance-why-feeling-bad-is-good

Slade, T., Johnston, A., Teesson, M., Whiteford, H., Burgess, P., Pirkis, J. and Saw, S. (2009). *The Mental Health of Australians 2. Report on the 2007 National Survey of Mental Health and Wellbeing*. Canberra: Australian Department of Health and Ageing.

Takayanagi, Y., Spira, A.P., Bienvenu, O.J., Hock, R.S., Carras, M.C., Eaton, W.W. and Mojtabai, R. (2015). Antidepressant use and lifetime history of mental disorders in a community sample: results from the Baltimore Epidemiologic Catchment Area Study. *Journal of Clinical Psychiatry* 76, 40–4.

The, A.M. (2014). *Leven met dementia: van verhalen naar inzicht*. Amsterdam: Universiteit van Amsterdam.

van der Gaag, M., Nieman, D.H., Rietdijk, J., Dragt, S,, Isingm, H.K., Klaassen, R.M., Koeter, M., Cuijpers, P., Wunderink, L. and Linszen, D.H. (2012). Cognitive behavioural therapy for subjects at ultra high risk for developing psychosis: A randomized controlled clinical trial. *Schizophrenia Bulletin* 38, 1180–8.

van der Gaag, M., Nieman, D.H. and van den Berg, D. (2013). *CBT for Those at Risk for a First Episode Psychosis: Evidence Based Psychotherapy for People with an At Risk Mental State'*. London: Routledge.
van Os, J. (2014). *De DSM-5 voorbij! Persoonlijke diagnostiek in een nieuwe GGZ*. Leusden: Diagnosis uitgevers.
Veenhoven, R. (2015). *Happiness in Netherlands (NL)*, World Database of Happiness, Erasmus University Rotterdam, The Netherlands. Viewed on 24 October 2015 at http://worlddatabaseofhappiness.eur.nl.
Whitaker, R. (2010). *Anatomy of an Epidemic: Magic Bullets, Psychiatric Drugs, and the Astonishing Rise of Mental Illness in America*. New York: Crown.
World Health Organization (2012). *Depression: A Hidden Burden*. Viewed on 24 October 2015 at http://www.who.int/mediacentre/factsheets/fs369/en/
Wunderink, L., Nieboer, R.M., Wiersma, D., Sytema, S. and Nienhuis, F.J. (2013). Recovery in remitted first-episode psychosis at 7 years of follow-up of an early dose reduction/ discontinuation or maintenance treatment strategy: long-term follow-up of a 2-year randomized clinical trial. *JAMA Psychiatry* 70, 913–20.
Yalom, I.D. (1980). *Existential Psychotherapy*. New York: Basic Books.
Zettle, R.D. (2005). The evolution of a contextual approach to therapy: from comprehensive distancing to ACT. *International Journal of Behavioral Consultation and Therapy* 1(2), 77–89.
Zimmerman, M., McGlinchey, J.B., Posternak, M.A., Friedman, M., Attiullah N. and Boerescu, D. (2006). How should remission from depression be defined? The depressed patient's perspective. *American Journal of Psychiatry* 163(1), 148–50.

INDEX

Note: Page numbers in **bold** refer to figures

22q11 deletion syndrome 68

Acceptance and Commitment Therapy (ACT) 160, 164
Allgemeine Psychopathologie (Jaspers) 116–17, 158
Alzheimer's disease: early stage 68; story bank 166
American Psychiatric Association 1, 7, 11
ancient domain 45–7, 48, 120, 126
Angermeyer, M.C. 30, 31
anti-stigma initiatives 30
antidepressant medication 23–7, 41, 107, 165–6, 121; increased use 15, 23; SSRI antidepressants 25–8
antipsychiatry 161
antipsychotic medication 46–8, 139, 153–4, 161–3; increased use 15, 23, 24; problems of 161; at-risk mental state (ARMS) 81, 87–8; side-effects 24; usefulness 30
antisaccade test 64–5, **66, 68**
anxiety 3, 8, 9, 40, 55–6, 69, 89, 101, 118–19, 156, 167; as disclosive state of mind 111, 113, 157; and stress 96; treatment 121, 123, 128, 139–45, 160, 166;
archetypes 125
Aristotle 127
ARMS cognitive behavioural therapy 89–93

art 2–3, 32–33, 43, 47, 104, 112, 121, 155; art-house films 38, 163 functions of 102, 165
Asch Paradigm 40
at-risk mental state (ARMS) 67–8; antipsychotic medication 81; benefits of intervention 87–92, 157; cognitive behavioural therapy (CBT) 89–93, 162; cognitive impairment 67–9, 78; criteria 66, 77; help seeking 87–8; immune function 81; medication 88; metacognitive training 67, 89–91; modular interventions 161–2; P300 event-related potential (ERP) amplitude 78–9, **79**; preventive treatment 87–8, 163; stigma 93, 157; transition to psychosis 77–8, 157
Attention-Deficit/Hyperactivity Disorders (ADHD): as construct 13; diagnosing 14–15; diagnostic criteria 10–11; effects of misdiagnosis 13, 17, 104, 151; environmental factors 105; medication 12–15
authentic existence 39–41, 102, 111
authentic self: Campbell, J. 114–15; Coelho, P. 115; constraints on 126–7; Csíkszentmihályi, M. 120; defining 127; Heidegger, M. 110–12; James, W. 115–16; Jaspers, K. 116–19; Jung, C.G. 125–6; Kierkegaard, S. 112–13; Nietzsche, F. 112; overview 110; and

recovery 138, 158–60; Rilke, R.M. 120–1; Sartre, J.P. 122; Spinoza, B. 113–14; synthesis of perspectives 126–8; Upanishads 113; Yalom, I. 123–5
autonomic nervous system 97

becoming who you really are 40, 45, 112
Beethoven, L. van 104
behaviour, medicalisation of 12, 104–5
behavioural experiment 142
Being and Nothingness (Sartre) 122
Being-in-the-world 111
being-with others 39, 40, 111, 121, 136
Belaise, G. 27
benzodiazepines 25–6, 98–9, 139
Biobank Cognition study 57, 70–2
biological markers 163–4; and clinical staging 60–2, **60**; cognitive remediation 71–3; context and overview 59; need for research 158; neuropsychological testing 62–3; research focus 61–2
biological-philosophical-art paradigm 156
biology, understanding mental illness 51
biomedical model 32–3; dominance of 23; effect on research 33; failure of 52; and prescribing practice 155; and prognosis 155
blame, for mental illness 31
bliss 114, 127, 138, 159
book: overall conclusion 167; structure and overview 2–3
brain: complexity of 48; effects of psychotropic medication 25–6; production of mind 51
brain-mind relationship 3, 32, , 50–2, 101, 117, 119
breathing 97–8, 142–3
Briefe an einem jungen Dichter (Rilke) 101, 121
Brodmann's area 46, executive functioning **67**, 68

Campbell, J. 44, 114–15, 127, 159
Campion, J. 163
Camus, A. 39, 124
Carmeli, C. 82
Cartesian dualism 50, 113
case conceptualisation, example **92**
case examples: ARMS 91–2; cognitive impairment 72–3; depression 133–8; diagnosis 17; diagnosis and treatment 146–54; environmental factors 106–7; Lizzie 139–45; Martin 146–54; mystic experiences 47–8; social interaction 41–2; SSRI antidepressants 28; stress–

relaxation continuum 98–9; Thomas 133–8; treatment process 139–45
Chakraborty, K. 13
Chan, K.Y. 105
children, and normality 104
Christianity 45
classification systems 7–10, 158
clinical staging 2–3, 67, 76–80, 155–7; and biological markers **60**–2; in psychiatry 61
co-morbidity 56
Coelho, P. 115
cognition: defining 62; disruption in psychiatric disorders **69**; in psychiatric symptoms 164
cognitive behavioural therapy (CBT): for psychosis 161–2; for ARMS 89–93; case-example 139–45; and risk of transition to psychosis 81
cognitive bias 90
cognitive impairment 62–71; ARMS phase 67–8; case example 72–3; early stage intervention 67–8, 69–70; executive functioning 64–8; longitudinal development 68; patients' wishes for treatment 63–4; selective attention 64, 66, 90; variance in 64; young people 66–7
cognitive remediation 71–3
cognitive therapy, success of 161; *see also* cognitive behavioural therapy (CBT)
Cohen, C.I. 119
comorbidity 8
Complex Figure of Rey 62–3, **63**
Comprehensive Assessment of At Risk Mental Stares (CAARMS) 67, 80
concealment 127
conformity 40
Corrigan, P.W. 93
costs, personal, social, financial 1
covariation bias 90
crying 101, 121, 134, 138
Csíkszentmihályi, M. 120, 143
Custance, J. 46

Dafny, N. 13
Dalsgaard, S. 12
Das Man 39, 40, 46, 111–2, 122, 126, 128
Das Stundenbuch (Rilke) 120
Dasein 110–11
death 101–2, 110, 120, 123– 4, 127, 136, 167
Dehue, T 12, 166
depression 24–5 , 50, 56–57, 87, 96, 98, 101–2, 105–7, 111–12, 159; case

example 41–42, 133–8; environmental factors 106–7; worldwide 166
Descartes, R. 50
despair 40, 102, 104, 112–3, 119, 121, 128, 137, 158, 164–7
diagnosis 1, 22–3, 31, 113, 157, 167; arbitrary 10, 107–8; categorisation 7–10; Jaspers' view of 117–9; overcoming categorical 55–7; personalised 77, 158; and treatment selection 8, 9
Diagnostic and Statistical Manual of Mental Disorders 1; broad categories 56; limitations 7–17, 155; need for alternatives 155, 167; *see also* classification systems
difference: benefits to society 104; defining as disorder 12–13
division of Child and Adolescent Psychiatry 14
dreams 117–8, 125, 127, 135
Dutch Health Council 14–15
Dutch Prediction of Psychosis Study 78, 79, 81

early intervention 67–8, 155, 156; ARMS cognitive behavioural therapy 89–92; benefits of 157; clinical staging 76–80; cognitive impairment 69–70; cost-effectiveness 88–9, 93; intervention success 92–3; meta-analyses 88; overview 76; predictive modelling 79–80; profiling 77; prognostic index 79–81; psychotherapy 89–92; risk stratification approach 78–80; transition to psychosis 77–8; underlying neurobiological mechanisms 81–2; video 90
Eastern philosophies 44, 48, 96
ego, relationship with Self 125
egocentricity 38
Einstein, A. 114
embodied condition, of mind 56
emotions, suppression/accepting 39, 42, 101, 121, 127–8, 137, 144–5, 157, 160, 166
environmental factors: case example 106–7; depression 106–7; health and illness 105–8; schizophrenia 105
epistemological debate 116
Erklären 51, 116–17, 121, 125, 158
European Prediction of Psychosis Study 79
event-related potential 78–9, 107
executive functioning 64, 66
exercise, for relaxation 98
existential psychotherapy 124, 164
Existential Psychotherapy (Yalom) 110, 123
existentialism 39, 116, 122

faith 118–19
fallenness 111
feel alive 123, 134, 159
fight-or-flight response 97–8
flow 120, 127
forgetfulness of being 39
freedom to choose 123
Freeman, D. 161–2
fulfilment 40, 120, 123, 138, 159, 160
funding 157
Fusar-Poli, P. 166

General Psychopathology (Jaspers) 116–17, 158
God: existence of 44–5, 147–8; and human nature 119, 126; Rilke's view of 102, 120–1; Spinoza's view of 113–14
government support 157
Grob, G.N. 7
Grover, S. 13

hallucination 24–5, 56, 71, 73, 89–90, 118, 139–142, 148, 152 161
happiness 38, 42, 160, 164–7
Hayes, S.C. 160
headspace centres 154, 156, 166–7
healing relationships 124
health, redefinition *see* redefinition of health and illness
Heidegger, M. 39, 110–12, 117, 126–7, 166
hell, Sartre's view of 122
help seeking: in low stigma settings 156–7; at-risk mental state (ARMS) 87–8
Hendriksen-Favier, A. 63–4
hereditary metabolic disorders, diagnosis 23–4
Hinduism 45, 97, 113
holocaust 136; human condition/existential situation 102, 104, 110
Huis clos (Sartre) 122
Huxley, A. 45
hybrid approach 116
hyperarousal 97–8

illness, redefinition *see* redefinition of health and illness
illumination 117
immune function, changes in 81
individual approach 157–9
individuals, manifestations of 117
individuation 125
ineffability 115, 118
inner resistance 117

integrity 111
insight, into illness 76, 118
International Statistical Classification of Diseases and Related Health Problems (ICD) 7–10
intuition 41, 45–6
isolation: in psychotic disorders 39, 102–3; types of 123–4, 154

James, W. 43, 46, 115–16, 118–19, 126
Jaspers, K. 51, 116–19, 121, 126, 158
jumping to conclusions 90, 162
Jung, C.G. 43, 46, 112, 125–7

Kahn, R. S. 68
Karanges, E.A. 15
Keefe, R.S. 68
Kerkhof, A.J.F.N. 165
Kessler, R.C. 23
Kierkegaard, S. 39, 112–13, 126, 166
Kingdon, D. 52
Kirov, C. 119
Kleinman, A. 52
Kraemer, M. 13–14
Kuhn, T. 32–3
Kusters, W. 46, 118

La Grande Bellezza (film) 38
Lavoie, S. 82
Law, H. 159–60
Law, W. 45
Le Noury, J. 26–7
L'Être et le Néant (Sartre) 122
life, as meaningless 124
listening 56, 128, 155–6, 162–3, 166
Lizzie 139–45
loneliness 40, 124, 164, 167
longitudinal studies, need for 157
love 38, 120, 124, 137, 160
low stigma settings 156–7, 166
lower mysticisms 43
Lukoff, D. 46
Luyn, B. 165

magnetic resonance imaging (MRI) research 16, 127–8
Martin 146–54
mass society 111
McGorry, P.D. 8, 9, 59–61, 77, 88, 156, 157, 162
meaning: need for 48, 124; search for 107
meaningful 38, 40, 42, 118, 121, 124, 138, 144, 155, 159, 160
meaninglessness 123–4, 159, 165
medicalisation, of behaviour 104–5

medication: antidepressant prescriptions 166; avoiding use of 41, 98, 156; non-compliance 24, 161; and recovery rates 98, 161; at-risk mental state (ARMS) 81, 88; and stress 98–9
meditation 98
mental illness: blame for 31; correlations with brain function 51; disruption of cognition **69**; increase in 22–3; subjective experience of 55–6; realism in 102, 118; reality of 59
metacognitive training 67, 89–91
methylphenidate *see* Ritalin (methylphenidate)
Milgram, S. 103
Millan, M.J. 55, 62, 64
mind: embodied condition of 56; production of 51
mind–brain problem: current science 51–2; overview 50–2
mind-brain relationship 32
mindfulness of being 39
misdiagnosis, effects of 13
Mitsein 111
Mohr, S. 119
Mojtabai, R. 166
Monism 50
monothetic classification 10
mood disorders, prognosis 24–5
moods, as states of attunement 111
Morein-Zamir, S. 72
Morrison, A.P. 159–60, 161
Morrow, R.L. 12
Müller, M. 93
mystic experiences 118–20, 42–4, 148, 155; case example 47–8; origin of 47, 115
mysticism, and human nature 43–4, 125–6

N-acetylcysteine 81–2, 163
National Institute of Mental Health 55, 163
need for care 9, 76
negative emotions, and personal growth 121, 123, 166
neurobiological mechanisms, and early intervention 81–2
neuroinflammation 60, 81
neurophenomenology 51, 56–8; case example 57
neuropsychological performance, phenotype clusters 70
neuropsychological testing, of visuospatial memory 62–3

neuroscience, promise of 50–1
neurosis, and psychosis 117–18, 119
Newton, M. 46
Nieman, D. 78, 87–90, 157
Nietzsche, F. 39, 104, 112, 126
No exit (Sartre) 122
noetic quality 115
normal distribution **103**
normality 103–5; and children 104
Nutt, D.J. 52

Obedience to Authority Study 103
obsessive compulsive disorder 28, 64, 66, 72
off-label polypharmacy 23
Olafson, M. 166
open dialogue approach 162–3
operationalized criteria, for ARMS 66–7
Other, as source of distress 122, 163

P300 event-related potential (ERP) amplitude 78–9, **79**, 82
pantheism 113–14, 116
paradigm shifts 32, 166–7
paradigms 22, 47, 51, 108, 110, 116, 118, 156; current paradigm 31–2; defining 32–3
parasympathetic nervous system 97
passivity 115
perennial philosophy 45, 118–20
personal growth 40–2, 48, 115, 121, 123, 125–7, 164; and negative emotions 166
personalised: care 77, 107, 159; diagnosis 158–9; prognostic value 2, 78; recovery 159
Pescosolido, B. 30
pharmaceutical companies: crime 27; marketing 27
phenomenology 56, 112; place in psychiatry 47; of psychiatric symptoms 43–4; understanding mental illness 51
phenylketonuria (PKU) 23–4
Philosophy of Madness (Kusters) 118
Physics II (Aristotle) 127
Pirsig, R. 147
Plotinus 46
polypharmacy 23
polythetic classification 9–10, 16, 128
Post Traumatic Stress Disorder 64–5, 68, 77
predictive modelling, early intervention 79–80
premorbid adjustment 79
Premorbid Adjustment Scale 78

prevalence 1, 22–3, 33 105, 156
Prevention of Mental Disorders (WHO) 87
prevention, secondary 9, 29, 33, 69, 70, 76, 81–2, 87, 164–5
preventive psychotherapy 89–90
preventive treatment: overview 87; at-risk mental state (ARMS) 87–8
primary prevention 164–5
profiling 2, 61, 76–8, 155, 158, 161
prognosis 1, 10, 16, 23–4, 70, 76, 81, 87, 155, 158, 162
prognostic index 78–81, **80**
psychiatric disease/illness *see* mental illness
psychiatric symptoms: awareness and knowledge 101–3; as brain dysfunction 102; cognition 164; development of 8–9; effect of classification 158; environmental factors 105–8; phenomenology 43–4, 134–154; stress relaxation continuum 96–9
psychiatry: criticism of 166; current paradigm 31–2; status and position 108
psycho-education 89–90; case example 91–2, 108, 162
psychoanalysis 126
psychosis: case examples 143–158; cognition 68; complexity of 48; environmental factors 105; mystic experiences 43–48; and neurosis 117–19; mental health care 29-30; new treatments 161–2; open dialogue approach 162; prediction 78–80; prevention 87–93, 162; transition 77
psychosocial impairment 77, 81
psychotherapy, at-risk mental state (ARMS) 89–92
psychotic disorders: isolation in 102–3; quality of care 29–30; transition to 77–8
psychotropic medication: convenience of 16; dispensing 15; effects on brain 25–6; increased use 22–4, 30, 108, 155–6; side effects 10, 14, 24–6, 30, 81, 153–4, 161; withdrawal effects 27–9
PsyMate 158
publication, as academic requirement 22, 33
publicness 111

quality of care, psychotic disorders 29–30

Radulescu, E. 16
realism, in mental illness 101–5, 107, 118, 167

recovery: authentic self 126–8, 158–60; defining 159; and medication use 161; natural 41–2; case example 137–42
redefinition of health and illness 155, 165–7; context and overview 101; as continuum 107; difference 104; environmental factors 105–8; individual perspective 108; medicalisation of behaviour 104–5; normality 103–5; psychiatric symptoms 101–3
relationships, positive and negative sides of 38–42
relaxation 96– 9, 108, 143–4, 159
religious adherence **44**
religious nature 43–8, 125
Research Domain Criteria project 55
researchers, isolation of 55
responsibility 123
rest-and-digest response 97
Rilke, R.M. 38, 39, 40, 46, 101–2, 104, 111, 120–1, 124, 126, 166
risk stratification approach 78–80
Ritalin (methylphenidate): cognitive impairment 72; prescribing 14–15; rebound and withdrawal effects 14; safety of 13–14; use of 12, 17
Rüsch, N. 93

safety bubble 105, 167
Sahakian, B.J. 72
Salinger, J.D. 47
Sartre, J.P. 40–1, 122
schizophrenia: 'The Abandoned Illness' report 29; cognitive impairment 68–73; environmental factors 105; patients' wishes for treatment 63–4; prevention 76–7, 81–2, 161; prognosis 24; and urbanization 105
Schizophrenia Commission 29
'Science in transition' 33
scientific method, limitations 124–5
scientific research 33
Seikkula, J. 163
Sein und Zeit (Heidegger) 110
selective attention 64, 66, 89–91
self-healing 40–1, 121, 125
Self, Jung's concept 125
self-knowledge 126, 127
self-labelling 93
self-stigmatization 93
self, understanding 32–3
social comparison 111–12, 165
social influence 39–40
social interaction 38–42; case example 41–2

solitude 38–40, 41–2, 104, 121, 128, 164
Sorrentino, P. 38
Spinoza, B. 113–14, 116
spirituality 45, 119, 126, 164
SSRI antidepressants 25–7, 107, 165; case example 28; withdrawal effects 27–8
Stafford, M.R. 88
stigma 30–1; minimising 156–7; at-risk mental state (ARMS) 92–3, 157
story banks 166
stress: effects of 9, 40–1, 59, 71, 81 89, 96, 127, 138, 144, 154, 158, 163; medication 98–9; psychiatric symptoms 96
stress–relaxation continuum 96–9; case example 98–9; physiology 97–8
stress–vulnerability model **89**
Study 329 26–7
study replication 33
sub threshold symptoms 9
subjective experience 3, 16, 51, 56–7, 62, 97, 110, 119, 128, 131
subjective experiences: attending to 155; non-classifiable 158
subliminal region 43, 115
suicide 25–6, 104, 136, 139, 154, 164–5
Swaab, D.F. 50
sympathetic nervous system 97
symptom dimensions 55–9, 70–1, 161, 164
symptoms: mix of 8, 61, 144; transdiagnostic approach 55–7, 61–2

target engagement 61
Taylor, I. 104
'The Abandoned Illness' report 29
The Alchemist (Coelho) 115
The Ethics (Spinoza) 113–14
The Herd 112, 126, 128
'The One' 46
The Perennial Scope of Philosophy (Jaspers) 118–19
the shadow 126
The Varieties of Religious Experience (James) 115
therapy, as healing relationship 124
Thomas 133–8
threshold, mental health to morbidity 56
Tolstoy, L. 102, 124, 137
transcendent experiences 43
transdiagnostic biomarkers *see* biological markers
transdiagnostic neuropsychological deficits 64–8
transdiagnostic, Biobank Cognition study 57, 71–2

transiency 115
treatment process, case example 139–45
truth 39, 40, 42, 45, 101–2, 108, 113, 115, 121, 125, 138, 160, 163, 167

unconcealment 111, 117, 123, 127
University of British Columbia (UBC) 12
Upanishads 113, 123–4, 127
urbanization, and mental health 105–6

van den Berg, D. 89–90
van der Gaag, M. 88, 89–91
van Heeringen, C. 165
van Os, J. 158
Veenhoven, R. 166
Verstehen 51, 116–17, 119, 121, 125, 158
visuospatial memory, neuropsychological testing 62–3
Vorstmann, J.A. 68
von Trier, L. 38, 163

Weinberger, D.R. 16
Wellness Recovery Action Plan (WRAP) 159–60, 164
Wellness Tools 159
Wessman, J. 70
Whitaker, R. 103, 104, 105, 166
Wieg, R. 28–9
World Health Organization (WHO) 7, 24, 87, 164

Wunderink, L. 24, 161
Yalom, I. 40, 104, 110, 123–5, 126, 137, 158
Yang, P.B. 13
Young, A. 51–2
young people, ARMS criteria 66–7
Yung, A.R. 66, 77

Zen Buddhism 45, 97
Zimmerman, M. 159

Taylor & Francis eBooks

Helping you to choose the right eBooks for your Library

Add Routledge titles to your library's digital collection today. Taylor and Francis ebooks contains over 50,000 titles in the Humanities, Social Sciences, Behavioural Sciences, Built Environment and Law.

Choose from a range of subject packages or create your own!

Benefits for you
- Free MARC records
- COUNTER-compliant usage statistics
- Flexible purchase and pricing options
- All titles DRM-free.

Benefits for your user
- Off-site, anytime access via Athens or referring URL
- Print or copy pages or chapters
- Full content search
- Bookmark, highlight and annotate text
- Access to thousands of pages of quality research at the click of a button.

REQUEST YOUR FREE INSTITUTIONAL TRIAL TODAY

Free Trials Available
We offer free trials to qualifying academic, corporate and government customers.

eCollections – Choose from over 30 subject eCollections, including:

Archaeology	Language Learning
Architecture	Law
Asian Studies	Literature
Business & Management	Media & Communication
Classical Studies	Middle East Studies
Construction	Music
Creative & Media Arts	Philosophy
Criminology & Criminal Justice	Planning
Economics	Politics
Education	Psychology & Mental Health
Energy	Religion
Engineering	Security
English Language & Linguistics	Social Work
Environment & Sustainability	Sociology
Geography	Sport
Health Studies	Theatre & Performance
History	Tourism, Hospitality & Events

For more information, pricing enquiries or to order a free trial, please contact your local sales team:
www.tandfebooks.com/page/sales

 | The home of Routledge books

www.tandfebooks.com